Studies on the Chinese Economy

General Editors: **Peter Nolan**, Sinyi Professor of Chinese Management, Judge Institute of Management Studies, University of Cambridge, and Fellow of Jesus College, Cambridge, England; and **Dong Fureng**, Professor, Chinese Academy of Social Sciences, Beijing, China

This series analyses issues in China's current economic development, and sheds light upon that process by examining China's economic history. It contains a wide range of books on the Chinese economy past and present, and includes not only studies written by leading Western authorities but also translations of the most important works on the Chinese economy produced within China. It intends to make a major contribution towards understanding this immensely important part of the world economy.

Titles include:

Thomas Chan, Noel Tracy and Zhu Wenhui
CHINA'S EXPORT MIRACLE

Sarah Cook, Shujie Yao and Juzhong Zhuang (*editors*)
THE CHINESE ECONOMY UNDER TRANSITION

Xu Dixin and Wu Chengming (*editors*)
CHINESE CAPITALISM, 1522–1840

Christopher Findlay and Andrew Watson (*editors*)
FOOD SECURITY AND ECONOMIC REFORM

Samuel P. S. Ho and Y. Y. Kueh
SUSTAINABLE ECONOMIC DEVELOPMENT IN SOUTH CHINA

Kali P. Kalirajan and Yanrui Wu (*editors*)
PRODUCTIVITY AND GROWTH IN CHINESE AGRICULTURE

Bozhong Li
AGRICULTURAL DEVELOPMENT IN JIANGNAN, 1620–1850

Alfred H. Y. Lin
THE RURAL ECONOMY OF GUANGDONG, 1870–1937

Dic Lo
MARKET AND INSTITUTIONAL REGULATION IN CHINESE INDUSTRIALIZATION

Jun Ma
THE CHINESE ECONOMY IN THE 1990s

Guo Rongxing
HOW THE CHINESE ECONOMY WORKS

Sally Sargeson
REWORKING CHINA'S PROLETARIAT

Ng Sek Hong and Malcolm Warner
CHINA'S TRADE UNIONS AND MANAGEMENT

Terence Tsai
CORPORATE ENVIRONMENTALISM IN CHINA AND TAIWAN

Michael Twohey
AUTHORITY AND WELFARE IN CHINA

Carl E. Walter and Fraser J. T. Howie
'TO GET RICH IS GLORIOUS!'
China's Stock Markets in the '80s and '90s

Michael Warner
CHANGING WORKPLACE RELATIONS IN THE CHINESE ECONOMY

Wang Xiao-qiang
CHINA'S PRICE AND ENTERPRISE REFORM

Xiaoping Xu
CHINA'S FINANCIAL SYSTEM UNDER TRANSITION

Yanni Yan
INTERNATIONAL JOINT VENTURES IN CHINA

Godfrey Yeung
FOREIGN INVESTMENT AND SOCIO-ECONOMIC DEVELOPMENT IN CHINA
The Case of Dongguan

Wei-Wei Zhang
TRANSFORMING CHINA

Xiao-guang Zhang
CHINA'S TRADE PATTERNS AND INTERNATIONAL COMPARATIVE ADVANTAGE

Studies on the Chinese Economy
Series Standing Order ISBN 0–333–71502–0
(*outside North America only*)

You can receive future titles in this series as they are published by placing a standing order. Please contact your bookseller or, in case of difficulty, write to us at the address below with your name and address, the title of the series and the ISBN quoted above.

Customer Services Department, Macmillan Distribution Ltd, Houndmills, Basingstoke, Hampshire RG21 6XS, England

Corporate Environmentalism in China and Taiwan

Terence Tsai
Assistant Professor
Department of Management
The Chinese University of Hong Kong, and
Senior Research Associate
Judge Institute of Management Studies
University of Cambridge

palgrave

First published 2002 by
PALGRAVE
Houndmills, Basingstoke, Hampshire RG21 6XS and
175 Fifth Avenue, New York, N. Y. 10010
Companies and representatives throughout the world

PALGRAVE is the new global academic imprint of St. Martin's Press LLC Scholarly and Reference Division and Palgrave Publishers Ltd (formerly Macmillan Press Ltd).

ISBN 0–333–73002–X

This book is printed on paper suitable for recycling and made from fully managed and sustained forest sources.

A catalogue record for this book is available from the British Library.

Library of Congress Cataloging-in-Publication Data
Tsai, Terence, 1964–
Corporate environmentalism in China and Taiwan / Terence Tsai.
p. cm.
Includes bibliographical references and index.
ISBN 0–333–73002–X
1. International business enterprises—Environmental aspects. I. Title.

HD62.4 .T77 2000
658.4'08—dc21

00–065261

10 9 8 7 6 5 4 3 2 1
11 10 09 08 07 06 05 04 03 02

Printed and bound in Great Britain by
Antony Rowe Ltd, Chippenham, Wiltshire

I dedicate this book to my parents and all the people who helped me along the process, especially the staff at the Faculty of Business Administration of the Chinese University of Hong Kong, the Richard Ivey School of Business at the University of Western Ontario, Canada, the Judge Institute at the University of Cambridge, and my beloved cat, Mao-mao, who died tragically in Boston a year after I left him.

Contents

List of Figures

List of Tables

Acknowledgements

This book is an account of the my findings based on a four-year international research project conducted under the auspices of the Centre for International Business and Management (CIBAM) at the Judge Institute of Management Studies, University of Cambridge in England.

I must thank Cambridge for increasing the breadth of my knowledge. St John's College was my initial host. Staff there know me well and I have been treated with kindness. Many thanks should go to my bedder Liz who took good care of me during my first three years there. Clare Hall elected me to a Research Fellowship in 1996. I must thank Professor Gillian Beer (President), Mr Ed Jarron (Bursar), Dr Chris Hope (Resident Fellow), and Dr Hugh Whittaker (Senior Tutor) for taking me in as a family member and for showing enough faith in my work. I later migrated to the Richard Ivey School of Business at the University of Western Ontario, Canada as an Assistant Professor. Dean Lawrence Tapp, Associate Deans (Professor Jeffrey Gandz, Professor Ken Hardy, Professor Jane Howell, Professor Larry Wynant,) and my Global Environment of Business Teaching Group Co-ordinator, Professor David Conklin, granted me ample freedom to pursue my work. Ivey MBA, Hong Kong EMBA, and PhD students and colleagues, among whom I must name Professor Don Barclay, Professor Paul Beamish, Professor Mary Crossan, Professor Joe DiStefano, Professor Tony Frost, Mr Trevor Hunter, Ms Diana Lee, Professor Fernando Olivera, have been more than supportive in many aspects. I have gained much more than I expected at Ivey. After Ivey, the Department of Management at the Chinese University of Hong Kong has kindly provided me with a comfortable home. Department Chairman, Professor Lau Chung Ming has given me ample support for my work. I also appreciate numerous brain storming sessions with Professor Peter Cheng (now at Hong Kong Polytechnic University), Professor Steven White (now at INSEAD), Professor Michael Young, and Professor C. S. Wong. I must also thank my teaching assistant, Ms. Mary Au for painstakingly checking the manuscript. My CUHK MBA, BBA, DBM, DVM, and APIB Executive Programme attendees have been a constant source of inspiration.

I am also grateful for the financial support furnished by the British Council, the Chiang Ching-kuo Foundation, Clare Hall, the Judge Institute, the Richard Ivey School of Business at the University of Western

Ontario in Canada, Faculty of Business Administration and Asia Pacific Institute of Business at the Chinese University of Hong Kong, St John's College, Sutasoma Trust, UK Government, and my wonderful parents, Mr Charles Tsai and Ms Amy Tsai.

Academically, I owe my supervisors a great deal. Professor John Child has been most kind and patient in supervising my work. I found his infinite wisdom to be the most intriguing. He is a real 'mastermind'. Dr Chris Hope never fails to give encouragement in times of need. He exemplifies what an academic should be. Professor Yuan Lu inspired me to the academic career and has always lent a helping hand. Professor Xinbao Dong of Tsinghua University in China was instrumental in arranging all the Chinese company visits and looked after me well in Beijing. Professor Bor-shiuan Cheng of National Taiwan University has given me much insight into the operations of Taiwanese businesses and kept me going when I was down. This list can go on and on. I am indebted to many people during my research career.

Last but not least, I want to thank my dear friends in Cambridge. My past and present office mates, Dr Christoph Nitsche, Dr. Stephan Henneberg and his lovely wife Ms Gamila Shoib. My buddies, Dr Thomas Ahnert, Dr Selwyn Blieden, Mr Stefan Eghbalian, Dr David Gibbons, Dr. George Hong, Mr Chris McCavit, Miss Ambika Gupta, Mr Markus Irngartinger, Dr Titus Moser, Dr Carola Niesler, Dr Thomas Niesler, Dr Piotr Romanowski, Dr Heinz Jurgen Schwering, Miss Irene Zia, and members of the Gang (Dr Steve Brenner, Dr Raphael Busso, Professor Tom Gallanis, Professor Mary Hannah Jones, and Dr Michael Jennings). I would not have survived Cambridge without their support. Special thanks also go to my siblings and in-laws, Ms Ming Tsai, Dr David Ling, Ms Freda Tsai, Mr David Wang, Dr Stella Tsai, Dr Frank Lin, and Mr Hans Tsai, for their unfailing love and care packages.

TERENCE TSAI

Abbreviations

ADL	Arthur D. Little
BACT	best available control technology
BAT	best available technology
CAC	command and control
CERES	Coalition for Environmentally Responsible Economies
CMA	Chemical Manufacturers' Association
COD	chemical oxygen demand
EMAS	Environmental Management Audit System (EU)
EPA	Environmental Protection Agency (US)
FDI	foreign direct investment
ICC	International Chamber of Commerce
IDA	International Development Association
ISO	International Standards Organisation
MNC	Multinational corporation
MoEA	Ministry of Economic Affairs (Taiwan)
NEPA	National Environmental Protection Agency (China)
NGO	non-governmental organisation
OSHA	Occupational Safety and Health Administration (US)
R&D	research and development
RCRA	Resource Conservation and Recovery Act (US)
SBU	strategic business unit
SCM	social contract model
SHE	safety, health and environmental
SOE	state-owned enterprise
TEPA	Taiwan Environmental Protection Association
TOSCA	Toxic Substance Control Act (US)
TVE	township and village enterprise
UNCED	United Nations Conference on Environment and Development
UNCTAD	United Nations Conference on Trade and Development
UNEP	United Nations Environment Programme
UNESCAP	United Nations Economic and Social Commission for Asia and the Pacific/United Nations Centre on Transnational Corporations, Joint Unit on Transnational Corporations
WCED	World Commission on Environment and Development

Part I
Background and Research Framework

1
Introduction

> Be fruitful and increase in number; fill the earth and subdue it. Rule over the fish of the sea and the birds of the air and over every living creature that moves on the ground.
>
> Genesis 1:28

> The earth dries up and withers, the world languishes and withers, the exalted of the earth languish. The earth is defiled by its people; They have disobeyed the laws, violated the statutes and broken the everlasting covenant. Therefore a curse consumes the earth; its people must bear their guilt.
>
> Isaiah 24:4–6 NIV

Ever since the industrial revolution, the natural environment has been under constant threat. The twentieth century has been scarred by highly publicised environmental disasters, such as those in Chernobyl, USSR; Bhopal, India (Union Carbide); and Alaska, USA (Exxon Valdez). In the 1990s, a decade characterised by the pursuit of material well-being and the fulfilment of self-interest, environmental protection proceeds slowly, competing against the 'not-in-my-backyard' mentality. The majority remain reluctant to make financial sacrifices in order to maintain an acceptable environment for future generations. Moreover, the globalisation of commercial activities, coupled with the intense desire of developing countries to increase their gross national products, places enormous stress on the environment:

> Environmental protection diverted real and financial resources from the production of conventional goods and services and hence slowed gross domestic product growth. . . . Developing countries, burdened

> by poverty, should strike a different balance, with more attention to growth and less to environmental protection.
>
> (United Nations Conference on Trade and Development (UNCTAD) 1992)

This poses a difficult political dilemma for the governments of developing countries: how can one maintain a stable and effective governance given the conflicting demands of rapid economic growth and environmental protection?

In response to the alarming state of environmental conditions and a general refusal to curb environmental pollution, Gro Harlem Brundtland and the World Commission on Environment and Development (WCED), a satellite organisation of the United Nations, pioneered the concept of 'sustainable development':[1]

> It modifies the conventional view of economic growth as GDP growth to incorporate a new balance between economic growth and environmental quality; it also recognises that environmental quality and economic growth can be mutually reinforcing at all income levels.
>
> (UNCTAD 1992)

The most significant breakthrough of the Commission, considering the disparate wealth of its international membership, was the development of proposals for institutional and legal change. A set of proposed legal principles for environmental protection and sustainable development was presented for public scrutiny (WCED 1987). Four main sections are included in this legal document:

- General Principles, Rights, and Responsibilities
- Principles, Rights, and Obligations Concerning Transboundary Natural Resources and Environmental Interferences
- State Responsibility
- Peaceful Settlement of Disputes.

The WCED has effectively produced ripple effects in the international environmental policy and law-making arena, as evident at the 1992 United Nations Conference on Environment and Development (UNCED) in Rio, where influential non-binding legal instruments such as Agenda 21 and the Rio Declaration on Environment and Development were presented. Based on the principle of sustainable development, the Rio Declaration strengthens international environmental law by merging it with international economic law and development law (Sands 1993).

While the sharp division between the North and the South exists, both parties, in light of the burgeoning commercial activities between the two, can no longer ignore the reaches of international decrees.[2] Several developing countries, under the guidance of international organisations such as the World Bank, embarked on instituting a programme to embrace the novel idea of sustainable development.

It is naive to think that international decrees can reverse the rate of environmental pollution. After all, environmental pollution is a by-product of industrialisation, and industrialisation goes hand-in-hand with increased commercial activities. In an increasingly competitive society, it is difficult for managers to invest in environmental protection when the return-on-investment cannot easily be realised. But Porter (1991) has correctly argued that 'the conflict between environmental protection and economic competitiveness is a false dichotomy. It stems from a narrow view of the sources of prosperity and a static view of competition'. The comforting news is that in McKinsey's recent survey (Walley and Whitehead 1994), '92% of CEOs and board members stated that the environment should be one of their top three management priorities, and 85% claimed that one of their major goals should be to integrate environmental considerations into business strategy'. Examining a domestic or national enterprise is less resource-exhaustive than studying a multinational corporation (MNC), but given the rapid internationalisation of the commercial world (Bartlett and Ghoshal 1989, Ohmae 1990, Tayeb 1992), there exists a need to understand the MNCs behaviour in developing countries, especially in such sensitive areas as safety, health and environmental (SHE) protection.

1.1 The role of multinational corporations in safety, health, and environmental protection

Multinational corporations play an increasingly important role in today's global economy, as demonstrated by the record foreign direct investment (FDI) flows recorded in 1996 at US$350 billion (UNCTAD 1997:xvi). In developing countries alone, FDI in 1996 rose to a record total of US$129 billion (UNCTAD 1997:6). 1996's record figures are part of an ongoing trend of increased MNC participation in developing country economies. Between 1981 and 1994, FDI to developing countries increased from US$13 to US$80 billion per annum, increasing fivefold between 1986 and 1993 (UNCTAD 1995:8). The World Bank further estimates that FDI to developing countries will grow at between 7% and 10% a year over the next decade (*The Economist*, April 22, 1995:7). It should be noted that a substantial portion of FDI is controlled by a small number of companies: 'the largest 100 (MNCs), ranked on the basis of the size of foreign assets, own US$1.7 trillion assets in their foreign affiliates, controlling an estimated one-fifth of global foreign assets' (UNCTAD 1997:xvii).

The rises in FDI to developing countries can be explained by two concurrent phenomena. First, many developing countries have replaced protectionist, import substitution-based policies emphasising capital formation in state-owned enterprises, with more liberal policies dependent on export-led growth, the attraction of FDI and MNCs, and the dynamics of the free market (Kruegar 1985, Daniel 1991). Second, MNCs are increasingly attracted to developing countries not only because they represent largely untapped and important markets, but also because of the potential for lower production costs and the presence of many of the world's most important unexplored natural resources within these countries.

The growth in the importance of MNCs in developing countries has been accompanied by increased concern about whether economic development, particularly in developing countries, occurs in a sustainable manner (WCED 1987, Gore 1992, Hawken 1993); that is to say, whether development occurs in a manner that not only results in economic growth, but also incorporates and accounts for any environmental and social costs that may accompany economic growth (Daly and Cobb 1994, Korten 1995, Welford 1995, Stead and Stead 1996). Since MNCs are at the forefront of many private-sector developments (UNCTAD 1996:xvii), their response to environmental and social issues is particularly important. With their international expertise and significant human, technical and financial resources (UNCTAD 1992:223), MNCs have a potentially wide-ranging influence – both positive and negative. Their response is especially critical given the role MNCs can play both as instruments of developing country state policy and as institutions in shaping developing country state actions and policies (Choucri, 1993:221, Moser and Tsai 1997).

1.2 The allure of China and Taiwan

China was selected as the focus of this research because of its fast pace of economic growth, its unique institutional structure, its substantial inflow of FDI, and most importantly, its early stage of environmentalism. In 1996, the growth of FDI inflows to China recorded an impressive figure of US$42.3 billion (UNCTAD 1997:306). A considerable portion of this FDI has been directed to China and towards pollution intensive sectors. According to government statistics, Chinese cities are among the dirtiest in the world. More than two-thirds of household and industrial waste water is dumped untreated into rivers, lakes and the sea. China also faces the problem of 'disconnection' between the provinces and the central government, since regional and district governments often fail to enforce Beijing's policy. Fear that tough pollution penalties might jeopardise economic growth and jobs discourages both the central and provincial governments from taking due notice of environmental problems (Tang *et al.* 1997). This is evident in the lack of environmental controls exerted over the mushrooming township and village enterprises (Maddox 1993).

Taiwan, while customarily regarded as a renegade province of China, has its own political agenda, retains an immense degree of autonomy, and its relationship with China can best be described as one of 'love–hate'. In fact, Taiwanese companies have invested more than $20 billion into China, with Taiwan thus becoming China's largest 'foreign' investor after Hong Kong (Reyes 1996). The investment is mainly driven by the rising business costs in Taiwan, including an inadequate labour supply, comparatively high labour charges, and the 'new' environmental protection demands. Pollution knows no boundary, and the well-recognised phenomenon of 'pollution transfer' from Taiwan to China is of particular concern bearing in mind the uneasy political situation between the two governments.

China, in comparison to Taiwan, which has acceded to the rank of newly industrialised countries (NICs), represents a new and budding market. The relative merits of the two markets, though not central to this research project, will be briefly discussed in later sections. Notwithstanding the pollution transfer from Taiwan to China, it is hence natural to contemplate whether MNCs, in their pursuit of cost efficiency, are leading such a movement. This research identified large MNCs in the pollution-intensive chemical sector as targets of investigation. This group of firms is expected to be more susceptible to the temptation of a 'pollution haven'. The chemical industry is one of the most important industries in the world; of the top 100 MNCs ranked by foreign assets in 1996, eleven are chemical companies (UNCTAD 1997:29–31). It is in developing countries that chemical MNCs are expanding most aggressively. The developing countries represent an excellent reserve of comparatively cheap labour, new sources of raw material and a vast untapped market. With the economic boom in the Greater China Region and the dominance of Taiwan and China in such areas as the electronic sector and in electronics chemical supplies,[3] it is increasingly difficult for MNCs to ignore the business opportunities there.

Despite an almost universal acceptance of the need for chemical products, the chemical industry has in recent years come under sustained criticism for its negative environmental impacts, particularly in developing countries. Bayer, for example, was met with large-scale protest in Taiwan for its billion dollar investment plan (Alperoxicz 1996). Just a few years ago, Du Pont experienced the same problem.

1.3 Four research questions

This book discusses the environmental management behaviour of MNCs and their subsidiaries within the aforementioned industrial sectors in China and Taiwan with respect to the following research questions:

1. How do MNCs balance their strategic intent and institutional constraints on SHE protection?
2. How do MNCs from industrialised countries respond and adapt to local institutional pressures for SHE protection in developing countries such as China and Taiwan?
3. What are the dominant modes of interaction between MNCs headquarters demands and the local needs in the realm of SHE protection?
4. How do the same MNCs respond under different institutional pressure in China and Taiwan? What are the similarities and differences in comparison with the local corporations?

Case study methodology, combined with semi-structured interviews and manufacturing plant visits were employed as the primary forms of investigation. The case companies involved in this study include three major MNCs – two US-based and one UK-based – with chemical manufacturing operations in China and Taiwan, one large-scale Chinese state-owned chemical producer (SOE) and one large-scale Taiwanese private chemical manufacturer.

Throughout the book, an emphasis is placed upon MNCs' ability to engage in strategic thinking in response to home and host country institutional demands. This, in turn, leads to the controversial and yet interesting debate on globalisation and localisation of MNCs' internal standards with respect to SHE protection demands.

1.4 The structure of the book

This book can be divided into three distinct parts: background and research framework, empirical results and analysis, and conclusion (see Figure 1.1). Chapters 1 to 4 fall into the first category: Chapter 2 renders a picture of the current state-of-the-art knowledge related to MNCs and SHE protection and identifies gaps in the scholarly literature; Chapter 3 sets the stage for the development of an analytical framework and provides new perspectives in dealing with SHE issues; and Chapter 4 describes the research methodology.

Chapters 5 to 9 form the core of Part II, empirical results and analysis, and are in direct response to the four research questions. Chapter 5

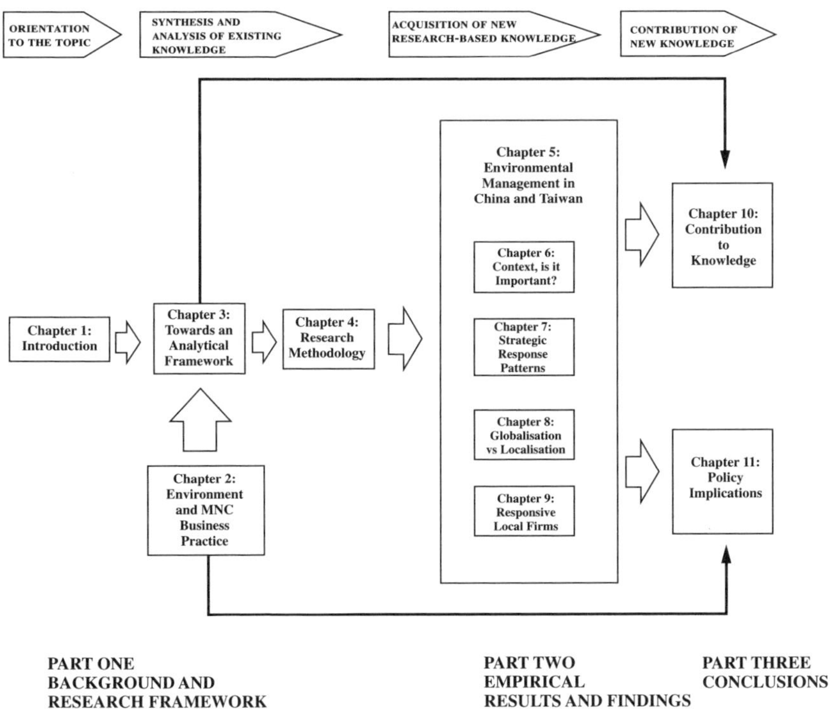

Figure 1.1 Organisation of book

provides a succinct summary of the Chinese and Taiwanese environmental management issues and highlights relevant policies and regulations. The findings from the research work on the three MNCs are streamed according to the four main themes. Wherever possible, the findings from China and Taiwan are compared and contrasted. Chapters 6 through 9 are 'data' chapters. The data set are a combination of viewpoints from not only the MNC managers and the principal research investigator but also from government officials, non-governmental organisation representatives and the MNCs' long-term business competitors. Analysis of the results will be presented in the final section of this book. It is intended that this section serves the function of story-telling.

Chapters 10 and 11 constitute the 'conclusion'. Chapter 10 targets the academic community and renders essential analysis to this study as well as suggesting a further research agenda. Chapter 11 prescribes means for managers to better adapt their businesses to unfamiliar conditions in a host country.

2
The Environment and Multinational Corporations' Business Practices

> With the globalisation of product production and marketing, and attendant expansion of intra-firm transfer of capital and technology, the role of MNCs in the next decade will become even more pivotal in shaping the nature and pace of technology transfer to developing countries.
>
> (Brown *et al.* 1993:3)

On 4 June 1994, the *Central Daily News* of Taiwan reported the following (author's translation):

> The US company RCA has long been dumping hazardous waste into deep wells located within its manufacturing plant. Groundwater and soil have been polluted as a result of this practice. The pollution has affected the health of the nearby population, which occasionally uses groundwater for drinking purposes. . . . RCA established its Taiwanese operations in 1970, producing electronic goods. The manufacturing plants subsequently merged with General Electric Company (GE) in 1986. In 1988, the French company Thomson purchased the plants from GE. According to former RCA employees, for over twenty years RCA has been disposing of hazardous waste into a number of 10-ft deep wells to avoid problematic and expensive waste management. Thomson was informed of such illegal practices and negotiated for a land purchase without buying the environmental liabilities. It then proceeded to conduct its own investigations by hiring environmental consultants Arthur D. Little and Bechtel. Eleven monitoring wells were installed onsite and four were installed offsite. Chemical analyses of groundwater yielded alarmingly high levels of contaminants. Thomson considered revealing the findings to the media. However,

the fear of unfavourable reactions, such as massive demonstrations of environmental activists and requests for unreasonably high compensation from the nearby residents, resulted in a 'do-nothing' approach. Thomson then made a decision to sell the land and seal all existing wells on site and commenced a gradual relocation to Thailand and China.

Cases such as this have become increasingly publicised and have placed into jeopardy the goodwill which corporations enjoy among the communities in which they operate. As a result, safety, health, and environmental (SHE) protection issues have come to be regarded as a key strategic management element in the modern boardroom (Steger 1993). Hutchinson (1992a & b) stated that environmental considerations should play a key role in strategic decisions such as policy formation. Interviews with representatives of the industrial giant Dow Chemical illustrated this pattern of 'strategic change' (Avila and Whitehead 1993). This overwhelming corporate endorsement of environmental criteria is a cause for some satisfaction on the part of environmentalists and green management scholars.

2.1 MNCs – the powerful and influential

In general, large MNCs such as GE, Thomson, and Dow Chemicals, have an immense potential impact on the global environmental, and on health and safety protection. The study of MNCs is a fairly well-established branch of management studies and the wealth of existing knowledge can certainly aid an understanding of the 'greening' phenomenon. In his world-wide best-seller *The Borderless World*, Kenichi Ohmae (1990) praised the virtues of MNCs and their roles in the world globalisation process. As developing countries are opening to the global economy, it is becoming easier and more lucrative for MNCs to take advantage of the profitable differences between localities with respect to wage structure, market potential, labour supply, taxes, local resources, and environmental regulations (Korten 1995: 126). The United Nations Conference on Trade and Development (UNCTAD) (1992:223–224) furnished an excellent summary of MNCs' influential characteristics:

- MNCs tend to be more mobile and to have greater discretion in the location of production than domestic firms, which suggests the possibility that MNCs have greater leverage in negotiating favourable environmental regulations, permits and exemptions with the host country.

- MNCs are extensively involved in environmentally significant activities. Moreover, MNCs are reported to have extensive involvement in most pollution- and hazard-intensive industries as measured by environmental control costs.
- MNCs tend to have financial, managerial and technological resources superior to those of local firms. The superior position both raises expectations and allows MNCs to exercise leadership in environmental protection.
- MNCs are in general more visible and vulnerable. MNCs are guests in the host country and, compared to local firms, often must strive harder to maintain good relations with host governments and local communities. MNCs also have a global image to protect and tend to be quite conscious of public and stockholder opinion, and of the potential for restrictive home country regulations, even for their foreign operations.

Dunning (1993) and Rugman and Verbeke (1998) added that MNCs have greater ability than the local or the other types of foreign companies to affect the location of environmentally sensitive activities, conduct trade in hazardous products, influence the environmental content of both production and consumption, and innovate new products and restructure activities in an environmentally friendly way. Levy (1995:1) argued that the behaviour of MNCs:

> is expected to differ from that of purely national firms. [MNCs] are faced with regulations and enforcement practices that vary across countries and have to make choices between standardised or differentiated responses [and], in the case of the former, which standards to follow.

It is known that MNCs have an important role to play in the sustainable development of developing countries (Hunt and Auster 1990, Greeno and Robinson 1992, Schmidheiny 1992, Smart 1992, Avila and Whitehead 1993, Levy 1995). Moser (1994) asserts that the need for more rigorous research in the area still prevails. He (Moser 1994:11–12) argues that:

> the majority of research is based upon a developed country context and focuses on such issues as the suitability of traditional management paradigms for achieving sustainable development (Commoner 1990; Allenby 1993; Ayres 1993; Ehrenfeld 1994; Gladwin, Kennelly and Krause 1995; Hart 1995; Shrivastava 1995), the ways in which

> companies in developed countries have responded to sustainable development (Gladwin 1975, Cairncross 1992, Hoffman 1994, Sharma and Vrendenburg 1994) and possible means by which corporations could behave in a more sustainable manner (Corbett and Van Wassenhove 1993, Elkington 1994, Cairncross 1995, Starik and Rands 1995).

The literature addressing the environmental role of MNCs in developing countries deals with four relevant research issues. The first relates to MNC behaviour in developing countries *vis-à-vis* local laws, regulations and political climate. The second discusses the internal MNC environmental standards relative to host-country industrial counterparts. The third explores the issues relating to MNCs' environmental protection technologies and skills transfer to developing countries. The fourth examines the role of the host country in influencing MNC technology transfer decisions and effects (Brown *et al.* 1993:7, Moser 1994).

The following sections give a concise review of the past research work in each of the aforementioned areas. As Brown *et al.* (1993:8) wrote, 'these studies mirror the evolution of MNC–host country relations during the past three decades', and inquiries have changed from the overly simplified classification and generalisation of 'good and bad corporate behaviour' to that of the 'debate about pollution havens and double (environmental) standards'. Despite this gradual transition from the 'basics' to 'sophistication', SHE remains very much an under-explored issue for MNC research.

2.2 MNCs and environmental management research

MNCs and the contextual constraints of host countries

MNCs and host country policy

The role of the host country in shaping MNC behaviour is best demonstrated by its laws and policies toward FDI. It can be argued that host countries' regulations exert a strong influence on MNCs' policy formation (as a manifestation and representation of strategic change) and response pattern *vis-à-vis* environmental protection issues. The work of Moser (Moser and Tsai 1997) in Colombia and Peru demonstrated that host-country environmental policies and regulations were considered to be most crucial in shaping the MNCs' response patterns. The research of Leonard and Morrell (1985), Morell and Poznanski (1981), Pimenta

(1987), Ural (1987) and White (1991) dealt with the development of host-country environmental laws and policies in relation to MNC. As a general trend, host developing countries are lagging behind and are relatively inexperienced in formulating and implementing environmental standards. In many cases, host government environmental law-making is dependent on the situation arising and serves as a response to crisis.

The pro-development mentality of the host developing countries, by nature, de-emphasises SHE protection. Inadequate environmental laws and policies not only reveal the shortage in trained environmental personnel but also imply the lack of commitment from the governments. International environmental management poses challenges for both governments and the MNCs (Cairncross 1992). Given the huge environmental costs, existing research has called for a more realistic evaluation of the cost and benefit associated with issuing new environmental decrees (Sandbach 1980; Pearce 1989, 1991, 1994, 1995, 1996). This bears particular relevance to host developing countries, which may enact laws and regulations in reaction to dealing with unfamiliar circumstances (both technical and organisational) with the MNCs (Moser and Tsai 1997).

MNCs and the 'Pollution Haven' Hypothesis

The anxiety associated with the negative impact of inadequate SHE laws and regulations gives rise to the 'pollution haven' hypothesis. Under this hypothesis, a motivation for MNC location in developing countries is that weak SHE law frameworks provide an incentive for dirty industry to relocate from developed countries where stricter environmental legislation prevails (Gladwin and Wells 1976, Richardson and Mutti 1976, Pearson and Pryor 1978, Knogden 1979, Walter 1982, Duerksen 1983, Castleman 1987, Leonard 1987, Leonard 1988, Johnston Hernandez 1992, Clapp 1994, Sorell and Hendry 1994). Castleman's (1987) study documents several cases of Japanese MNCs exporting pollution-intensive product and production methods while failing to consider the adverse health and social effects of these actions.

Opposing the dominant perspective, Harrison (1994) and Moser (1994) questioned the importance of weak environmental frameworks as the motivating factor for MNCs' relocation of industry to developing countries. Auty and Warhurst (1993) further argued that some corporations even choose voluntarily to exceed local environmental standards. Furthering the debate, Moser (1994:12) outlined a number of possible factors to support this claim. These include access to advanced technology with accompanying economic and environmental efficiencies, fears of expropriation, and retroactive environmental penalties, often on a world-wide scale, for 'poor' environmental behaviour. MNCs are also keenly aware of the threats posed by the future environmental legislation and are routinely in compliance with the relevant 'green' conditions for new project financing. Other factors include stricter regulatory requirements and greater public awareness in the home nation, and the opinions of environmentally conscious shareholders (Auty and Warhurst 1993, Birdsall and Wheeler 1992). Choucri (1993:211) provided yet another explanation for the shift in corporate location of activities. He attributed the relocation to 'growth and industrialisation in the developing countries' and to the 'policies of site exclusion' rather than to the 'movement of world environmental legislation' and argued that, as of 1988, 'pollution havens' had not become apparent.

Studies of landmark pollution tragedies at MNCs' facilities in developing countries form another line of inquiry (Bowonder, Kasperson, and Kasperson 1985; Castleman and Purkavastha 1985; Gladwin 1985; Morell and Poznanski 1981; Bowonder and Linstone 1987; Gladwin 1987; Lagadec 1987; Shrivastava 1987; Weir 1987). These authors contributed to the understanding of the 1984 accident in the Union Carbide pesticide plant in Bhopal, India. Union Carbide's extensive array of hazardous chemical operations and weak corporate environmental policies were highlighted. This group of studies clearly portrayed the reactive corporate mindsets in the 1980s and analysed the associated corporate SHE practices that, combined with the accumulation of unfavourable economic, regulatory, infrastructural and management conditions, resulted in thousands of casualties.

Responses of MNCs

MNCs and negotiation/bargaining

Leonard (1985, 1988) and Pintz's (1987) work on negotiation between host countries and multinational corporations regarding environmental issues added a new dimension to the existing literature. Their case studies covered highly polluting industries such as mining, chemical production and energy generation in Papua New Guinea, Mexico, Ireland and Spain. Brown *et al.* (1993), whose work built upon the tradition of negotiation, critiqued Leonard (1985, 1988) and Pintz's (1987) findings as limited in both the process of negotiation and in the 'actual performance of the new enterprises', leaving many questions 'at the nexus of MNC–host country interactions'. Brown *et al.*'s (1993) own research centred on MNC (Xerox, Du Pont and Occidental Chemicals) subsidiaries in India and Thailand and examined the topic relating to technology-transfer-induced negotiation with the host countries. Their case studies yielded the following major findings:

- MNCs display leadership as initiators of SHE dialogue and negotiation
- MNCs are responsible players in the industry
- While SHE considerations are absent during the negotiation between the MNCs and the host countries, they are prominent during the negotiation between the MNCs and their respective joint venture partners. The absence of SHE negotiation is attributed to procedural,[4] institutional,[5] and conceptual/historical[6] factors (Leonard 1985, 1988).

The relative importance of each factor at each stage of negotiation is analysed and the relatively good image of the MNCs is more an outcome of the intricate interplay of the factors than of good corporate planning.

MNCs and technology/skill transfer

Technology and skills transfer is perceived to be a key means by which MNCs can contribute to sustainable development within developing countries. According to Agenda 21 (UNCTAD 1992):

> Multinational companies, as repositories of scarce technical skills needed for the protection and enhancement of the environment, have a special role and interest in promoting co-operation in and in relation to technology transfer, as they are important channels for such transfer, and for building a trained human resource pool and infrastructure.

As such, in return for access to developing countries' markets and natural and human resources, MNCs undertaking business in developing countries reciprocate by helping the countries reach their development goals in an environmentally responsible manner (ECLAC 1991, Wescott 1992).

There appears to be little empirical analysis of the issue of technology transfer and most evidence remains case-study-based and anecdotal. The limited number of studies can be divided into three sub-groups of investigation (Brown *et al.* 1993:7). The first analyses corporate policies for implementing SHE systems in MNC facilities in developing countries (Gladwin 1977, Morrison 1991: 16–17, UNCTAD 1991, Rappaport and Flaherty 1992). In their exploratory case study on the large MNCs, Rappaport and Flaherty (1992) investigated the corporate responses of five companies to environmental challenges. 'Interviews were conducted at each case company's corporate headquarters, a domestic manufacturing facility, and at one or more of the company's overseas manufacturing facility'. Their preliminary findings are summarised as follows:

- Corporations are concerned about whether they are perceived by the public as environmentally responsible.
- The profitability of a company does not correlate with the quality of its environmental programmes.
- Top management commitment is important to developing and implementing effective environmental programmes.
- Physical distance from the corporate headquarters does not affect the quality of the environmental programmes at subsidiaries (including foreign).
- Association with a highly publicised incident does not result in the development of aggressive environmental programmes.

The second study focuses on the organisational behaviour of MNCs in host country settings (Gladwin and Walter 1976; Gladwin and Wells 1976). Gladwin and colleagues presented five major case studies – Dow Chemicals, Gulf Oil, F. Hoffmann-La Roche, International Telephone and Telegraph, and Rio Tinto-Zinc – to illustrate conflict management involving nine subject areas of terrorism, human rights, politics, questionable payment (bribes), marketing, labour relations, environment, technology, and economics/finance. The authors drew heavily on the organisation theories to account for the observations, and the research represents a departure from the purely descriptive studies.

The third study devotes itself to the implementation of international SHE guidelines at MNC facilities in developing countries (ILO 1984). Implementation of international guidelines signifies a certain degree of knowledge transfer from the MNC home countries, usually industrialised, to the host developing countries. Such knowledge transfer may be mismatching local needs. Developing country conditions serve to hinder the implementation of ordinarily desirable guidelines. The pros and cons of adopting international SHE guidelines are discussed in these studies. In the more recent studies, Wescott (1992) proposes that MNCs can be, and are, instrumental in the transfer of developed country environmental technology and skills. Other authors, including Ashford and Ayers (1985), Pintz (1987), Amba-Rao (1989) and McKerron and Cogan (1993), provide examples of circumstances under which MNCs do not always apply developed country expertise and technology to a developing setting.

Globalisation and localisation of MNCs

A further research inquiry deals with the comparative analyses with respect to SHE protection of MNC subsidiaries performances in developed versus developing countries (Knogden 1979, Royston 1979, Hassan *et al.* 1981, ILO 1984, Ives 1985, Brown *et al.* 1993). The studies identified and summarised conflicts and problems within MNCs when confronted with inconsistent and unfamiliar external demands. MNC subsidiaries in developing countries are in many ways subjected to tougher operating conditions. The ambiguity of SHE laws and regulations, the difficulty in understanding the needs and thinking pattern of the local staff, and the lack of SHE infrastructure support combine to lower the standard of performance. The findings from this group of studies are descriptive and not overly theoretical. Several interesting management issues are raised but these are in need of theoretical grounding.

MNCs relative to developing country counterparts

A comparison of MNC performance with local private-sector and state-owned enterprises suggests that MNCs have higher environmental standards than their local counterparts (Royston 1985; Castleman 1987; Pearson 1987; Pimenta 1987; UNESCAP 1988, 1990; Warhurst 1994). It is argued that this is because of the access MNCs have to superior technological, human and financial resources. MNCs are also leaders in technological innovation, institutions of technological change and agents of commercialisation for new technology (both organisational and mechanical) (Choucri 1993). Hence they are believed to hold keys to economic upgrading of the host countries in the developing rank.

Since, by default, MNCs tend to engage in the manufacturing of a wide range of product lines and are responsible for a broad spectrum of hazardous and pollution-intensive activities, host developing countries often exhibit a love–hate attitude towards their presence. The keen suspicion by the host country governments manifested by the closer scrutiny directed towards compliance with environmental standards than towards their local counterparts, is an example of such a paradoxical relationship (Warhurst 1994). The 'foreignness' of MNCs in host countries have propelled them to act cautiously and more sensitively to the local concerns. This behaviour is especially pronounced if the MNCs are contemplating additional investment in the same host countries. The high visibility of MNCs in the international market place further serves to encourage responsible behaviour. The financial penalties, as well as other negative impacts, experienced by Union Carbide, Exxon, and Shell as a result of their landmark environmental tragedies, were sufficient to keep the MNCs at bay.

2.3 Links to business management

The absence of research on developing countries is a reflection of how the general academic community perceives the broad, new, and fast evolving field of environmental management. For that reason, the definition of the field is somewhat ambiguous. For different people, 'environmental management' conjures up different images. Three broad categories prevail:

- Environmental resource economics and management
- Environmental health management
- Environmental management and business strategy.

The first category is primarily concerned with the efficiency of managing natural resources and is a well-established branch within the realm of applied economics (Tietenberg 1988; Pearce 1989, 1991, 1994, 1995, 1996). An extension of the research area covers environmental policy analysis and experienced academics in this discipline are often retained by governments as senior public and economic policy consultants. The second category focuses on the management of public health in relation to detrimental environmental effects. The emphasis is on building a reasonable cause-and-effect relationship and finding management solutions for environmental problems. The third category represents an attempt to integrate environmentalism into the current theories of strategic management in the business sphere and has been adopted in this research. Most of the past research, technically orientated to a large extent, has failed to satisfactorily apply various strategic business management theories in explaining peculiar manifestations of environmentalism in businesses (Taylor and Welford 1993; Azzone and Manzini 1994). The methodologies employed were predominantly exploratory and descriptive case studies.

An impressive number of cases describing the environmental, health and safety programmes at various business corporations have been collected by different researchers and management practitioners (Willums 1990, Smart 1992, Willums and Goluke 1992, Hopfenbeck 1992). Some broadly incorporated the notion of strategic management and appeared as 'handbooks' with step-by-step instructions for practitioners (Kinlaw 1993; Welford and Gouldson 1993). All the texts stressed the need for integrated strategic management, yet few specified what this means (Walley and Whitehead 1994).

Corbett and Van Wassenhove's (1993) ongoing research project in INSEAD (France) presents an interesting theoretical discussion of internalising environmental issues within a corporation. They adapted Wood's (1991) framework for corporate social performance and restricted it to corporate environmental performance. The revised framework consists of four major components: environmental issues, the process of corporate environmental responsiveness, principles of corporate environmental responsibilities, and the outcomes of corporate behaviour. The relationship among these components is shown in Figure 2.1.

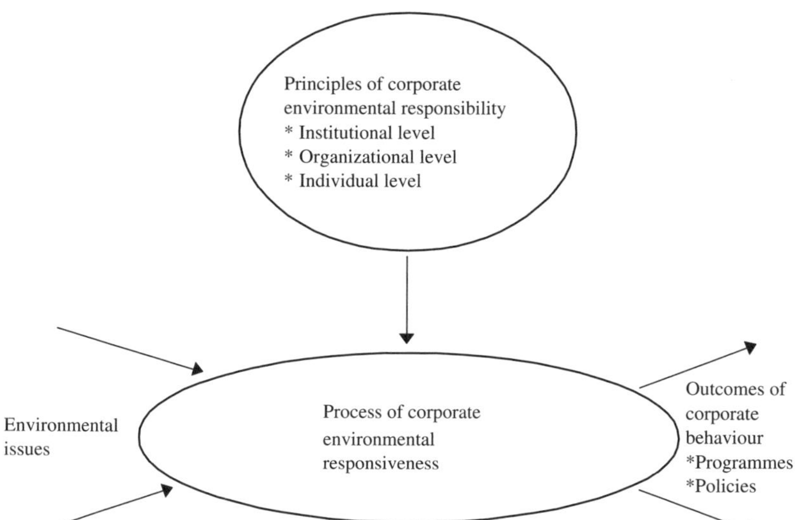

Source: Corbett and Van Wassenhove 1993

Figure 2.1 Corporate environmental performance: a framework

'Precisely how these processes work depends on the specific environmental issues concerned and on the motivation driving the firm to do anything at all.' Three different levels of principles of corporate environmental responsibility were identified, each providing its own motivation to act. At the institutional level, social legitimacy is the main driving force. At the organisational level, public responsibility is the primary driving force. At the individual level, it is managerial discretion that determines how firms act. Corbett and Van Wassenhove argued that whenever a firm takes an environmental action, it is motivated by some combination of these principles. Which principle will dominate, depends on the specific environmental issue, the firm's strategy, its structure, its culture, the people working for it, and the amount of managerial discretion. It should be noted, however, that Corbett and Van Wassenhove devote little attention to the process of corporate environmental responsiveness, especially when compared to the discussions on principles of corporate environmental responsibility and outcomes of corporate behaviour.

2.4 Summary

By assessing previous research, one can easily recognise the urgency of theory building in the field of environmental management and business strategy. This section presents the predominant thinking that a MNC is mighty and all influential; it then proceeds to summarise the past environmental management research on MNC. Four broad areas have been identified:

1. MNCs and the contextual constraints of host countries with the associated issue of pollution transfer
2. Responses of MNCs as manifested in the negotiation with host government and the transfer of technology and skill
3. Globalisation and localisation of MNC operations standards
4. Comparison of MNCs with their developing country counterparts.

The section concludes by reviewing representative research linking greening to the more mainstream management issues.

In the light of the past research effort, this study has been designed with two goals in mind:

- to avoid addressing issues that have been covered in past research or work in progress
- to place equal weight on both theory development and testing.

In Chapter 3, relevant management theories will be examined in constructing an analytical framework.

3
Towards an Analytical Framework

> The point of social contract thinking is not to dig up the historical causes of, say, the Sumerian or Egyptian kingdoms. It is, rather, to clarify the proper moral presuppositions of organisational existence. The strategy is to engage people in a thought-experiment that will utilise reason and intuition in a manner calculated to achieve moral insight. The point of applying social contract reasoning to business is to clarify the moral foundation of productive organisations, of which corporations happen to be one kind.
>
> Donaldson 1989:47

The field of environmental management has an urgent need for definition and theory building, as firmly established and debated in Chapter 2. In response to the greening trend in business, Gladwin (1993) pleaded for the application of organisational theory to clarify this phenomenon. He believed that 'sociological theory pertaining to organisation holds the greatest promise for improving our understanding of how greening works'. To this end, he cited institutional theory as a probable source of 'guidance on the why, how, and when of greening'. Westney (1993:54) supported the adoption of an institutionalisation paradigm for the study of MNC responses, in particular for examining the extent to which MNC behaviour is universally uniform (operating country independent) or locally variable (operating country dependent). Rothenberg and Maxwell (1992) employed institutional theory in their examination of the Volvo Group. In a reply to Mintzberg's (1979:293) statement that popular business trends (in the present case, different manifestations of greening) exert a strong influence on the techniques of corporate management, Rothenberg and

Maxwell offered reasons based on DiMaggio and Powell's (1983) work to account for this phenomenon.

This particular application and adaptation of institutional theory seemed plausible. However, more extended applications of institutional and complementary theories are required for a more complete analysis. Such studies are timely and topical in the light of the long-standing accusation that institutional theorists have, to a certain degree, ignored the fact that organisations may exhibit different responses to environmental issues, and that the role of organisational interpretations and innovation is omitted (Greenwood and Hinings 1993, Penner 1994, Jennings and Zandbergen 1995, Halme 1996). This research proposes an adaptation of Oliver's (1991) model, which combines both institutional- and resource-dependence theories, with the complementary perspectives of strategic choice and bargaining power to explain corporate greening phenomena. The introduction of the model, with due consideration rendered both to SHE protection and to MNCs, provides a means to examine green strategic change from an organisational studies perspective. The respective merits of institutional and complementary theories will be analysed and assimilated in the ensuing sections with the intent of offering a framework for further theory development.

I. Synthesis

3.1 Green strategic change

The interdisciplinary nature of environmental issues and their inseparable links with various facets of society dictate the choice of a systemic paradigm to provide a ground for analysis. Based on Granovetter's (1985) 'embeddedness' theory, systemic theorists propose that the objectives and practices of strategy depend on the particular social system in which strategy-making takes place.

> Strategists often deviate from the profit-maximising norm quite deliberately. Their social background may give them other interests than profit – professional pride, managerial power, or national patriotism perhaps. The pursuit of these different objectives, even at the cost of profit maximisation, is therefore perfectly rational, even if the rationale may often be disguised.
>
> Whittington 1993:4

Granovetter and Whittington's viewpoints echoed the earlier work of Child (1972, 1997) on the strategic choice model, which suggested that specific strategic choices reflect how the dominant coalition perceives environmental constraints in relation to its definition of the organisation's objective. Continuing along this train of thought, Pettigrew (1987:4) stated that:

> The management of strategic change involves consideration of not only the content of a chosen strategy, or even of the analytical process which reveals various content alternatives, but also the management of the process of change, and the context in which it occurs. Two aspects of context are considered: the inner and outer contexts of the firm. 'Inner context' refers to the structure, corporate culture and political context within the firm through which ideas for change have to proceed. Outer context refers to the economic, business, political and societal formations in which firms must operate.

With reference to Pettigrew's (1987) model, this book proposes that strategic change with respect to environmental protection challenges is highly dependent on the 'context', which can be further differentiated into 'outer' and 'inner'. The outer context may include elements such as laws, policies, and law-enforcement mechanisms, whereas the inner context may include economic feasibility and considerations such as corporate attitudes and beliefs.[7] Corporate attitudes and beliefs are collectively a substantive isomer of business ethics and their insertion into the theoretical consideration offers a fresh dimension to strategic environmental management. Business ethics, when completely rid of self-interest, encompass the popular definition of environmental ethics[8] (Sorell and Hendry 1994). It is likely that business ethics hold partial responsibility for the various company-initiated environmental protection programmes.

Institutional and the complementary contextual (or environmental, as commonly referred to) adaptation theories, in the case of green strategic change, appear to be promising in offering a satisfactory explanation. In this research, a distinction is made between two aspects of strategic change undertaken by MNCs:

- strategic change in positioning in response to greening demands
- strategic change in positioning upon entering a new territory, i.e. globalisation versus localisation.

3.2 The greening of business ethics: the 'virtuous' and 'virtual' dimensions

In the preceding section, it was proposed that business ethics can produce company initiatives to protect the environment. It is then perfectly reasonable to inquire what the term 'business ethics' means. Business ethics is a new discipline of academic research that emerged approximately 20 years ago from studies of 'business and society'. Outside academe, the discussion of business ethics can be traced back to Aristotle:

> He argued that goods should be exchanged for their 'real value', their costs, including a 'fair wage' for those who produced them, but then he concluded, mistakenly, that any profit (that is, over and above costs) required some sort of theft (for where else would that 'surplus value' come from).
>
> Solomon 1992

Stakeholder, social contract models, and all-inclusive approach – to ecocentricity

Principles of business ethics can also be derived from Kant and the tradition of ethical egoism (Sorell and Hendry 1994), even though most of the ancient Western philosophers questioned the intrinsic morality of business transactions (e.g. the theses of Immanuel Kant and St Thomas Aquinas, among others). The most influential approach in management studies, however, has been the stakeholder model (Freeman 1984, Freeman and Gilbert 1988, Hosmer 1994). The model states that 'when business interacts with society, a shared interest and interdependence develops between a company and other social groups. When this occurs, corporate stakeholders are created. Stakeholders are all the groups affected by a corporation's decisions, policies, and operations' (Frederick *et al.* 1992). Through this model, a company is held accountable to the non-market factions (or secondary stakeholders) within the society. Local communities, social activist groups, and media all fall within this category. Fineman and Clarke (1996:727) examined the 'greening of management' in four different UK industries – supermarkets, automotives, power generation and chemical production – and concluded that their 'pro-environmental' responses 'are in the main, accounted for by just a few external stakeholders – campaigners[9] and regulators'. Fineman and Clarke (1996:729) further added that

> their influence is acknowledged only if expressed through the language of more 'legitimate' interests (e.g. creditors, customers, regulators) or through the alliances, such as between campaigners and the media. Generally, the environmental 'conscience' of industry is constructed within a small network of self-serving stakeholders.

An integrated approach (other than maximising profit and including effects of corporate ethical reasoning) that answers the concerns of the stakeholders to a certain satisfactory level is, therefore, needed in order to ensure the smooth operation of the company.

Influential as it is, the stakeholder model is not perfect. Donaldson (1989:45) pointed out that the

> stakeholder model has serious problems. The two most obvious are its inability to provide standards for assigning relative weights to the interests of the various constituencies (e.g. regulators and campaigners versus customers and supplies), and its failure to contain within itself, or make reference to, a normative, justificatory foundation.

He proposed instead to use a social contract model (SCM) to account for ethical considerations in business. The SCM views all productive organisations as engaging in an implied contract with society. 'Productive organisations' here refers to the organisations rooted firmly in a moral foundation. A set of reciprocal obligations exists on both sides of the organisation/society divide, and the existence of a productive organisation is justified on moral grounds. For international 'productive' business organisations such as the MNCs, three culture-neutral conditions must be imposed because of the cultural variability of implied constraints:

- That a productive organisation should enhance the long-term welfare of employees and consumers in any society in which the organisation operates.
- That a productive organisation should minimise the drawbacks associated with moving beyond the state of nature to a state containing productive organisations.
- That a productive organisation should refrain from violating minimum standards of justice and of human rights in any society in which it operates.

In studying the competitiveness of the British companies, the Royal Society for the Encouragement of Arts, Manufactures and Commerce launched an inquiry, *Tomorrow's Company*. The RSA report (1995), based on the inquiry's results, clearly embodies an ethical dimension in its advocation of an inclusive approach to business leadership, people, investment need, and society. The case for change in the management approach reflects more 'fundamental' corporate transformation in response to the legitimacy of maintaining a 'licence to operate'. The inquiry cited law/regulation, industry and market standards, industry reputation, media, individual attitudes (customers, suppliers, consumers, employees, investors and community), pressure groups, public opinion/confidence, and political opinion, as the change agents and cautioned that 'a company which undermines its licence to operate by the wrong behaviour exposes itself to a range of sanctions' (RSA 1995:5). The licence to operate is thus closely linked to competitiveness, and an inclusive approach constitutes a plausible new guiding principle for action.

The framework of an inclusive approach for *Tomorrow's Company* (RSA 1995:8):

- defines and communicates its purpose and values
- develops a unique success model and applies it through matching measurements
- places a positive value on each of its relationships
- works in partnership with stakeholders
- maintains a healthy reputation.

The three models described here deal primarily with the issues of business ethics in the traditional sense. Shrivastava (1995) advances the models further to include the 'Earth' as the ultimate stakeholder in his ecocentric management paradigm. Central to this paradigm is the concept of equality between humans and nature. The ecocentric view of the firm calls for a revision of management's basic ideas of organisational objectives and strategy. The new concept of strategy should emphasise co-alignment of an organisation with its environment and 'address the issues of impacts of the firm's activities on the natural and social environment, and it must provide avenues for renewal of environmental resources that the organisation use' (Shrivastava 1995:134). To this end, he proposed seven organisational guiding principles (Shrivastava 1995:131):

- Organisational goals should emphasise sustainability, quality of life, and stakeholder welfare.
- Organisational values should reflect the importance of the central role of Nature as well as the importance of intuition and understanding.
- Organisational products should be designed to be more ecologically sensitive.

- Organisational production systems should use less energy and fewer resources and produce fewer wastes.
- Organisational structures should be less hierarchical, more participative and decentralised, with lower income differentials between managers and the workforce.
- Organisational environment should be interpreted to reflect the finite nature of the Earth's ability to provide energy and resources and to absorb wastes.
- The basic organisational business functions of marketing, finance, accounting, and human resource management should reflect consumer education, long-term ecologically sustainable growth, accounting for full environment costs, and a safe, healthful, and fulfilling work environment.

Definition of corporate ethics

As defined earlier in the chapter, business ethics in the corporate sense (henceforth termed corporate ethics) encompasses corporate culture, attitudes, values and beliefs. Pettigrew (1987:4) believed that the 'inner context consists largely of the structure, culture and politics of an organisation'. Culture, according to him, 'includes the beliefs, meanings and rationales used for legitimate action, together with the languages, codes and rules that inform those actions'. Frederick *et al.* (1992:7) further added that 'the strategy of a business involves basic decisions about its mission, purpose, and reason for being. These are value-laden decisions, affected by the values and ethics of management'. Corporate ethics is a subset of business ethics in the sense that it is narrower in scope. Sorell and Hendry (1994) used the terms *narrow* and *broad* business ethics to distinguish between the two. They also offer a set of definitions, and the relationship between business and corporate ethics is depicted in Figure 3.1.

A code of ethics for a firm is narrow when its provisions concern only those employed in the business or, in addition, only groups who are directly concerned financially, such as shareholders or current customers. By contrast, a code of ethics for a business is broad when it assigns responsibilities not only to all those implicated by a narrow code, but also to the community or society in general, or to the (natural) environment.

Corporate ethics reflects what an organisation considers to be morally and financially sound. Within this framework of thinking, Goodpaster (1991) categorised corporate ethics into the following three types (see also Figure 3.2):

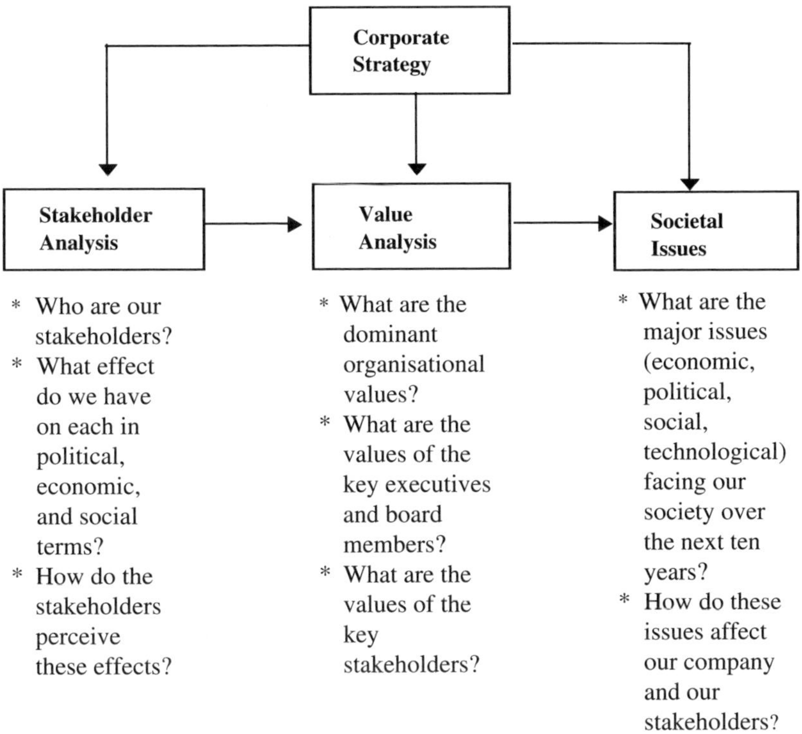

Source: Freeman 1984:92

Figure 3.1 Strategy and social responsiveness

- *Type 1*: Ethics as a guide to self-interest (self-interested rationality) – ethical values are managed solely with an eye to rational self-interest as the overarching value, e.g. 'issues management' and 'public relations'.
- *Type 2*: Ethics as a systemic constraint – ethical norms are incorporated not through the logic of self-interest but through systemic constraints on the choice of business goals. There are two sub-types:
  — Type 2A: The invisible hand pattern (market ethics) – ethical values are already programmed into the business system, making supplementary efforts foolish, even morally suspect.
  — Type 2B: The hand-of-the-law pattern (law ethics) – ethical values are secured through non-economic forces outside the organisation, without direct managerial involvement.

Type 2a: Market ethics	**EXTERNAL**	Type 2b: Law ethics
COMPETITIVE		**CO-OPERATIVE**
Type 1: Self-interested rationality	**INTERNAL**	Type 3: Ethics of respect

Source: Goodpaster 1991:98

Figure 3.2 Depiction of typology in a 2 × 2 matrix

- *Type 3*: Ethics as an authoritative guide (ethic of respect) – managerial accountability for ethics goes hand-in-hand with a recognition of its authority.

Type 3 embraces moral obligation completely, while the rest do so conditionally. Type 1 and 3 are internal (or actor-centred) action guides, while Type 2 is an external (or system-centred) action guide. Type 3 thinking can thus be regarded as true business ethics thinking. It is expected that all four types of corporate mindset are present among the MNCs.

Modes of ethical reasoning

Conflicts often exist in incorporating social factors into strategic change, i.e. policy formation. It is to be expected that if a corporation is profitable and has satisfied the needs of its primary stakeholder to an acceptable degree, as determined by the majority, it is in a position to evaluate its social obligation. The expectation of the society is usually higher than the corporation's willingness to meet that expectation. Hence, there exists a gap of social legitimacy. Environmental laws and policies, together with institutions, are external, but powerful, forces responsible for narrowing the gap. Mylonadis (1993) argued that external values and beliefs, especially with regard to environmental protection, have a significant role in determining the operations of an organisation. For example, some primary stakeholders of the corporation may bear dual roles as members of various institutions, i.e. inter-organisational penetration; this will offer incentives for the corporation to be more socially and environmentally responsible. However, if corruption exists within the institutions and the mindset of the stakeholders is entirely profit-seeking, the gap will widen as there is little motivation for the corporation to behave ethically. A corporation's ethical reasoning may follow the guidelines set forth in Table 3.1.

Ethical reasoning of an inward-looking company is expected to be different from an outward-looking one. The mode of reasoning is also dependent on whether the perspective is local, regional or global (Figure 3.3). For MNCs, the headquarters may be fully outward-looking, while its foreign subsidiaries may be completely inward-looking due to organisational disconnection or autonomous status. The effect of greening on corporate culture and values has aroused disputes among management scholars (Shrivastava 1992, 1995; Throop *et al.* 1993; Sharma and

Table 3.1 Three methods of ethical reasoning

Method	*Critical determining factor*	*An action is ethical when . . .*	*Limitation*
Utilitarian	Comparing benefits and costs	Net benefits exceed net costs	1. Difficult to measure some human and social costs 2. Majority may disregard rights of minority
Rights	Respecting rights	Basic human rights are respected	Difficult to balance conflicting rights
Justice	Distributing fair shares	Benefits and costs are fairly distributed	1. Difficult to measure benefits and costs 2. Lack of agreement on fair shares

Source: Frederick *et al.* 1992:87

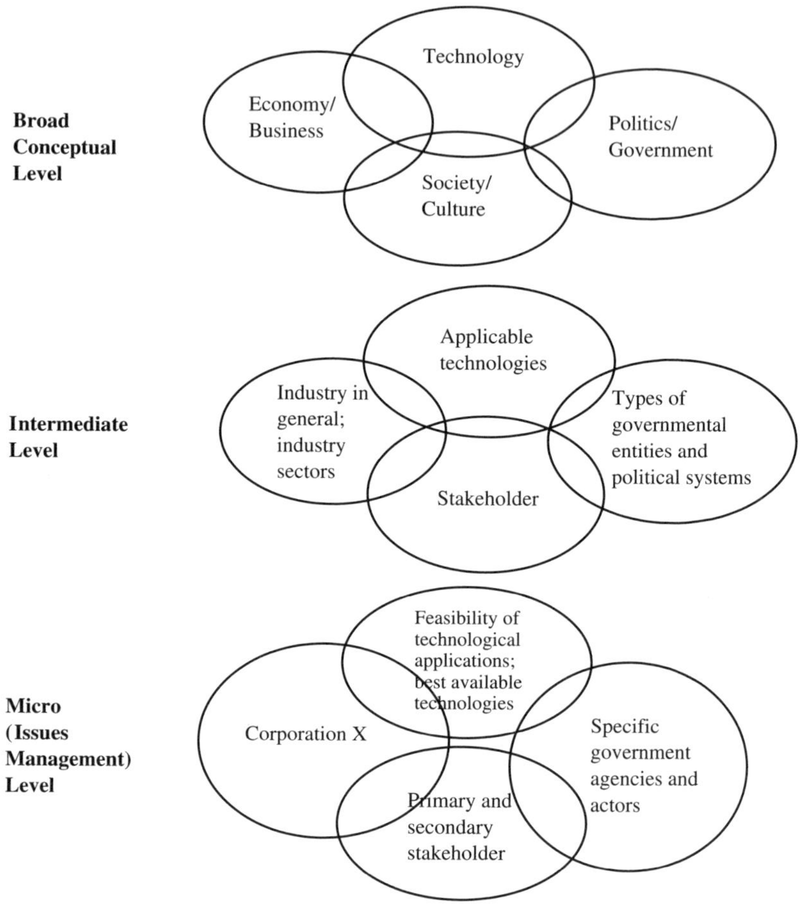

Source: Frederick *et al.* 1992:6

Figure 3.3 A range of levels at which to conceptualise business, institution and society

Vredenburg 1994; Soderbaum 1994; Meima 1995; Welford 1995). Despite this, empirically based studies are rare (Ehrenfeld and Hoffman 1993, Halme 1995).

Business and corporate ethics is a difficult area in which to conduct research. Ethics, which is inherently philosophical, culture-based and paradoxical, deserves far more attention than it receives in the present academic study. Its implications for business management have begun to shed light on further research.[10] The cultural perspective of ethics represents an immense challenge for management scholars. The most widely cited management ethics literature, such as the work of Donaldson (1989), Freeman (1984), and Freeman and Gilbert (1988), have their roots in the western philosophical tradition. Yu's (1987) work on modern religious and commercial ethics in China has led to a substantial following in the Chinese academic community, and proved to be a much-welcome addition to a field lacking cultural diversity. Devotion to business ethics can in itself generate an interesting dissertation. However, for reasons of scope limitation and consistency with the chosen paradigm, business and corporate ethics are treated in this research as an *inner* contextual factor (Pettigrew 1987) and will be accounted for in the following discussion on institutional theory.

3.3 The greening of institutional theory

'Institutional arrangement constrains individual behaviour by rendering some choices unviable, precluding particular courses of action, and restraining certain patterns of resource allocation' (Powell and DiMaggio 1991:10). Gladwin (1993:48) offered a succinct summary of institutional theory with relevance to the green strategic change. 'Institutions', according to the sociological schools, is defined as a collective and regulatory complex consisting of political and social agencies that dominate other organisations through enforcement of laws, rules and norms ('formal rules' and 'informal constraints') (Schenk 1988, North 1990, Powell and DiMaggio 1991, Lu and Lake 1997). Isomorphism[11] with public opinion, educational systems, laws, courts, professions, regulatory structures, awards, and certification and accreditation bodies offers a variety of advantages for organisational survival – for example, greater stability and predictability (DiMaggio 1988), enhanced legitimacy and status (Oliver 1990), greater ease of access to resources (Pfeffer and Salancik 1978), and greater invulnerability to questioning (Meyer and Scott 1983). Greening can thus be viewed as a process of normative conformity and/or external legitimisation.

The impact of organisational conformity on the norms and interests of external bodies has been described by Powell and DiMaggio (1991:13) in terms of the 'shadowland of informal interaction' – influence patterns, coalitions and cliques – both to illustrate how the informal structures deviate from as well as constrain aspects of formal structure, and to demonstrate the subversion of the organisation's intended, rational mission by parochial interests. They also described organisations as 'embedded in local communities, to which they are tied by the multiple loyalties of personnel and by inter-organisational treaties ['co-optation'] hammered out in face-to-face interaction'. The institutional pressures thus encourage organisations to mimic successful examples as well as to 'enhance their legitimacy' (Gladwin 1993).

Institutional isomorphism

Coercive, normative and mimetic isomorphism (DiMaggio and Powell 1983) can be observed in a corporation's effort to protect the environment and improve its occupational health and safety records. Isomorphism to greater public environmental awareness, rapid promulgation of environmental regulations, and increasing demands from environmental pressure groups, *impose, authorise* and *induce* corporations to institute sets of measures to protect the environment. This can be considered an effect of outer or 'exogenous' pull (Lu and Lake 1997). By the same token, corporations also experience inner or 'endogenous' pull to be isomorphic and to *acquire, incorporate* or *bypass* their internal environmental policies and expectations (Scott and Meyer 1989, Westney 1993). The trend of green strategic change, which usually commences in a particular industrial sector (e.g. chemical production) and spreads first among the competitors, is a form of normative conformity and mimicry.[12] For example, Du Pont, which has long been recognised by governments and environmental professionals as a leader in industrial and occupational safety, often found itself in a position to establish industrial standards for others, including its competitors, to follow. In extreme cases, securing the legitimacy to remain in business may largely depend upon a corporation's ability to conform to the superior environmental standards implemented by such leading edge companies. In developing countries, where environmental protection is in the budding stage, governments frequently utilises large, reputable corporations such as Dow Chemicals, ICI and Du Pont's codes of environmental protection conduct as examples on which to base regulation (Tsai and Child 1997). This propagates the belief in mimicry and normative conformity even further. Government attitudes also induce mimicry among competitors in the same industrial sector, which can be viewed as an attempt to gain greater social legitimacy.

Supplementing the attention given to the external entities, North (1990), DiMaggio and Powell (1991), Greenwood and Hinings (1993) focused on internal elements such as shared beliefs, as exemplified by corporate culture and values (or mental models), of the organisations. North (1990) proposed that institutions, organisations and the 'mental models of actors', i.e. managers in a company, interact to produce institutional change. The mental model of the actors, having been conditioned by the complexity of the environment, by the limited feedback from the consequences of actions, and by the inherited cultural bias of the players, determines the perceptions, which in turn determine the strategic choice (Halme 1996). The sources of change, according to Halme (1996:97):

> are the opportunities perceived by decision makers. They stem from either external changes in the environment, or the acquisition of learning and skills and their incorporation in the mental constructs of the actors. The acquisition of learning and skills will lead to the construction of new mental models by decision makers to decipher the environment.

Even though different actors, or managers, may hold varying degrees of perception, there is a set of fundamental corporate values, that may be the belief that 'being green is good for business', that managers adhere to (Pfeffer 1981, Donaldson and Lorch 1983, Shrivastava and Schneider 1984, Spybey 1984, Etzioni 1988, Johnson 1992, Schein 1992).

3.4 The addition of resource dependency theory

Institutional theory instils a sense of passivity into the phenomenon of greening. It appears as if, without institutional rules, norms or values, there could be no strategic change. It is altogether a non-choice behaviour, since in order to be a legitimate member of the society, conformity to all institutional conditions is expected. Institutional theory has increasingly been 'criticised for its lack of attention to the role of organisational self-interest and active agency in organisational responses to institutional pressures and expectations' (Perrow 1985, Powell 1985, Covaleski and Dirsmith 1988, DiMaggio 1988, Oliver 1991). Oliver (1991:1) argued for a combination of the resource dependence and institutional perspectives, and further proposed that 'institutional theory can accommodate interest-seeking, active organisational behaviour when organisations' responses to institutional pressures and expectations are not assumed to be invariably passive and conforming across all institutional conditions'.

Convergence and divergence

Sociologists have increasingly portrayed institutional theory as complementary to the paradigm of resource dependency (Pfeffer and Salancik

1978, Westney 1993). In parallel with Pettigrew's (1987) model, Oliver (1991) presented her thesis first by analysing the 'context' and 'motive' of organisational behaviour using the convergent and divergent perspectives of institutional and resource dependency theories. With respect to 'context', institutional and resource dependency theories converge to the following assumptions:

- Organisational choice is limited by various external pressures (Pfeffer and Salancik 1978, Friedland and Alford 1987, Meyer and Rowan 1992).
- Organisational environments are collective and interconnected (Pfeffer and Salancik 1978, DiMaggio and Powell 1983, Powell 1988).
- Organisations must be responsive to the external environment in order to survive (Meyer and Rowan 1977, Pfeffer and Salancik 1978).
- Organisations seek stability and predictability (Oliver 1991).

Resource dependency theory diverges from institutional theory in its focus on the task environment rather than on the institutional environment (Pfeffer and Salancik 1978). It also tends to emphasise environmental uncertainty rather than the certainties associated with a strong external normative order. Another contrast lies in resource dependency theory's emphasis on proaction designed to cope with dependencies on the external providers of key resources, which are problematical because they furnish those resource providers with levers with which to control the organisation (Thompson 1967, Pfeffer and Salancik 1978, Scott 1987, Oliver 1991). This is a significant departure from contemporary institutional theory's failure to recognise proactive organisational behaviour, and its emphasis on conformity for survival, isomorphism, and on adherence to norms and values as an act of organisational continuity. For institutional theorists, organisational behaviour is driven by 'preconscious acceptance of institutionalised values or practices and not by processes of interest mobilisation' (DiMaggio 1988). Moreover, new institutitonalists fail to acknowledge the ability of a leading 'institution', such as Du Pont when regarding safety standards, to shape or build the institutional norms and standards, and, in turn, profit from this form of 'proactivity' in raising the expectation of stakeholders. This ultimately changes the competitive dynamic of the market and threatens the survival of the non-conformers. The 'interest seeking' behaviour could create further profit financially from its norm-setting practices and programmes by the institution offering training courses and consulting services.

In assessing 'motives' for organisational behaviour, both theories converge to the assumptions that organisations are interest-driven and keen on seeking legitimacy and stability (Dowling and Pfeffer 1975, Pfeffer and Salancik 1978, DiMaggio and Powell 1983, Meyer and Scott 1983, Zucker 1986, DiMaggio 1988, Oliver 1991). However, for institutional theorists, interests tend to be socially and institutionally defined rather than politically calculated (Scott 1987, Hinings and Greenwood 1988, Oliver 1991). The advantages of conformity for the sake of self-interest are manifold, and include 'increased prestige, legitimacy, social support, internal and external commitment, access to resources, attraction of personnel, fit into administrative categories, acceptance in professions, and invulnerability to questioning' (Oliver 1991). Resource dependency theorists, on the other hand, have focused on resource mobilisation and strategising to 'alter the situation confronting the organisation to make compliance less necessary' (Pfeffer 1982).

Institutional and resource dependency theories complement each other in their description of existing environmental management practices. In seeking social legitimacy, a corporation will abide by all essential environmental regulations, be they formal, such as environmental laws, or informal, as in the case of non-governmental organisations' (NGOs) environmental protection demands. However, in compliance, various cost-saving strategies may be used. This is evident in the petrochemical industry's waste minimisation programme (e.g. Dow Chemicals' Waste Reduction Always Pays Programme (WRAP)), whereby technical experts were consulted to minimise or recycle waste in each stage of the production cycle. For Dow:

> WRAP is carrying a 55 percent return of investment (compliance) for 1992 . . . Working alone as a company, or an industry, or a nation, acting only in response to external pressures, we can be seen as self-serving and defensive. But if we have the courage voluntarily to mandate for ourselves global environmental standards, then I think we will get well ahead.
>
> Avila and Whitehead 1993

Porter and Linde (1995) further add that tough environmental regulations (a form of institution) force companies to be more innovative in all aspects of their operations, i.e. in pursuit of greater resource productivity, while aiming to reduce the cost of compliance.

Despite acknowledgement by resource dependence theorists that organisations may mobilise resources to counteract external dependencies, it is the case that both institutional and resource dependence perspectives tend to assume an asymmetry of power between organisations and environmental bodies. Modern institutionalism (Powell and DiMaggio 1991) highlights ways in which external structures are mapped onto organisational forms, and external norms and regulations are reflected by organisational practices. The main focus of the resource dependence perspective is on the power which the external providers of financial, technical and other resources thereby enjoy over the policies and on the conduct of the organisations they service (Pfeffer and Salancik 1978). It is true that 'old institutional theory' did take account of political initiatives by organisational leaders, such as the successful lobbying and co-option strategies of the Tennessee Valley Authority (Selznick 1949). It is also the case that Pfeffer and Salancik recognise there may be some scope for organisational managers to exercise a degree of strategic choice in negotiation with external resource providers, a possibility to which Pfeffer gives rather more attention in recent writing (Pfeffer 1992). Nevertheless, the availability of proactive options to organisational leaders in their dealings with environmental bodies is generally underdeveloped within the two perspectives.

Complementary theories – the need for 'proactive' perspectives

It is here that a contribution is made by two further theoretical perspectives which more explicitly draw attention to the need for inclusion of proactive as well as reactive options among the range of strategic responses to external demands. These are the 'bargaining power' and 'strategic choice' perspectives. The 'bargaining power' perspective can be regarded as a strategic response to institutional pressure and was advanced as a modification to resource dependence theory. It has been developed with particular reference to the assumption that resource provision, especially that of capital, necessarily furnishes a basis for control over the policies of the receiving organisation. It suggests instead that the control implications of resource dependence may be mediated by the bargaining powers and skills of an organisation's management. The bargaining power perspective posits that management can negotiate to obtain a more favourable agreement with resource providers on the basis both of the assets that it commands and the 'general trends' that may be in its favour (Blodgett 1991). The assets at its command could include 'softer' items, such as technical expertise, while favourable general trends might include the support of public opinion for the pursuit of environmentally friendly policies, even though these are at the expense of returns to external stakeholders in the short term at least.

Hence, the bargaining power perspective warns against an assumption that the impact of resource dependence is entirely deterministic.

The strategic choice perspective draws attention to a more general range of proactive strategies that organisational leaders may be in a position to adopt *vis-à-vis* their environments. These include two main possibilities: first, that organisational leaders can select the environments in which their organisations will operate (sectors, markets and countries); second, that within the selected environments they may have some scope to negotiate and agree accommodations with external institutions and resource providers. These are the possibilities for exercising 'strategic choice' (Child 1972, 1997).

The strategic choice perspective accepts that environments have properties that cannot simply be enacted or negotiated by organisational actors. This lends considerable importance to the question of whether they can select an attractive environment in which to operate. Organisational leaders may, for example, consider an attractive environment to be one in which social or political pressures are not as extreme as elsewhere. Strategic choice analysis also recognises that it may be possible to accommodate at least some external expectations through personal interaction between organisational actors and their external counterparts. In other words, it sees key organisational actors as seeking to realise their goals both through selection *between* environments, and through seeking accommodation and co-operation with groups *within* given environments.

The possibility of co-operation between organisations and external parties is given rather little attention in the institutional and resource dependence perspectives. Both imply that the leaders of organisations come under pressure to comply with external demands, and hence that the relationship may be one of antagonism and even resentment rather than one of positive co-operation. The 'prisoners' dilemma' theorem (Axelrod 1984) reminds us that two parties in a relationship will often better secure their objectives in the long term through co-operation than by attempting to maximise short-term gains at the expense of the other party. Thus, the aspirations of environmental policy may be more effectively met through co-operation between regulatory agencies and enterprises, especially when the latter are, as a result, willing to contribute their technological expertise to the attainment of environmental goals, and at the same time the enterprises are better able to realise their business objectives in the absence of legal distractions and with the aid of a more measured timetable for the introduction of environmental improvements. Co-operation therefore needs to be included within the range of possible strategic responses to external expectations.

3.5 The greening of strategic responses

This section addresses strategic responses with respect to environmental/contextual constraints. Oliver (1991) presented an exhaustive set of strategic responses based on the assimilation of institutional and resource dependency theories:

A. Acquiesce – Habit (following invisible, taken-for-granted norms)
Imitate (mimicking institutional model)
Comply (obeying rules and accepting norms)
B. Compromise – Balance (balancing the expectations of multiple constituents) Pacify (placating and accommodating institutional elements)
Bargain (negotiating with institutional stakeholders)
C. Avoid – Conceal (disguising nonconformity)
Buffer (loosening institutional attachments)
Escape (changing goals, activities, or domains)
D. Defy – Dismiss (ignoring explicit norms and values)
Challenge (contesting rules and requirements)
Attack (assaulting the sources of institutional pressure)
E. Manipulate – Co-opt (importing influential constituents)
Influence (shaping values and criteria)
Control (dominating institutional constituents and processes)

Oliver's scheme does not, however, include the co-operative strategic response to which we just drew attention. This might be added as option F in her scheme, and involves joint problem solving, and even a willingness to integrate objectives, as indicative behaviours. As we shall note in Table 3.3 below, Kirchgeorg (1993) includes co-operation as a form of implementing an environmental strategy designed to achieve adaptation.

Oliver's (1991) strategic response model was developed as a part of theory development without explicit intent for any specific application other than to classify broadly the probable reactions of organisations to institutional demands. The preceding sections of this book have argued that the greening phenomenon is brought about by the contextual pulls of various institutions. Greening strategies, in this book, refer to the strategies enabling a company to achieve a set of well-defined objectives, usually to increase resource productivity (Porter and Linde 1995), while at the same time being environmentally friendly. Greening strategy is thus a form of business strategy. Given the similar contexts, a business strategic response should approximate a green strategic response. The adoption of the model to illustrate green strategic responses is hence plausible but may require field verification. Nevertheless, if institutional and resource dependency theories address the phenomenon of green strategic change in a satisfactory manner, the model should predict green strategic responses with a high degree of accuracy. A review of the existing environmental management literature could furnish an indication of the integrity of the model.

Organisational strategic options in the environmental literature

The work of Porter (1985) (focus, overall cost leader, differentiation) and Miles and Snow (1984) (prospectors, defenders, analysers, reactors) have greatly influenced the system of business strategy classification. In the field of environmental management, Hass (1996) advocated a classification scheme of strategic typology models[13] based on their underlying structure: (a) stages along a type of continuum/progression or (b) categorical.

The continuum/progression models. Using various criteria, the continuum/progression models evaluated response/attitude/postures of companies along a time line which is characterised by distinctive stages. For instance, the Greeno (1991) (or A. D. Little) model assessed companies based on: (a) primary purpose, (b) primary motivation, and (c) vulnerability to environmental issues. The Newman (1993) (or Booz•Allen and Hamilton) model used only two criteria: (a) view of risk management and (b) view of opportunities. Hunt and Auster (1990) adopted four main evaluative criteria: (a) degree to which programme reduces environmental risk, (b) commitment of organisation, (c) programme design, and (d) involvement with legal counsel, public relations, manufacturing/production and product design. Roome (1992) differed from the aforementioned models by using 'standards of compliance with legal requirements and responses to social pressures' in the first three stages of his model and then added 'operating to standards of managerial excellence and state-of-the-art environmental management, as practised by the leading edge companies in their sectors' in his last two stages. The resultant typologies are presented in Table 3.2. A major flaw of this system of classification is the difficulty and the ambiguity in assigning stages to companies in a continuous time frame with respect to different criteria, and aggregation of these evaluations (Hass 1996).

Table 3.2 Selected continuum environmental management strategy model typologies

Source	*Model stages or categories*				
Hunt and Auster (1990:9)	Stage 1 'Beginner'	Stage 2 'Fire fighter'	Stage 3 'Concerned citizen'	Stage 4 'Pragmatist'	Stage 5 'Proactivist'
Greeno (1991:17)	Stage 1 Problem solving	Stage 2 Managing for compliance		Stage 3 Managing for assurance	
Newman (1993:32)	Reactive	Proactive		Innovative	
Roome (1992:18)	Non-compliance	Compliance	Compliance plus	Commercial and environmental excellence	Leading edge

Source: Hass 1996: 61

The categorical models. The categorical models operate under the assumption that: (a) a rating process along the specified dimensions is possible, and (b) the dimensions which define the axes will differentiate between the companies (Hass 1996). Steger (1993), using a company's potential for market opportunities resulting from an environmental protection stance and the level of environmental risk inherent in a company's activities, produced a theoretical typology of four possible generic strategies – offensive, innovative, indifferent and defensive. This strategic typology was derived from the 1991 Forschungsgruppe Umweltorientierte Unternehmensführung (FUUF) study of 592 German companies of all sizes in all branches of industry, including service, trading, financial service and manufacturing. Rondinelli and Vastag (1996) in their study of international environmental standards, such as ISO 14000 and the European Union's Eco-Management and Audit Scheme (EMAS), employed two dimensions of endogenous[14] and exogenous[15] environmental risks to classify companies into the following categories: proactive, strategic, reactive and crisis prevention. Schot's model (1992), which is empirically based, used the following classification criteria: (a) general response/attitude to regulations (specifically emission), (b) top management support of environmental policy and its implementation, and (c) approach towards environmental problems, i.e. external/internal, technical/organisational, problem/search for solution. Five management strategies – dependent, defensive, offensive, innovative, and niche – emerged as a result. Kirchgeorg's (1993) empirical study examined environmental 'strategy alternatives' and how companies select them. He suggested five different strategy alternatives:

- Innovation (Innovation)
- Adaptation (Anpassung)
- Retreat (Rückzug)
- Passivity (Passivität)
- Resistance (Widerstand).

Five criteria – organisational and strategic objectives, intensity of environmental adjustment, time of strategy development/realisation of measures, type of strategy development, and accomplishment of strategies/form of implementation – were devised to categorise companies into one of the five strategic alternatives (Table 3.3).

Kirchgeorg (1993) then surveyed 197 companies in eight industries and identified four homogeneous clusters – selective environmental-orientation (20%), passive (30%), internally oriented active (27%), environmentally oriented innovators (23%) – based on the five strategy alternatives.

The categorical approach suffered from the 'impossibility' of being exhaustive and mutually exclusive in its classification (Bailey 1994). Schot (1992) noted that it was difficult to place companies into categories because elements of different strategies exist in different combinations or companies were in transition between two categories. Notwithstanding the pros and cons of both schemes, it is felt that the management strategy models advanced by various researchers, either based on pure conceptual exercises or derived with empirical data, bear a striking resemblance to Oliver's (1991) 'strategic response model'. This gives strong support to the view that a combination of institutional, resource dependence, strategic choice and bargaining power perspective offers a relevant framework for understanding the phenomenon of green strategic change and the policies adopted by firms towards it. This framework draws primarily from Oliver's (1991) model with two modifications. First, the need to take account of proactive as well as reactive strategies. Second, the need to include co-operation as a further strategic response.

II. Derivation

3.6 Application to MNCs

The credibility of Oliver's (1991) model has been established through comparison with other green strategic models. Applying Oliver's (1991) model to account for the behaviour of MNCs can be equally feasible

Table 3.3 Kirchgeorg's five environmental strategies and his criteria

Strategy characteristics	*Kirchgeorg's environmental strategies*					
Criterion	*Resistance*	*Passivity*	*Retreat*	*Adaptation*	*Innovation*	*Examples*
Strategy objectives	Market/society (external)	NA	Company (market)	Company (market)	Company/ market/ society	Internal: focus on the company External: additional focus on other marketers
Intensity of environmental adjustment	Passive	Passive	Adaptive	Adaptive	Innovative	Passive: no long-term environmental strategies and no realisation on operative level Active: own initiative
Time of strategy development/ realisation of measures	Mainly reactive	NA	Normally reactive	Reactive	Proactive	Reactive: environment only taken into account when company is directly affected Proactive: acting after recognising first signals
Type of strategy development	Isolated	NA	Isolated	Isolated	Integrated	Isolated: partial approach limited on some products or divisions Integrated: total, coherent for whole company
Accomplishment of strategies/form of implementation	Normally co-operative	NA	Individual	Individual/ co-operative	Individual	Individual: strategy implemented only in the company Co-operative: joint-initiatives

and can provide a welcome interpretation to an area, i.e. the greening of international businesses, which is in need of further theorising. Gladwin (1993) advocated an institutional theory-based model to answer why MNCs go green at different rates and in different forms within different countries. The observation is interpreted as a form of 'structural isomorphism between structures of states and organisations operating under their jurisdiction' (Carroll *et al.* 1990; Gladwin 1993). The host countries may exhibit a rather confusing and contradictory 'love-hate' behaviour in their dealings with MNCs. Most governments in developing countries welcome foreign direct investments for the potential economic gains and technology transfer. However, 'the extent to which an (MNC) is willing to transfer environmental-related practices to another country, and how far it is prepared to adapt these practices to meet the particular needs of that country, depends on what is required of the foreign subsidiary as well as on the costs and benefits involved' (Dunning 1993:541). On the other hand, since MNCs represent 'foreignness', governments often watch and supervise with extreme vigilance (Lu and Lake 1997). In China, the demand for MNCs to be in compliance with environmental regulations is exceedingly strong, as evident in the regulatory agencies' requirements for more than sporadic environmental inspection. Certain policies, such as the import chemical tax, were targeted at MNCs and other foreign investors. The Chinese government granted MNCs a fair amount of bargaining power in siting their manufacturing plants, while simultaneously imposing a set of more stringent environmental standards than the ones observed by Chinese state-owned enterprises of similar sizes and operations (Tsai and Child 1997).

From Rappaport and Flaherty's (1992) findings,[16] MNCs appeared to share similar behaviour traits with national corporations. Key elements in Oliver's (1991) model, such as active choice behaviour, isomorphism with respect to national systems, normative conformity, and organisational mimicry with the ultimate motive of seeking greater social legitimacy can readily be observed. Despite the similarities, MNCs face greater challenges in conforming to unfamiliar foreign environmental laws, professional values and social norms. In China, the inconsistency of law enforcement among the coastal and inland provinces often surprises the MNCs. The poorer inland provinces are more than willing to sacrifice environmental well-being for greater material wealth. Consequently, the effort undertaken by the MNCs to protect the state of the environment is perceived to be 'unnecessary, too costly and an unacceptable form of extra-territoriality' (Dunning 1993:538, Tsai and Child

1997). The absence of a certain infrastructure in the 'host' country also limits the choice of strategic responses. The presence of great uncertainty thus forces the MNCs to place prime attention on risk aversion (Miller and Quinn 1993).

Universalistic and particularistic standards – a cyclic relationship

The same MNC in different countries is likely to exhibit similar strategic responses *vis-à-vis* identical environmental issues. Most big MNCs possess a set of internal global, i.e. universalistic, environmental standards for process design, waste treatment and disposal and take much pride in implementing them in different countries. The slogan for most is: 'we will use the more stringent environmental standards'. It is indeed true that the adopted global environmental standards for a large, reputable MNC, in most cases, exceed the ones in a developing 'host' country. The difficulty comes when the universalistic standards are unachievable in a certain country, due to the absence of appropriate technology. Dow Chemicals may be setting an industrial standard by building an incinerator for hazardous waste treatment in its Thailand plant (Avila and Whitehead 1993), but not every MNC is willing to imitate it. Mimicry by the competitors as a function of normative conformity can prove to be extremely expensive. MNCs in China were routinely asked to lay their own pipelines for wastewater discharge and/or to contribute towards building a waste water treatment for the local community in addition to their own in-house pre-treatment facilities. Such inadequacy in the host country's infrastractural support creates unexpected burdens in MNCs' corporate headquarters. The inability to discharge a certain amount of hazardous process waste water calls for process re-design and hence increases the budget for research and development.

The exercise is not entirely without benefit because a thorough examination of the current production cycle may reveal excessive commitment of resources and aid in capturing re-cyclable wastes. Thus, non-passive conformity to environmental regulations, as opposed to paying fines or halting production of a certain product, can be self-interest serving. Porter (1991) has argued that

> the conflict between environmental protection and economic competitiveness is a false dichotomy. It stems from a narrow view of the sources of prosperity and a static view of competition.

It is observed that though stringent and consistent with the universalistic standards, the content of MNCs' environmental programmes

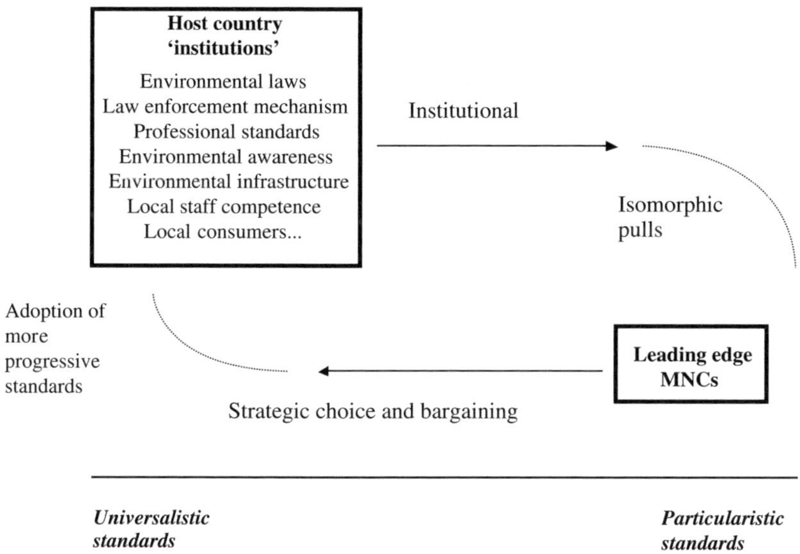

Figure 3.4 The cyclic relationship of universalistic and particularistic standards[17]

differ slightly from one country to another, and these particularistic standards are attributable to different institutional environments.[17] In certain cases the particularistic standards are more advanced and progressive due to the innovation that originates in the local subsidiaries as a response to the different institutional pressures (Tsai and Child 1997).

Different institutional climates spur innovation, and innovation often results in greater resource productivity (Porter and Linde 1995). In an age when MNCs are in intense pursuit of competitive advantage, advances made in achieving greater resource productivity through environmental protection measures certainly enhance the corporation's ability to compete. The particularistic standards implemented in one subsidiary can rapidly be adopted as universalistic standards, after a feasibility evaluation is performed by the corporation's environmental professionals (see Figure 3.4). This form of cyclic dynamic is commonly found in leading edge MNCs that conduct business operations in developing countries, where the institutional demands are unfamiliar and unpredictable.

An example of strategic response typology – regulations in a developing country

Environmental regulations are major institutions that exert isomorphic pulls on MNCs. Environmental law- and policy-making is a fairly recent phenomenon. The first major international convention[18] was presented in 1940 and came into force in 1942 (Sands 1993). However, by 1989, the United Nations Environment Programme (UNEP) Register of International Treaties and other agreements already had 140 entries, and they can roughly be classified into three categories: (a) conventions on transboundary pollution, (b) conventions on resources shared between two or more states in a region, and (c) conventions on the use of resources of the 'global common' (North 1992). Table 3.4 presents a selection of agreements relevant to international business managers.

With constant improvements in transportation and telecommunication technology, the influence of international laws can be far reaching. The United Nations (1993:36–37) advised MNCs to 'follow, as a matter of practice, developments in international environmental law at the global and regional levels, in addition to those in respect of the national legislation of the relevant home and host states'.[19] Such developments, according to the UN, can have a 'direct impact on foreign direct investment decisions, including siting decisions and regulatory compliance (through increasingly stringent environmental impact assessment requirements), and environmental conditions attached to public and private project finance)'. In particular, that may affect 'the costs of production (through the imposition of environmental taxes and other fiscal and economic instruments), the removal of certain national subsidies, the adoption of a preventative approach and cleaner production techniques, and compliance with increasingly stringent natural resource standards'.

In addition to the challenges posed by international environmental laws and policies, the differences in environmental quality regulations between countries are becoming problematic for international business managers. North (1992:23) observed that

> companies from industrialised countries will have to decide (or will be forced to decide by the Green movement) if they want to build their profitability on the comparative advantage of lower environmental standards in developing countries. Companies from developing countries might find an increasing number of trade barriers as their products do not meet the rigid environmental standards of industrialised countries. Recycling regulations may force producers

Table 3.4 Selected international agreements in the field of the environment

General environmental concerns
- Stockholm Declaration (1972) *Non-binding*
- UNEP Principles of Conduct in the Field of the Environment for the Guidance of States in the Conservation and Harmonious Utilisation of Natural Resources Shared by Two or More States (Nairobi, 19 May 1978)
- UNEP Goals and Principles of Environment Impact Assessment (Nairobi, 17 June 1987)
- Convention on Environmental Impact Assessment in a Transboundary Context (Espoo, 25 February 1991)
- Treaty on European Union (Maastrict, 17 February 1992)
- North America Free Trade Agreement (Washington, Ottawa and Mexico City, 8, 11, 14, 17 December 1992)
- Agenda 21 (Rio de Janeiro, 1992) *Non-binding*
- Rio Declaration on Environment and Development (Rio de Janeiro, 1992) *Non-binding*

Nature and living resources
- International Convention for the Regulation of Whaling (Washington, 2 December 1946) as amended
- Convention on International Trade in Endangered Species of Wild Fauna and Flora (Washington, 3 March 1973) as amended
- International Tropical Timber Agreement (Geneva, 18 November 1983)
- Convention on Biological Diversity (Rio de Janeiro, 5 June 1992)

Atmosphere
- United Nations/ECE regulations concerning gaseous pollutant emissions from motor vehicles, pursuant to the 1958 agreement concerning the Adoption of Uniform Conditions of Approval and Reciprocal Recognition of Approval for Motor Vehicle Equipment and Parts (Geneva, 1 August 1970, as amended and supplemented in 1991)
- Convention on Long-range Transboundary Air Pollution (Geneva, 13 November 1979)
- Vienna Convention for the Protection of the Ozone Layer (Vienna, 22 March 1985), and Montreal Protocol (16 September 1987)
- United Nations Framework Convention on Climate Change (New York, 9 May 1992)

Hazardous substances and processes
- European Agreement Concerning the International Carriage of Dangerous Goods by Road (Geneva, 30 September 1957) as amended
- Vienna Convention on Civil Liability for Nuclear Damage (Vienna, 21 May 1963) and related protocol
- European Agreement on the Restriction of the Use of Certain Detergents in Washing and Cleaning Products (Strasbourg, 16 September 1968)
- OECD Procedures and Requirements for Anticipating the Effects of Chemicals on Man and in the Environment (Paris, 7 July 1977)
- OECD Decisions on the Mutual Acceptance of Data in the Assessment of Chemicals (Paris, 12 May 1981) and related recommendations
- FAO International Code of Conduct on the Distribution and Use of Pesticides (Rome, 19 November 1985) as amended
- UNEP London Guidelines for the Exchange of Information on Chemicals in International Trade (Nairobi, 17 June 1987) as amended
- UNEP Cairo Guidelines and Principles for the Environmentally Sound Management of Hazardous Wastes (Nairobi, 17 June 1987)
- Basel Convention on the Control of Transboundary Movements of Hazardous Wastes and their Disposal (Basel, 22 March 1989)
- UN/ECE Convention on the Transboundary Effects of Industrial Accidents (Helsinki, 17 March 1992)

Source: North, 1992:23–4; Sands, 1993:248–51

to take used products back and dispose of them in their country of origin. Product liability regulations vary greatly from country to country. Products which are banned in one country, such as pesticides, are still allowed in other countries. In addition, a producer may be liable for future damage caused by a product considered 'harmless' today.

In countries with more advanced legal systems, open dialogue usually exists between regulatory and regulated communities. Moreover, there is a constant exchange of environmental legal expertise between the two communities, as a natural result of 'demand and supply' in the employment market. The interaction can be explained by two popular models of law- and policy-making: technology-based (also known as command-and-control (CAC)) and market-based. 'Polluter pays' principles have become intrinsic to both models (OECD 1975).

CAC and market-based models. According to Dudek *et al.* (1993), the CAC model relies on uniform, inflexible, technology-based standards issued by the central government.[20] The acronyms BAT (best available technology) and BACT (best available control technology) are firmly rooted in US practices (Porter and Linde 1995). The use of this model results in high compliance costs, restricts innovation, and discourages efficient use of resources. However, for the regulated community, the CAC model has the advantage of saving time and effort in alternative pollution abatement proposals and technology evaluations. For the regulatory community, the CAC model leaves little ambiguity regarding compliance and requires less manpower to administer. The market-based model, on the other hand, emphasises environmental performance, leaving the choice of specific response and compliance strategies to each individual enterprise (Dudek *et al.* 1993). The regulated community often favours the market-based model for its implied reduction in compliance costs. As for the regulatory community, the model removes the burden of identifying and authorising the best available control technology.

Four principal types of market-based environmental protection instruments are in existence. Subsidies, usually from government, provide incentives for environmentally positive activities. Taxes, such as resource-depletion taxes, and charges, such as effluent/emission and input charges, if set at a right level and administered properly, discourage undesirable behaviour. Tradable pollution permits make environmentally damaging activities illegal without a specially created right, which must be bought and can then be traded. Refundable deposits reward environmental care by returning deposits and penalise damage by confiscating it. All these instruments have been implemented with much success, except tradable pollution permits, which have been controversial. Such permits might allow very high discharges in some places, compensated by very low emission elsewhere, which will often be unacceptable; to be effective, permits have to operate with 'backstop' regulations setting maximum discharge rates (Jacobs 1991; Cairncross 1995).

The CAC and market-based models entice different strategic responses from MNCs. In a developing country, however, there exists another hindrance in the choice of strategic response – the ambiguity and the fast-changing nature of environmental laws and regulations. In addition, market-based models, even if implemented, are almost invariably destined to failure due to the low experiential level of the regulatory community. In China, environmental law enforcers often lack the necessary technical knowledge to handle the actual implementation of newly enacted laws and rely from time to time on leading-edge MNCs to provide environmental protection training classes and render expert advice on environmental health and safety. The communication 'break down' between the central and local governments complicates matters further.

Strategic response typology. Figure 3.5 provides a strategic response typology of leading edge MNCs in the Greater China region. Depending on the regulation category, CAC or market-based, and the enforcement level by the host governments, the responses can be quite varied. A *defiance* response is sometimes chosen if the regulations are taken out of context from a set of comprehensive US or European environmental regulations and deemed unsuitable for the situation in the host countries, for example, the requirement for lab-certified chemical analysis results when the lab certification practice is absent, and the inappropriate use of modelling parameters without considering country-specific climatic and geographic factors. In response to the recently instituted chemical registry tax, fashioned after US's TOSCA laws but without implementation details or a grace period, a group of reputable MNCs in China chose to challenge the authorities.

The *manipulation* strategy to influence law making and attract a favourable interpretation of mandates is rendered redundant in most tightly controlled countries; public participation in legislation is unheard of and not solicited, even if the intention is to recommend adopting more progressive standards. Since leading edge MNCs operate

	Regulation High	**Regulation** Low
CAC model	**Acquiesce** Habit Imitate Comply **Defy** Dismiss Challenge Attack **Manipulate** (Possible but rarely)	**Manipulate** Co-opt Influence Control
Market-based model	**Acquiesce** Habit Imitate Comply **Compromise** Balance Pacify Bargain Buffer **Manipulate** (Possible but rarely) **Co-operate**	**Compromise** Balance Pacify Bargain Buffer

Figure 3.5 Strategic response typology – environmental regulations in the Greater China region

under a set of progressive universalistic standards, they would certainly like to ensure that the local companies abide by the same standards on the grounds of fair competition. Leading edge MNCs may choose to *compromise* if (within the scope of the law) they foresee no unpleasant consequences as a result of this action. In the case of Chinese chemical registry law, after the failure of a defiance strategy, the MNCs decided to bargain for a lower chemical registration fee while at the same time pacifying the authorities so as not to jeopardise their future business prospects (Tsai and Child 1997). *Acquiescence* is the most straightforward response but may involve substantial compliance costs in the beginning.

Virtually no leading edge MNCs will opt for *avoidance*. In a rapidly shrinking business world, and with advances in media technology, maintaining a good image as a global citizen can be extremely beneficial for business. Union Carbide, after the Bhopal tragedy, operated in the red for a good number of years. Selecting an avoidance response will undermine the legitimacy of a firm to compete in the global market place. In an unfamiliar situation full of uncertainty, MNCs of same stature often choose to form a coalition to discuss their common concerns and formulate similar strategic responses – an interesting phenomenon of 'norm' formation among peers and a form of acquiescence response (Tsai and Child 1997). Much of this 'norm' formation can be attributed to the phenomenon of Benchmarking Consulting and its resultant codes of practice, such as ISO 14000, the International Chamber of Commerce (ICC) Business Charter, the Chemical Manufacturers' Association's (CMA) Responsible Care programme, and the Coalition for Environmentally Responsible Economies (CERES) principles (Nash and Ehrenfeld 1996). This particular response can also be regarded as one of *co-operation* among business rivals, and between the regulated and the regulatory communities. In the Asia-Pacific region, the American Chamber of Commerce, acting on behalf of all the major MNCs, works closely with different governments and the interested local chemical manufacturers to achieve a uniform adoption of the Responsible Care programme (Tsai and Child 1997).

3.7 The next step

The preceding sections have demonstrated the feasibility of applying a modification of Oliver's (1991) general approach to analyse the specific phenomenon of corporate greening. It has been applied satisfactorily to MNCs, based on comparisons with other field-based studies. However, in-depth research is required to validate further the specific model developed in this chapter. Actual site visits and interviews with senior managers (as employed by Rappaport and Flaherty (1992)) can provide insightful observations on an operating organisation. Comparative studies between countries at different development stages can be useful in understanding MNCs dilemma of globalisation versus localisation, and can contribute to composing a more 'advanced' environmental strategic typology.

A note on country-specific analysis

The vibrant commercial environments of China and Taiwan provide a fertile ground for examining the proposed analytical framework. The work of Orru, *et al.* (1997), which advances institutional theory in an East Asian setting, provides an interesting reference point. This research, while not pursuing the question of organisation forms and country-specific enterprise group comparison, stresses the same issue of concern, organisational isomorphism. Orru *et al.* (1997:154) advance the concept of competitive and institutional isomorphism convergence and argue, based on their research findings in Japan, Korea and Taiwan, that 'institutional pressures can contribute to the emergence and maintenance of market order both within and between competitive organisations'. They further comment that:

> each economy rests on institutional principles that provide a coherent logic for competitive economic action. Socially constructed, accepted models of correct behaviour shape interfirm relations, prompting firms to behave with and against each other in characteristically homogeneous ways. To be 'technically efficient', firms must consider and comply with the institutional settings in which they are embedded.

It must be added here, in line with Parsons' (1953) organisational stratification, that managerial isomorphism could also play a role in MNCs strategic response, especially under joint venture arrangements in an unfamiliar setting, where vulnerability and high visibility impel the foreign managers to compete for 'control'. China and Taiwan each present a set of challenging institutional constraints or 'pulls', and such pulls are increasingly being rationalised through the action of the state and support the development of distinct sets of organisational behaviour (Meyer and Rowan 1977). Zucker (1977:726) posited that 'social knowledge, once institutionalised, exists as a fact, as part of objective reality, and can be transmitted directly on that basis'. MNCs which straddle different fields (countries and industries) are likely to experience a variety of distinct and potentially contradictory isomorphic pulls – regulative, normative, and cognitive (Scott 1995:34–62) – in different operating environments (Westney 1993:60–1). A summary of Scott's framework is presented in Table 3.5 and as an illustration of his theories, a graphic analysis of MNC's relocation rationale, is presented in Figure 3.6.

However, according to the new Institutionalists DiMaggio and Powell (1983), organisations in the same environment become structurally similar as they respond to the identical sets of institutional pressure (or specific cultural patterns present in their environment),[21] which in turn

Table 3.5 Elements of institutions

	Regulative	*Normative*	*Cognitive*
Basis of compliance	Expedience	Social obligation	Taken for granted
Mechanism	Coercive	Normative	Mimetic
Logic	Instrumentality	Appropriateness	Orthodoxy
Indicators	Rules, laws, sanctions	Certification, accreditation	Prevalence, isomorphism
Basis of legitimacy	Legally sanctioned	Morally governed	Culturally supported, conceptually correct
Carrier			
Culture	Rules, laws	Values, expectations	Categories, typifications
Social structures	Governance system, power system	Regimes, authority system	Structural isomorphism, identities
Routines	Protocols, standard procedures	Conformity, performance of duty	Performance programmes, scripts

Source: Scott 1995:35, 52

shape the forms of isomorphism. This is also due to the fact that they carry with them their own isomorphic organisation, culture and routines. If so, MNCs in China and Taiwan will evolve to be identical, given a sufficient time span. A discussion at a different level should focus on China and Taiwan's common cultural lineage and conflicting political traditions.

As Hamilton and Biggart (1997:113) stated 'organisational practices, instead, represent strategies of control that serve to legitimate structures of command and often employ cultural understanding in doing so' and 'practices diffuse along lines of social relations, but also to other actors broadly considered similar' (Strang and Meyer 1993:492). In order to appreciate fully the management issues in China and Taiwan, a thorough understanding of the respective political as well as cultural climate is a prerequisite. The political ideologies of China and Taiwan are as far apart as they can be. Since the political/regulatory sphere often dictates the predominant isomorphic pull in environmental protection (Nitsche 1997, Moser and Tsai 1997) and taking into account North's (1990:54) statement that 'enforcement is undertaken by agents whose own utility

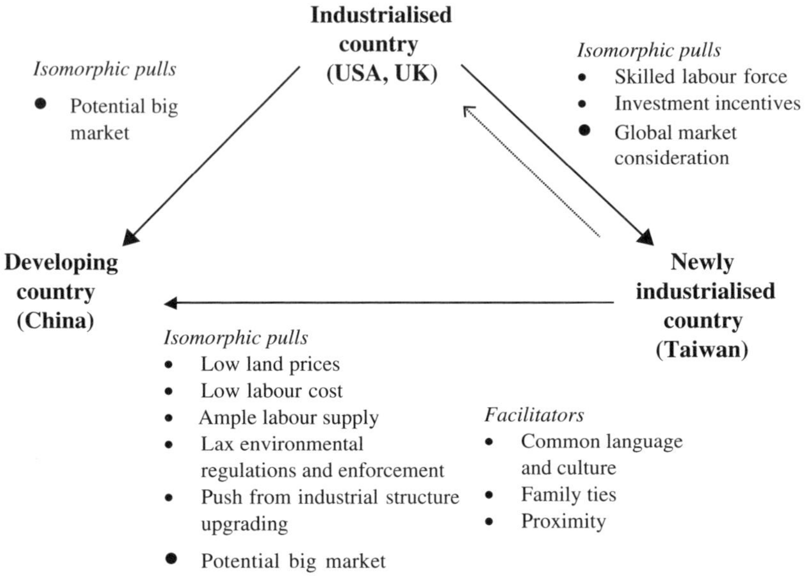

Figure 3.6 Rationale for relocation

functions influence outcomes', there might be a need for MNCs to revisit this treatment of both localities under the same strategic planning unit of a 'Greater China region'.

The globalisation of environmental issues and the strategic nature of the responses[22] further lead to a query whether MNCs are strategically responding to involvement in changing field boundaries or participation in multiple fields (Westney 1993). Jennings and Zandbergen (1995) maintain that institutional fields can be further differentiated into societal and organisational, in analogy to the general and the task environments. Societal fields, with particular reference to the greening values and practices, are 'shaped by at least three factors: (a) the nation state, (b) social movements, and (c) innovations among sets of organisations, such as industries' (Jennings and Zanbergen 1995:1028). The prominent role of the State in the arena of environmental protection was again recognised: 'the State has an impact through its framework for governance,[23] which sets up different types of organisations involved in sustainability within societal fields. In addition, the State has an impact through the type of enforcement or sanctions it uses, such as litigious or penal styles of enforcement versus consensual or conciliatory styles' (Jennings and Zanbergen 1995:1029). Organisational fields, as defined by DiMaggio and Powell (1991) or Meyer and Scott (1983),[24] are therefore considered sub-fields within the broad societal fields, and have the tendency to grow, proliferate and become linked. The end result is the birth of a 'suprafield' for global ecological sustainability. The significance of societal and organisational fields is evident in the connection of macro- and micro-processes to allow for diffusion of learning and innovation across different units (Jennings and Zanbergen 1995:1030–1031). Senior managers in China and Taiwan increasingly have a shared consensus of how the environmental protection effort can best be operationalised and the core (but not the details) of these model practices varies little with geographic locations[25] (Tsai and Child 1997). Besides the earlier deliberation of institutional perspectives, adaptation of transaction cost theory with a particular emphasis on 'social and relational contracting' (Donaldson 1989:47–64; Williamson 1975, 1985, 1991, 1994; Boisot and Child 1996) may provide a complementary explanation for the greening phenomenon of MNCs in China and Taiwan.

Summary

Environmental management is an emerging field of scholarly inquiry. Since this discipline is in its early stages of evolution, it calls for definitions and theoretical development. The analytical framework for this research adopts organisation theories, in particular, the environmental adaptation theories, to examine the recent trend of greening phenomenon in multinational corporations.

The rationale is based upon the conviction of the inseparability of an organisation from its immediate environment, as emphasised by the term 'embeddedness'. It is further stipulated that greening is a form of systemic strategic change, and as such is dependent and shaped by various contextual factors. Business or corporate ethics, with the models of stakeholder social contract and an inclusive approach, is perceived as an influencing factor. Other environmental constraints, as exemplified by the essence of new institutional theory, determine the behaviour of an organisation to a large degree. This relates to the first research question of how MNCs balance their strategic intent and institutional constraints. In seeking stability, legitimacy, ease of access to resources, and invulnerability to questioning, an organisation is certain to exhibit coercive, normative and mimetic isomorphism with the constraining institutions. The addition of resource dependency theory, strategic choice, and bargaining power perspectives produce a set of strategic responses

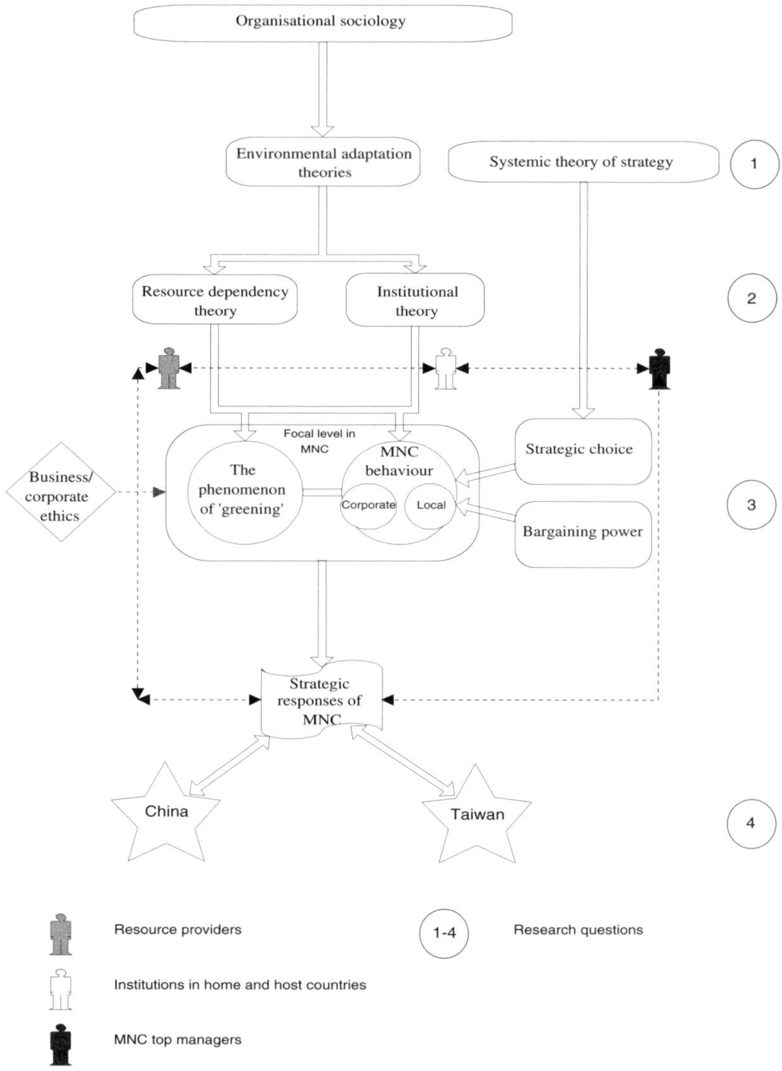

Figure 3.7 Analytical framework – a graphical representation

that aim to counter the criticism of passivity assumed by the institutional theory alone. The predictive responses are compared to the empirically derived response typologies in the environmental management literature. The essence of research question two, which deals with the adaptation and responses of MNCs to the institutional constraints of environment, is emulated here.

An example was given to predict MNCs' response to the command-and-control and market based models of policy making. Attention was also drawn to the development of MNCs' universalistic and particularistic standards in safety, health and environmental protection, and a complementary line of analysis to study the conflicts of globalisation versus localisation in MNCs was proposed. This supplies an answer to research question three. The chapter ends with a note on country-specific analysis to echo the issues raised in research question four, in which accentuation was given to the local conditions of China and Taiwan. Figure 3.7 depicts the analytical framework.

4 Research Methodology

> . . . the subjectivity that originally I had taken as an affliction, something to bear because it could not be foregone, could, to the contrary, be taken as 'virtuous'. My subjectivity is the basis for the story that I am able to tell. It is a strength on which I build. It makes me who I am as a person and as a researcher, equipping me with the perspectives and insights that shape all that I do as a researcher, from the selection of topics clear through to the emphasis I make in my writing. Seen as virtuous, subjectivity is something to capitalise on rather than to exorcise.
>
> Glesne and Peshkin 1992:104

The seed for conducting this research was sown during my association with the General Electric Company (GE) Corporate Environmental Programmes in 1989–1990. Fairfield, Connecticut and Albany-Schenectady-Troy, New York proved to be fertile grounds for the continued growth of the budding ideas. GE is a true industrial giant and I began to appreciate the far-reaching power of a hefty multinational corporation (MNC). I was placed as a corporate consultant in charge of developing a new environmental management system, and GE senior managers granted me their precious time for in-depth interviews and stimulating discussions. I later joined CH2M HILL Inc., the largest environmental consulting company in the United States, if not internationally. In addition, I was retained by the Massachusetts Department of Environmental Protection as a policy/regulation advisor. My job obligation brought me in touch with several Global 500 corporations, state governments, the US Environmental Protection Agency officials and leaders of major environmental groups. Before I commenced my full-time research in Cambridge in the fall of 1993, I travelled extensively both within the

United States and world-wide to fulfil different project needs. Close association with various multinational corporations elicited my interests in their internal management guidelines and policies concerning environmental protection. I became familiar with various corporate global environmental standards, and through different project assignments, I had the chance to test them against a myriad of disparate US state environmental laws and regulations. I was intrigued by the efficacy, resource, and influence of multinational corporations within their own home countries. Given the size of my projects, which seldom fell below the million dollar mark, I started to wonder whether MNCs were as responsive to the greening demands in their foreign subsidiaries. A past project with a major US chemical client operating in the Czech Republic suggested fairly responsible behaviour, as evident in the MNC's desire to apply its home country pollution abatement practices. In this case, the MNC was relatively sensitive to international 'greening' pressure as well as the host government's perception of its image. I arrived at the Judge Institute with this experiential knowledge and, as befitted Strauss's (1987:11) recommendation that the 'experiential data should not be ignored because of the usual canons governing research (which regard personal experience and data as likely to bias the research), for these canons lead to the squashing of valuable experiential data. We say, rather, "mine your experience, there is potential gold there!"', I proceeded with the fine-tuning of my pre-conceived 'notions' and formally launched my research design.

4.1 Selection of research method

My past experience with environmental modelling and risk analysis/assessment trained me to 'reason' beyond the numbers. Uncertainty analysis performed at the end of each project, unfortunately, often casts shadow on the conclusions drawn. Though comfortable with quantitative methodologies, I was determined to experiment with the qualitative paradigm to complement my sphere of understanding. The strength of qualitative research, as described by Maxwell (1996:17), derives 'primarily from its inductive approach, its focus on specific situations or people, and its emphasis on words rather than numbers'. He cites five research purposes – understanding the meaning, the particular context, and the process, identifying unanticipated phenomena and influences, and generating new grounded theory about the latter, and developing causal explanation – as particularly suited for qualitative studies.

These rationales coincide with my four main research questions focusing on the context and response of MNCs' greening phenomena in China and Taiwan. My ontological, epistemological and methodological stance for this research project leaned *slightly* towards interpretivist-constructivist, while still under the influence of my positivistic upbringing, i.e. as an engineer and technical manager, and as evident in my pursuit of conventional benchmarks of rigour: internal validity, external validity, reliability, and objectivity (Guba and Lincoln 1994:105, Yin 1994:33–8). I, like many positivists and postpositivists, subscribe to the viewpoint that several paradigms can be accommodated in a single conceptual framework (Guba and Lincoln 1994:115). In Chapter 3, I attempted to convey my thinking process in developing an analytical framework for this study. Suffice to state that inherent in my framework is the firm belief that what is often assumed to be objective knowledge is actually the result of a particular perspective, which is shaped by various contextual factors. I found constructivist thinking intriguing, and somewhat parallel to my framework, in its interpretation that

> what is at stake for the constructivist are systems of representations, social and material practices, laws of discourses, and ideological effects. In short, constructivists are concerned above all with the production and organisation of differences, and they therefore reject the idea that any essential or natural givens precede the process of social determination.
>
> (Fuss 1989: 3)

Guba and Lincoln (1989:71) added that the nature and quality of a construction, much like the central thesis of bounded rationality (Simon 1947, 1957, 1960; March and Simon 1958; Cyert and March 1963), depends largely on the 'the range and scope of information available to a constructor, and the constructor's sophistication in dealing with that information'. This explanation reinforces the significance of experiential data, as a more informed and sophisticated construction often accompanied by a vicarious experience (Guba and Lincoln 1994:112). The research inquiry advances through a dialectic of iteration, analysis, critique, reiteration, and re-analyses and ultimately coalesces in a consensus (or a 'joint construction' of a case) between the investigators and the sample subjects. This case can then be evaluated for its fit with the related data and information, its credibility, its relevance and its modifiability (Guba and Lincoln 1989:179). Such a construction or case is invariably 'embedded' in the social context, as I have proposed in Chapter 3 using Granovetter's (1985) theory and supported by Gergen's 'social constructionism' (Gergen 1985, Gergen and Gergen 1991), which placed emphasis on the collective rather than the individual generation of meaning and regarded constructions as dictated by conventions of language and other social processes. Gergen (1986:143) claimed that 'there are no independently identifiable, real-world referents to which the language of social description are cemented'. The crucial roles of language and social processes in this research design will be acknowledged later in the chapter.

In constructing the cases, I used case study methods. This was well suited to my goal of generating and building theory in an area where little data or theory exists, and I could use 'controlled opportunism' to respond flexibly to new discoveries made in collecting new data (Eisenhardt 1989:539, Dutton and Dukerich 1991). Yin (1994:1) considered the application of case study to be the most optimal 'when "how" and "why" questions are being posed, when the investigator has little control over events, and when the focus is on a contemporary phenomenon within some real-life context'. The technical definition of case study, according to him (Yin 1994:13), is an empirical inquiry that 'investigates a contemporary phenomenon within its real-life context, especially when the boundaries between phenomenon and context are not clearly evident.

The case study inquiry:

- copes with the technically distinctive situation in which there will be many more variables of interest than data points, and as one result,
- relies on multiple sources of evidence, with data needing to converge in a triangulating fashion, and as another result,
- benefits from the prior development of theoretical propositions to guide data collection and analysis.

His authoritative handbook *Case Study Research* (Yin 1994) was taken as an important point of reference throughout this study, which can be considered exploratory in nature. I followed the principles of Yin's (1994:44–53) multiple-case design. Studying three MNCs of similar scale using a pre-defined theoretical/analytical framework could be considered to have fulfilled the criteria for both *literal* and *theoretical* replications.

The examination of MNC subsidiaries in China and Taiwan further qualified the design of this research as what Yin referred to as an *embedded* multiple-case replication. The prevailing and differing characteristics among the cases will be distilled from data analysis. Noting the deficiency in case study methodology with respect to linking data to propositions and setting criteria for interpreting the findings, I supplemented my analysis exercise with certain desirable features, namely the systematic data preparation and management of grounded theory (Glaser and Strauss 1967; Strauss 1987; Strauss and Corbin 1990, 1994). In relation to the case study approach, grounded theory has been criticised for its accentuation on the immediate and observable environment of behaviour and its distrust of social structural concepts and the associated forms of analysis (Layder 1993). Moreover, the assumption of structural conditions being necessarily relevant to the 'interactional/processual phenomena under study' (Strauss 1987:80) needs to be amended. A properly designed case study incorporating contextual factors for a situated event could hence constitute a viable 'corrective measure'.

On another level, I also conceded to Layder's (1993:53–70) call for assimilating strands of general theory. Layder argued that 'grounded theory should draw on other research perspectives as resources for theory construction . . . and not assume such theories [as] "speculative" and unconnected with the empirical world', as 'some aspects of such theories (a concept, or several, or a segment of the whole theory) may be very useful in ordering fieldwork data, or in stimulating ideas or lines of thoughts about new concept or theoretical insights'. My undertaking in this research could therefore be viewed as an attempt to integrate the boundaries of the two distinct research strategies. The characteristic trait of grounded theory in avoiding a specification of theoretical prepositions at the outset of an inquiry was in this instance 'violated' by my inclusion of a case study analytical framework[26] (Yin 1994). However, here I noted Strauss and Corbin's further (1994:273) elaboration that in grounded theory methodology 'theory may be generated initially from the data, *or*, if existing (grounded) theories seem appropriate to the area of investigation, then these may be elaborated and modified as incoming data are meticulously played against them' and with such consent, my effort could be justified as a step in the right direction. Even though possessing an existing framework aided in saving resources, as I was forced to delineate clearly and concentrate solely on the scope of my investigation, I also realised its shortcoming of restraining my imagination. The merger certainly facilitated my detachment from the *ideological hegemony*, i.e. the existing literature and the assumptions embedded in it, and provided a new way of framing the phenomenon (Maxwell 1996:34). Bearing in mind the aforementioned statements, I must clarify that my approach was more akin to sensitising concepts (Blumer 1954) and a theoretical description development than substantive and formal theory building, though wherever feasible, I would endeavour to follow Glaser and Strauss's (1967) 'out-and-out theory constructing' (Layder 1993:49).

4.2 Selection of the case companies

A good understanding of the critical phenomena relies on choosing a case well (Patton 1990, Yin 1994). In selecting the case companies, I placed emphasis on the ease of obtaining access and the potential for a continuous, trusting relationship (Maxwell 1996:66). It was no surprise that my past clients sprang to mind. Researching my past clients eliminated the need for acquiring information about their SHE protection effort in their respective home countries, as such information was already part of my experiential data. I composed a list of ten chemical MNCs with which I had associated in at least three major environmental projects in an industrialised country setting. Through electronic database research and by eliminating companies without manufacturing facilities in either China or Taiwan or both, I shortened this list to five. I then exercised my connections and started negotiating with the Asia-Pacific or the Greater China regional managers for access. Even with the past association, approval did not materialise easily.

I concur with Punch (1994:86–87) in his discussion of the politics of fieldwork, that the nature of the research topic, researcher's competence, status, institutional background, and personality, the 'sympathy' of the gatekeepers, and the organisational expectation in terms of result feedback, all played a role in access negotiation. I submitted a full, rather than the customary abridged, version of my case study protocol (Yin 1994:63–73) to the senior management for scrutiny, and detailed the expected managerial time commitment. It was my intention, as an integral part of trust building, to be frank and sensitive to the management concerns and thus avoid the pitfall of mutual deceit (Punch 1994:93). I also attempted to solicit input from the corporate SHE directors, and they co-operated by distributing the study proposal to the plant level for review and comments. Phone calls and facsimiles were exchanged on a frequent basis. I made two trips, during November-December 1993 and July 1994, to the MNCs regional headquarters in Hong Kong and Taiwan for the purpose of clarifying questions and formally presenting the research project. The entire negotiation process lasted close to a year (from November 1993 to August 1994), and this closely reflected the decision-making duration within the MNCs. Through much persuasion, final approvals were obtained from three (two US-based, one UK-based) out of the short-listed five. The other two declined to participate, almost at the beginning of my fully-fledged negotiation effort, on the ground of the sensitivity of the research issue and that they had never collaborated with any external researcher.

The three companies studied were enthusiastic about the pioneering nature of my proposed study, and as an MNC Regional SHE Manager noted, the research was first of its kind to be conducted in the Greater China Region and the company would benefit much from being the first audience of the research dissemination. For the case participants, in observation of the ethical codes of conduct for researchers and in gaining the utmost level of trust, I promised full confidentiality of their identities. Historical and financial data, manufacturing processes, specialised products, precise site locations, and organisational charts, which might lead to disclosure of the company identities and was deemed irrelevant to the main research questions, would be concealed in the case reports and analyses. The current practice in the research community dictated that 'settings and respondents should not be identifiable in print and that they should not suffer harm or embarrassment as a consequence of research' (Punch 1994:92). In spite of my intended pursuit of reality and the desire to report it, I felt strongly about the limit of the public or scholarly 'right to know' (Stake 1994) and had volunteered to submit drafts of my case reports to the participants for checking of accuracy. Several took up the offer and were, in general, quite satisfied with how they were portrayed. This could also be regarded as the first step in constructing the validity of my findings (Yin 1994:33–35).

Two large chemical firms, a Chinese state-owned enterprise (SOE) and a Taiwanese private corporation, were included in the comparison group. Access to the Chinese SOE, which had been designated by the government as the SHE model company in the chemical industry, was handled and achieved by a colleague in China. His criteria of selection were the scale of manufacturing operation, the proximity to his institution of affiliation, and the existing institutional connection. Access negotiation in China was an art by itself. *Guanxi* and the political status and affiliation of the researchers were highly valued. Although official recommendation letters from a recognised Chinese institution were routinely requested, support from the senior management could only be harnessed via excellent *guanxi*. Once the threshold had been crossed, I found the Chinese managers to be hospitable and relatively open. The

Taiwanese firm, which had won the Taiwan Environmental Protection Association (TEPA) outstanding environmental protection award for consecutive years, granted full access with minimal effort on my part. This particular firm had enjoyed the largest global market share for a specialised chemical product, and was perceived by many leading Taiwanese management scholars as an 'atypical' business. Not only were the senior managers supportive of academic research, they also possessed a strong sense of business ethics and social values. I followed the same procedures of routing the research proposal and assuring confidentiality of identity to the Chinese and the Taiwanese counterparts. The design was, on the first level, to compare the local best to the MNCs, and on the second level, to contrast the firm behaviour at the two culturally related and yet politically distinct localities. Figure 4.1 presents a schematic design of the research.

4.3 Data collection

Data collection was organised into several phases. The pre-fieldwork phase (October 1993–September 1994) was marked by an intensive effort of gathering background material from multiple sources, often via archival (electronic databases) research and monograph survey, especially the 'formal studies and evaluations of the same targeted sites' (Yin 1994:83–84). Newspaper and popular magazine clippings, both in Chinese and English, for the past ten years were consulted for reports on significant MNC investment projects in China and Taiwan. I then wrote to the MNCs for their annual reports (general, corporate, regional, and environmental) and SHE publicity documents covering the period from 1988 to 1993, as most of the MNC chemical investment in China did not materialise until a year or two after the Tiananmen Square incident in 1989. Layder (1993) in his discussion of research on situated activities, attached prominence to time scale and history in addition to context and setting, which form the institutional features of social life and 'differ in terms of their durability and continuity'. Archival research, hence, enhanced the understanding of the time-varying event settings in relation to a given social context, which is 'generally less responsive to localised pressure for change than immediate settings' (Layder 1993:13). Besides the 'historical' sources, my past consulting projects bequeathed an up-to-date working library of MNC internal SHE guidelines, handbooks, project and audit reports. I have also maintained a collection of international environmental codes, EU directives, US Environmental Protection Agency (EPA), Occupational Safety and Health

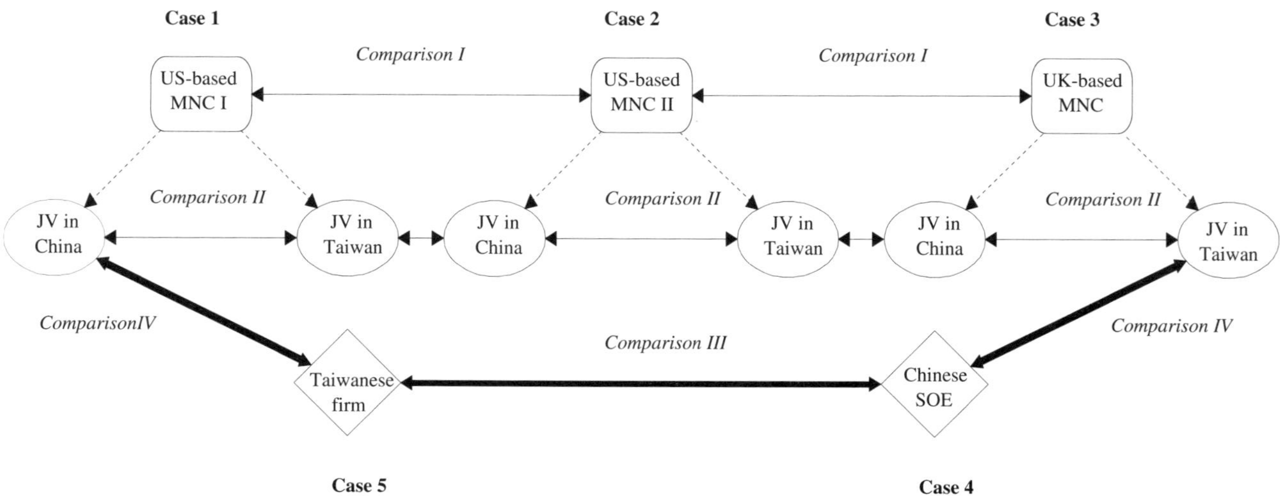

Figure 4.1 Research design – a schematic representation

Administration (OSHA) and various US state guidance documents for SHE protection.

In November and December 1993, a senior academic at the Judge Institute and I were invited by TEPA to deliver a series of lectures and workshops in Taipei and at the National Taiwan University (NTU). Several MNCs sent representatives to participate in the workshops. Their involvement and the information exchange certainly broadened the horizon of my research inquiry and enhanced my project database. The trip opened the access to TEPA and NTU library resources, and TEPA was kind enough to provide different publications on environmental regulations and policies. Throughout my stay in Taipei, in an attempt to gather an impression of the regulators on the MNCs in Taiwan, I interacted and consulted with TEPA senior officials and interviewed high-ranked officers from the Industrial Bureau[27] and the Labour Administration[28] of the Executive Yuan. In July 1994, I undertook another journey to Hong Kong and Taiwan in pursuance of the case companies and, during the process of ascertaining our 'mutual fits', was given the opportunities to conduct informal interviews with the regional managers. The 'pilot interviews' done prior to the final articulation of the study's theoretical propositions, provided considerable insight into the issues being studied and helped in further refinement of my research (Yin 1994:75).

The fieldwork phase formally commenced with semi-structured interviews with MNC regional managers in October 1994. This technique had the dual benefit of enabling the researchers to stay focused and concurrently permit freedom in investigating topics of interest in greater detail, should the situation oblige such action. The informants retain the liberty to respond in any way they choose, and their own interpretations and meanings freely surface in the interview data (Layder 1993:41). The questions (see Table 4.1) first considered SHE protection initiatives and led directly to strategic intents, institutional constraints, strategic response, and globalisation and/or localisation of such initiatives. Next, depending on the responses given, interviews proceeded to explore related themes, such as corporate environmental policies and guidelines, senior management's attitude towards SHE protection, the level of strategic importance, perception of competitors' SHE performance, and the resources (financial and human) devoted specifically for SHE protection. The same interviews, i.e. exploration of the identical themes, were also conducted at the plant level with operations managers and plant SHE managers/co-ordinators. A four-hour quick on-site audit was administered following the interviews. For the Chinese SOE and the Taiwanese chemical company, due to the structure of the organisation and the co-location of corporate and manufacturing facilities, the first level interviews were rendered redundant.

I spent the first four months (October to January 1994) of the fieldwork in Taiwan, covering MNC subsidiaries and regional headquarters in Taipei, Taichung, Hsin-chu, and Kaohsiung. The next four months (February to May 1995) were occupied by interview trips to Hong Kong, Beijing, Shanghai, Ningbo, and Guangzhou. A further four months (June to September 1995) in Kaohsiung were devoted to preparing feedback to MNC regional headquarters in Hong Kong, MNC regional managers, and SHE regional directors in the Greater China regional headquarters. The participants in the study, classified by the types of organisation or regulatory role, are as follows:

- *MNCs*: 3 business directors, 3 Asia-Pacific regional managers, 3 Asia-Pacific regional SHE directors, 3 Greater China SHE managers, 6 plant managers (or deputy manager), 6 plant operations managers, 6 plant SHE managers, and 12 shopfloor workers.
- *Chinese SOE*: 1 general manager, 1 SHE manager, 2 chief engineers, and 2 shopfloor workers.
- *Taiwanese Firm*: 1 general manager, 1 deputy manager, 1 assistant manager, 1 SHE manager, and 2 shopfloor workers.
- *'Formal' Regulators*: 1 National Environmental Protection Agency (NEPA) deputy administrator, 1 TEPA administrator, 3 NEPA department directors (Departments of Policies, Laws, and Regulations, Pollution Control, and International Co-operation), 2 TEPA division chiefs (Divisions of Pollution Control, and Science and Technology Advisors), 6 officers at the Chinese and Taiwanese local Environmental Protection Bureau (Beijing, Shanghai, Kaohsiung, etc), 2 department heads at the Taiwan Industrial Bureau, Chairman and Senior Advisor of the Foreign Investment Evaluation Council, Ministry of Economics in Taiwan.
- *'Informal' Regulators*: 4 Taiwanese NGO representatives,[29] 10 Chinese and Taiwanese academics, 4 contractors, 2 suppliers, 3 business competitors.

The tape-recorded interviews were then supplemented with quick one-hour on-site audits (observations) and reviews of plant SHE records. I paid, on the average, at least three visits to the participating organisations and for the case companies, the frequency was even greater. The interviews were conducted in Mandarin and Amoy Chinese or English.

I conversed with the participants in the language with which they felt most comfortable. The language, both spoken and body, extruded certain cultural contexts and social connotations. I made constant reference to my background, i.e. the 'self as an instrument' approach (McCracken 1988), either as a Western-trained consultant or a Chinese patriot, in easing the participants into a trusting mode. Thereupon, I assessed the quality of our 'social interaction' (Easterby-Smith *et al.* 1991) and decided whether to lend a sympathetic ear, or undertake other modes of questioning. In all cases, I restrained myself from making excessive comments on their responses. The protocol was to give them a simple, value-free question and allow for a fair amount of 'personal' reflection and reconstruction of the case event. In four of the five case companies, I discovered during the first interviews that there existed 'SHE critical incidents' and as the questionnaire was semi-structured, I followed the leads with the critical incident technique (Easterby-Smith *et al.* 1991: 83–84). The narrative was rich in details, as the incidents were mostly recent[30] and greatly publicised by the local media, and amply illustrated the essence of SHE protection issues, which in turn tied in nicely with my research objectives. Participants' rationalisations of the events were reduced to the minimum through later interviews with various sources and more direct questions focusing on the same events.

Besides the scheduled interviews, I continued my archival research in the field. The small but well-organised library of the Taiwan Environmental Protection Alliance, a NGO, was a gem. There I freely pursued Chinese newspaper and magazine clippings covering SHE issues on both sides of the Strait. The libraries of Tsinghua University in Beijing, notably the environmental-engineering department library, possessed a wonderful collection of environmental-protection related journals, case studies, and official publications. The China Environmental Science Press in Beijing was another good depository of information. My collection on Chinese environmental laws and policies grew tremendously during the fieldwork phase. The quest of multiple sources of evidence to develop converging lines of inquiry was not only a means of triangulation, but also a collateral effort to construct validity for the study.

The post-fieldwork phase (October 1995–June 1997) involved additional visits to the Greater China region for information updates. Two formal visits, one in December 1995 and another in July 1996, to the case companies were made to present the preliminary findings and collect new internal SHE publications. The trip in December 1995 to

Taiwan was taken with two senior academics at the Judge Institute in the form of research seminar presentations, and further information on MNCs management practices was obtained via active dialogue with both the academic and the business communities. The trip in July 1996 aimed to gather the new versions of environmental laws and regulations and concluded satisfactorily with an unanticipated acquisition of a monograph on the history and success story of my Taiwanese case as well as numerous other official publications. From August 1996 to April 1997, I participated in several academic conferences to solicit external expert reviews on my 'chain of evidence' (Yin 1994:98–99) and was fortunate enough to receive insightful comments from a colleague who had just finished a similar study on one of my case companies in Thailand. Her results added a new dimension to my construction of case validity, as well as confirming data reliability, and contributed much to my case report composition. Throughout this phase, I sustained dynamic communication channels with the informants, in particular, the companies studied. They gave much encouragement, and patiently went through several iterations of interview transcripts. In data collection, I conformed to Patton's (1987) rules[31] – triangulation of data sources (data triangulation) and among different evaluators (investigator evaluation). His other rule on triangulation of perspectives on the same data set (theory triangulation) will be addressed in the data analysis section and Chapters 6 to 9.

4.4 Data analysis

The case study database resulting from this work was immense. Multiple sources of data collection undoubtedly increased the work load of data analysis. The tape-recorded interviews were transcribed verbatim into an electronic format. The task was both lengthy and tedious. Each recorded hour of the English interviews required on average six hours of non-stop transcription. The Chinese ones, because of the simultaneous interpretation and transcription, took more than nine hours. The concentration and time devoted to the tape transcription, though much resented, assisted in my internal integration and examination of various theoretical propositions raised in Chapter 3. Chinese to English interpretation was exceedingly difficult due to the contextual and ideological issues surrounding these two distinct languages. Word-to-word translation was therefore impossible, but every attempt was made to eliminate excessive subjective interpretation. The translation was checked by a non-specialist professional interpreter to ensure its accuracy and then cross-examined by both of us to minimise subjective interpretation.

The electronic files were then coded according to the four main themes of analysis, parallel to the research questions – strategic intent versus institutional constraints, response and adaptation, globalisation versus localisation, local firms (with their own subsets of strategic intent, institutional constraints, strategic responses and adaptation). Under each main theme, sub-topics (clusters) and associated key words (factors)[32] were formulated (see Table 4.1).[33] This was congruent with Miles and Huberman's (1984) techniques of putting information into different arrays, making a matrix of categories, and placing the evidence within them. I adopted for the analysis Yin's (1994:103) recommended strategy of relying on theoretical propositions, as outlined in Chapter 3. In strengthening the internal validity of the case studies, I used pattern-matching on *non-equivalent* dependent variables as a pattern as the mode of analysis (Cook and Campbell 1979:118, Trochim 1989, Yin 1994:106). The unit of analysis was the SHE protection initiative (and critical incident, wherever applicable), but in achieving both the theoretical and literal replications, for each of the three case MNCs, there existed two embedded cases, one in China and one in Taiwan.

Analysis protocol

In analysing the data, both inductively and deductively founded on the techniques of generative, constructive and illuminative analyses, I subscribed to Huberman and Miles' (1994:431–432) viewpoint that 'analysis will be undifferentiated and disjointed until the researchers has some local acquaintance with the setting', and Layder's (1993:70) opinion that the definition of grounded theory should be expanded to include

> theories which are guided by, rather than simply limited by empirical data. Such theories attempt to depict structural features of social life, which may be difficult to observe in an immediate way . . . these theories depict explanatory models of the setting and contexts in which activity take place.

I found Huberman and Miles' (1994:432) 13 tactics for generating meaning particularly enlightening and extended them by four additional stages (Easterby-Smith *et al.* 1991:108–111):

1. *Familiarising with the data transcripts*: during the tape transcription, I had the chance to internalise the issues, as the time required was

Table 4.1 Interview and analysis guide

Themes/clusters/factors	*Illustrative questions*
Strategic intent vs institutional constraints (MNC and local)	
Context	Why do you engage in SHE protection initiatives? Please list the factors. (*Factor eliciting question*)
Outer	
SHE regulations/laws/policies	How important are SHE regulations/laws/policies in forming your company's SHE initiatives?
Law enforcement mechanism	How effective do you think is the SHE law enforcement mechanism in China/Taiwan?
Non-governmental	Did you have any dealings with SHE NGOs? If so, why?
Organisations (Taiwan Only)	
Contractors	Did local contractors obey your SHE standards?
Suppliers	Have you ever organised a SHE training course for your suppliers?
Competitor	Are you familiar with your competitors' SHE programmes? List names (MNC or local) and types of the programme.
Inner	
Ethics	What is your definition of SHE ethics? Is there a company ethics and/or environmental mission statement?
Culture	Can you observe any country-specific SHE-related practices?
Economic considerations	How does your budget for SHE protection come about? Is there a maximum annual figure?
Strategic intents	What are the strategic benefits of your SHE protection initiatives?
Time horizon	What is the time frame of your strategy making? (*Scale: Long, mid-range, short*)
Response and adaptation (MNC and Local)	How do you react to greening demands? Do you consider your environmental protection initiatives as a direct response to such demands?
Globalisation vs localisation (MNC only)	Do you have corporate-wide standards? (*Factor eliciting question*)
Engineering standards	Are there inconsistencies between the host and home country design codes?
Management standards	Can you tell me about your home internal management standards?
SHE standards	Have you ever encountered any local regulatory conflicts with your internal standards?

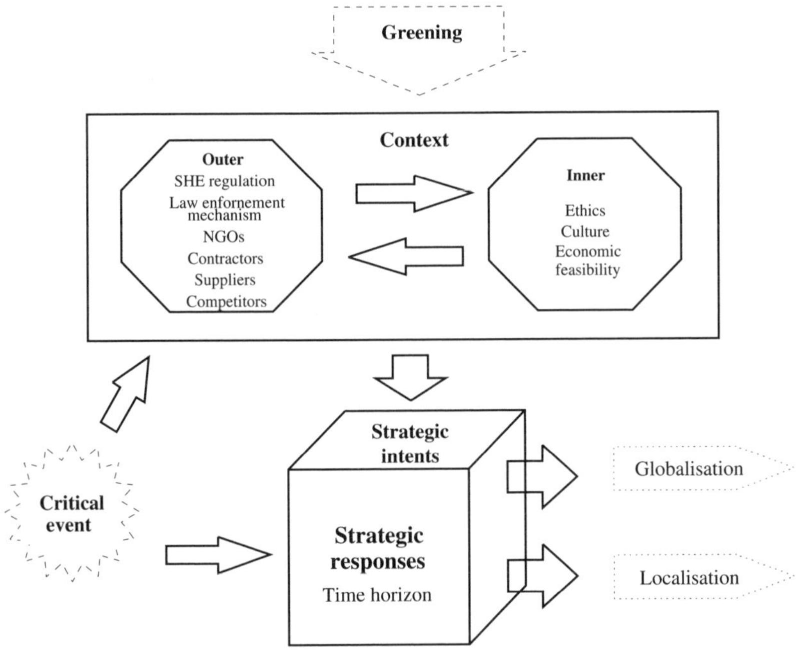

Figure 4.2 Conceptual map for analysis

exceedingly long and the effort tedious. After tape transcription, I collected all the data files in three file holders marked: MNCs, China, and Taiwan. I first applied the strategy of distancing myself from the data set for at least a month. I then went back to read all the data files twice without stopping. A total of 10 readings were done to decipher the key messages.

2. *Reflecting*: Each reading was done at an interval of at least a week to allow for reflection. That also allowed for the reading of company literature and a world-wide web search on recent happenings at the companies studied.
3. *Noting patterns and themes*: themes and patterns gradually emerged and were re-defined after each time of reading. The main themes were developed as part of the analytical framework. The purpose of this exercise was to clarify if I had made wrong assumptions regarding the corporations' behaviour.
4. *Seeing plausibility – making initial, intuitive sense*: each emerging pattern was checked against the intuitive sense to determine its plausibility.

5. *Clustering by conceptual grouping* (see Table 4.1 & 4.2).
6. *Creating metaphors*: I achieved more integration among diverse pieces of data by using the mind construct of metaphors. Simple metaphors were used in this exercise.
7. *Counting to see what is there and to keep oneself honest*: I resisted the temptation of imposing my preconception onto the 'data'.
8. *Recoding – venturing backwards to see what was actually said*: I re-read the interview transcript in relation to my conceptual clusters.
9. *Making contrast and comparisons*: I made contrast and comparisons between cases and geographic localities.
10. *Partitioning variables*: I unbundled variables that have been prematurely grouped.
11. *Subsuming the particulars into the general, shuttling back and forth between first-level data and more general categories.*
12. *Factoring* (see Table 4.1).
13. *Noting relations between variables*: I used the network approach to identify the linkages.
14. *Finding intervening variables.*
15. *Building a logical chain of evidence*: I used the software which I thought was appropriate and followed a time-line approach.
16. *Linking and making conceptual/theoretical coherence*: I did this via comparison with the framework presented in Chapter 3.
17. *Re-evaluating*: started writing-up process to consolidate my thinking.

In combining the strengths of case study and grounded theory methodologies, I have in fact adopted a hybrid methodology combining entry to the field with an analytical framework and deriving insights in an open-ended manner from the data. A pre-defined framework enabled me to draw upon my past experience in structuring my thoughts and provided credibility in interviewing the informants. 'Knowing the issues' is crucial in gaining access to conduct the research and contributes to the development of depth in formulating questions during the interview. Within this broad pre-defined structure, I allowed respondents the freedom to voice their viewpoints and restricted myself from influencing their patterns of thinking. This gave me the opportunity to develop and refine the theory in a grounded manner. In the course of subsequent analysis, informants' responses were used to verify and re-define the framework as well as to establish emerging patterns. This procedure thus amounted to a process of methodological 'structuration' between an existing framework and new, grounded insights

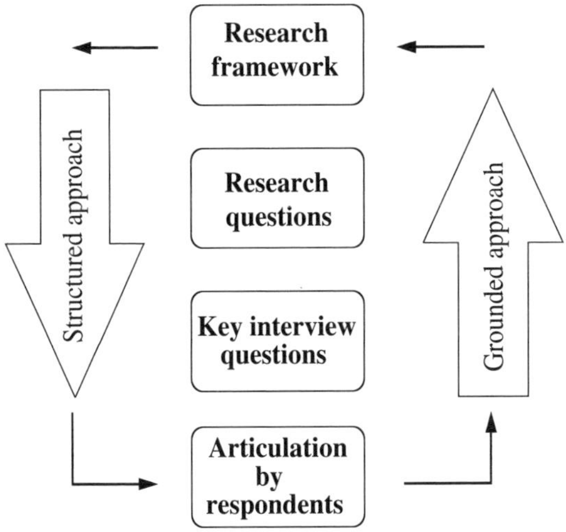

Figure 4.3 Methodological structuration

(see Figure 4.3). The methodology can thus be termed 'case-based theory grounding'.

In the case of 'reporting', I essentially emulated the order of analysis with, first, the central themes and then the sub-topics of interest, but alerted myself to the dangers of methodolatry[34] (Janesick 1994). I consciously tried to balance description and interpretation, while noting Denzin's (1989) suggestion that thick description makes deep interpretation possible, and Van Maanen's (1988) seven criteria of realistic, impressionistic, confessional, critical, formal, literary, and jointly told. The 'stories' I tell are fairly similar and consistent for the three case MNCs (Chapters 6 to 8). The tales for the Chinese SOE and the Taiwanese firm, which shared less commonality with the MNCs, are grouped together in Chapter 9. Minimal interpretation is rendered in the 'data' chapters (Chapters 6 to 9). The analysis will be presented in Chapters 10 and 11.

4.5 Summary

This chapter presents the methodology employed for the research discussed in this book. As the subject of investigation falls in an emerging field of research, I consider it appropriate to adopt in-depth case study as the principle means of investigation to draw upon the richness of details. Three MNCs, each with manufacturing operations in China and Taiwan, a Chinese state-owned enterprise, and a Taiwanese corporation were chosen as the cases. The study employed semi-structured interviews and more than 90 people were consulted over a period of four years. The chemical industry was selected as the sector of study and the data analysis was based on the grounded-theory approach within the broad structure of my research framework.

Part II
Empirical Results and Findings

5
Environmental Management in China and Taiwan

> In spite of our achievements over the years in the protection of environment, breaches of law and regulations are still much in evidence. What is more, there is no law to go by in many aspects. Therefore, it is imperative to establish a new order in environmental protection.
>
> Li 1989:7

This chapter is the first of five where findings are presented. The content, as in the other four, focuses on telling 'stories' – in-depth analysis will be presented in Chapters 10 and 11. Two main sections cover the country profiles of China and Taiwan and the profiles of the five companies studied. A brief summary is included at the end of each section.

I. Country profiles

The 'big emerging markets', among them the Chinese economic area, or the Greater China region, including China, Hong Kong and Taiwan, are the ten areas designated by the Clinton administration as the most attractive for US exports and investments (McCoy 1996). China itself has been lauded as the fastest growing economy in the world for the past twenty years (*The Economist* 1996). To the second quarter of the 2001 fiscal year, China boasted a GDP growth[35] of 7.8% and its industrial production was up by 8.1% in August; the figures for Taiwan are –2.4% and –5.9% in July (*The Economist*, 15 September 2001:90). From 1975 to 1993, UNCTAD's statistics (1996) showed that from 1991–95, the post-Tiananmen years, China's average annual GDP growth was 12%. This figure is particularly impressive considering the trade sanctions against China. If political stability can be guaranteed, China's current growth is sustainable for another twenty years (T*he Economist*, 17 August 1996 and 28 June, 2001).

The above figures represent several times the pace of GDP growth in the US, Europe and Japan (Jacob 1995). The growth has come mainly from manufacturers, often foreign, who took advantage of the country's immense pool of cheap labour, where wages average around RMB 752.76 a month (Chinainfobank 2001; equivalent to US$90.95 based on the Exchange Rate: US$100 = RMB 827.70). Alongside the cheap labour force, the thought of potentially the world's largest untapped market attracted an ever increasingly number of investors from the wealthy North. All major multinationals have established their presence in China, frequently through the popular means of joint ventures, and are getting 'impressive access in key sectors, with 80% of car sales, 90% of PCs, and almost 100% of telecom equipment' *(Business Week* 1996a:3). It may be difficult to assess how much the 'untapped market' has been realised due to the Chinese insistence on a high export percentage of the production. It is known that China, as a dynamic trader, has garnered US$5.04 billion trade surplus with the US, US$4.02 billion with Japan, and more than US$3.69 billion with Europe (EIU Country Forecast 2001). By June 2001, accounting for the latest twelve months, the trade surplus stood at a healthy US$19.9 billion (*The Economist*, 28 July, 2001:92)

Taiwan, the twin brother of China, has long been considered a solid representative of the Asian economic miracle and hence, together with Hong Kong, Singapore, and South Korea, nicknamed one of the four little dragons. Taiwan ranks eighteenth in the world's per capita gross national product list, and has achieved US$12 000 of GNP per person. It's foreign currency reserves, comparable to its larger brother's, are consistently ranked among the highest in the world, with China boasting an impressive US$183.9 billion[36] and Taiwan, US$110.1 billion[37] (*The Economist*, 15 September 2001:90). Foreign investment into Taiwan from 1952 to 1994 totalled US$19 billion, and in 1994 alone, the figure was an impressive US$1.6 billion (Ministry of Economic Affairs 1994). Foreign and overseas Chinese enterprises brought approved investment in Taiwan to a new record for the year of US$7.607 billion in 2000, 79.79% more than in 1999, according to statistics released by Taipei in late January 2001. (Taipei Representative Office, 2001)

Foreign investors, who were first drawn to Taiwan by its cheap labour force, much as in China, are now investing for other reasons. Taiwan has, in recent years, shed its past image and transformed itself into a

Mecca of advanced technology. The combination of American know-how and Asian can-do, coupled with the ability to adapt quickly to market changes, has turned Taiwan into one of the world's leading producers of computer-related electronics. In fact, Taiwan has passed Germany and moved into third place among the world's leading producers of information technology products. Taiwanese companies produced 70% of the world's motherboard and keyboards, 53.7% of its monitors, and over 50% of its notebook and desktop computers, scanners, network and graphic cards, mice, and switching power supplies (Bradbury 1996, Republic of China – Government Information Office, 2001). Seizing the window of opportunity, Philips has decided to move the headquarters of its computer monitor business from Eindhoven in the Netherlands to Taiwan (Corporate Location 1996). Eyeing the booming market, major upstream foreign electronic companies,[38] are building their plants near Hsin-chu Science Park, the hotbed of the Taiwanese electronics industry (Hunter 1996). Other foreign investors, while not entirely confident in engaging China, and appalled by the wide-spread piracy of intellectual property there, have chosen Taiwan as a strategic base for targeting the vast Chinese market. Bayer, United Parcel Service, MTV, Ogilvy & Mather and J. Walter Thompson are prime examples (Kilburn 1996, Moore 1996, Alperowicz 1996, Tripathi 1996).

With the surge in its electronics industry, the Taiwanese government has firmly established an agenda to develop the information sectors as strategic industries in gaining international competitiveness (Kim 1996) and simultaneously exerts a push for industrial structure upgrading. The Ministry of Economic Affairs (MoEA) issued a statement advising Taiwanese chemical manufacturers, again an industrial sector the government considers strategic, either to introduce advanced chemical technology from abroad or develop their own high-end technology to strengthen their global competitiveness. The MoEA also wants the industry to boost research and development (R&D) spending from 1.2% of industry sales in 1995 to 3% by 2002, and reduce the number of chemical companies from 12000 in 1995 to 10500 by 2002 and employees from 420000 to 400000 (Roberts 1996).

Confronted with the pressure to upgrade manufacturing technologies, and the rising cost in production due to ever escalating land prices and local labour shortages, an increasing number of Taiwanese firms are looking towards China for an immediate solution (Baum 1996). The common cultural and language linkages and geographic proximity serve as a magnet for a sizeable migration of Taiwanese enterprises (Liu 1994,

Chinese Security Company 1994). New laws passed in 1994 allowed easy remittance of profits to Taiwan and accelerated Taiwan–China market integration (Myers and Chao 1994). Taiwan-based Yue Yuen, the world's leading purveyor to such brand name footwear as Nike, Reebok and Adidas, now controls 97 production lines in China and, in 1995, netted US$87 million on sales of almost US$512 million (Sender 1996). Taiwanese firms transfer not only investment capital but also pollution. Most Taiwanese investment in China is from small- and medium-sized enterprises seeking refuge from the tougher environmental regulations in Taiwan (Chinese Security Company 1994). Taiwan's investment in pollution-intensive industries, i.e. chemicals, textiles and machinery, ranked second in the world behind Hong Kong at US$261 million and accounted for 11% of the total number of foreign investment in this category again the second highest (Xia 1995).

Prior to the policy change in 1997, a fair number of foreign investors were taking advantage of free import duty to equip their manufacturing plants with machinery phased out by industrialised countries for efficiency and environmental protection reasons. Several engaged in the production in China of internationally banned chemicals, including CFCs. The pollution-intensive industries very much follow the general pattern of foreign investment, with a disproportionate concentration in the coastal provinces. Guangdong alone accounted for 23.47% of total pollution-intensive investment and 21.89% of the approved cases. With the inclusion of three special economic zones, the percentages increase to 36.61% and 35.13%, respectively. Jiangsu, Shandong, Zhejiang, Shanghai, Liaoning, Fujian and Xiamen are other popular destinations (Xia 1995). This trend demonstrated the importance of geographic proximity in the selection of investment location. Guangdong is a stone's throw away from Hong Kong and Fujian and Xiamen are close neighbours to Taiwan.

In recent years, because of its ability to attract foreign investment, China began to tighten its environmental regulations in the coastal provinces. Taiwanese investors, usually owners of small- to medium-sized enterprises, were comparatively mobile and employed a 'hit-and-run' strategy in responding to the increasing demand for environmental protection. Inland provinces, often eager for foreign investments, provide even more incentives for relocation of businesses and manufacturing facilities. There is hence a 'pollution locus' in formation from the coast to inland. The common language and cultural linkages made joint ventures with township and village enterprises (TVEs)[39] relatively effortless and induces a even wider spread of environmental pollution.

5.1 The Chinese environmental management system

Historical perspectives – China

What then is the Chinese environmental management system? Is it stringent enough to ensure a satisfactory degree of sustainable development? There are no easy answers to these questions. The concept of living in harmony with the natural environment took early root in China. Laozi, the prominent ancient philosopher and the founder of Taoism, stressed the importance of cohabiting in 'unity' with the 'heaven', an umbrella term for the nature. The environmental protection movement in the People's Republic of China (founded in 1949) was not properly instigated until 1973 with the First National Environmental Protection Conference as a response to the 1972 United Nations Human Health Convention. Before 1970, environmental consideration was very much a by-product of agricultural and industrial policies. Scarcity of resources for agriculture and industry triggered environmental campaigns to conserve water, clean-up pollution and kill pests.

In 1956, the government produced the Sanitary Standard for Designing Industrial Enterprises, which contained the sanitary standards for air, water and soil in the production and dwelling-place environment. In 1959, the Sanitary Regulations for Drinking Water were adopted to further protect natural resources and the health of the working population (Wu 1987). In 1970, a mass campaign for recycling urged people to maximise the use of 'three wastes' – waste materials, waste water and waste gas (waste heat was occasionally added to the list as the fourth waste). In all, resource conservation was emphasised, rather than profit or technical production (Sandbach 1980). In 1972, after China prepared for and took part in the Stockholm Conference on Human Environment, the principles of environmental protection and the principles of the 'three simultaneousness'(*sic*)[40,41] were laid down. This signified the beginning of the environmental era in China. The First National Environmental Protection Conference in China passed several regulations on environmental protection and improvement in trial implementation, commonly termed 'the three old mandates' and formulated a 32-word guideline on environmental protection, aimed at combating the problem arising from three major waste streams. Besides the 'three simultaneousness', the systems of discharge/emission charges, including financial incentives for environmental protection, and environmental impact assessment were the other two main components covered under the old three mandates.

However, the latter part of the Cultural Revolution put a halt to progress until Deng Xiaoping came to power in the late 1970s. Deng formulated new strategies for economic and social development, and regarded environmental protection as an integral component of his modernisation project. Several environmental laws/policies have been successfully promulgated, the most significant being the adoption of Article 11 of the Constitution of the People's Republic of China in 1978. The article stipulates that: 'the state protects the environment and natural resources, and prevents or eliminates pollution and other hazards harmful to the public' (Wu 1987). The Second National Environmental Protection Conference convened in 1983 and laid the foundation for 'three constructions, three synchronisations, and three unities'.

The new policy united planning, implementation and development with economic growth, urban and rural construction, and environmental protection to achieve greater efficiency in resource utilisation. This forms the nucleus of the 'three major policies' in environmental protection – implementing 'preventive measures first to attain the unity of prevention and treatment', instituting the polluter-pays principle, and emphasising administrative management, as manifested in the 'eight management systems'. The systems combine the 'the three old mandates' with the 'five new measures' – establishing protection target responsibility (an essential duty of each local government, with performance being assessed in annual reviews), encouraging an integrated approach to environmental evaluation and audit (five categories, including air, water, noise, solid waste and greening of cityscape, and 21 indices), inaugurating permits for emission and discharge (based on the concept of total quantity or aggregate control), centralising control of pollution (for economy of scale consideration), and prioritised timetables for control and treatment (for large and seriously polluted industries).

Since the 1980s, environmental protection has been incorporated into the Five-Year Plan for national economic and social development. In the eighth Five-Year Plan period (beginning 1991), 24 concrete targets[42] were adopted for realisation by 1995, including the treatment of 'three industrial wastes' and the discharge and removal volume of SO_2 and dust. Yearly objectives were developed by the State Planning Commission to ensure proper implementation of the plan (PRC National Environmental Protection Agency and State Planning Commission 1994). In 1992, after the United Nations Conference on Environment and Development, the Central Committee of the Communist Party of China and the State Council approved the 'ten countermeasures' (Table 5.1) to ensure sustainable development (Wu and Flynn 1995, Zhang 1994, PRC National Environmental Protection Agency and State Planning Com-

Table 5.1 The ten countermeasures

1. To implement the strategy of sustainable development.
2. To adopt effective measures to prevent and control industrial pollution.
3. To conduct comprehensive treatment of urban environment and eliminate the 'four harmful elements' in cities (smog, sewage, garbage, and noise).
4. To increase energy consumption efficiency and improve the energy consumption structure.
5. To introduce eco-farming, persevere afforestation and effectively strengthen biodiversity protection.
6. To promote vigorously scientific and technological progress, strengthen environmental research, and develop the environmental protection industry.
7. To apply economic means to protect the environment.
8. To strengthen environmental education and consistently raise the environmental consciousness of the whole nation.
9. To perfect the environmental legal system and intensify environmental management.
10. To formulate China's action plans in the spirit of the UNCED.

Source: PRC National Environmental Protection Agency and State Planning Commission, 1994

mission 1994). The official publications, *China Agenda 21* and *Environmental Action Plan (EAP) of China: 1991–2000*, authored by the National Science Council, State Planning Commission, Ministry of Finance, and the National Environmental Protection Agency, were produced under the auspices of the International Development Association (IDA), a branch of the World Bank, to demonstrate China's commitment to becoming a global citizen.

China's environmental protection system is far from simple, and consists of intricate webs of national, provincial, county and city subsystems (Figure 5.1). The order of command is not entirely clear to the general public, and foreign investors often face difficulty in distinguishing relevant policies and regulations. The system, which employed close to 75 000 people in 1992 (Wu and Flynn 1995), can trace its roots back to 1982. Following the Second National Environmental Protection Conference, the National Environmental Protection Commission was established under the jurisdiction of State Council. In 1988, the National Environmental Protection Agency (NEPA), which replaced a similar organisation founded in 1984, was set up by the State Council to supervise the effort.[43] NEPA employs over 300 professionals (Li 1993) and has under its umbrella institutions such as the Chinese Research Academy of Environmental Sciences, China National Environmental Monitoring Centre, National Environmental Management Training Centre and the

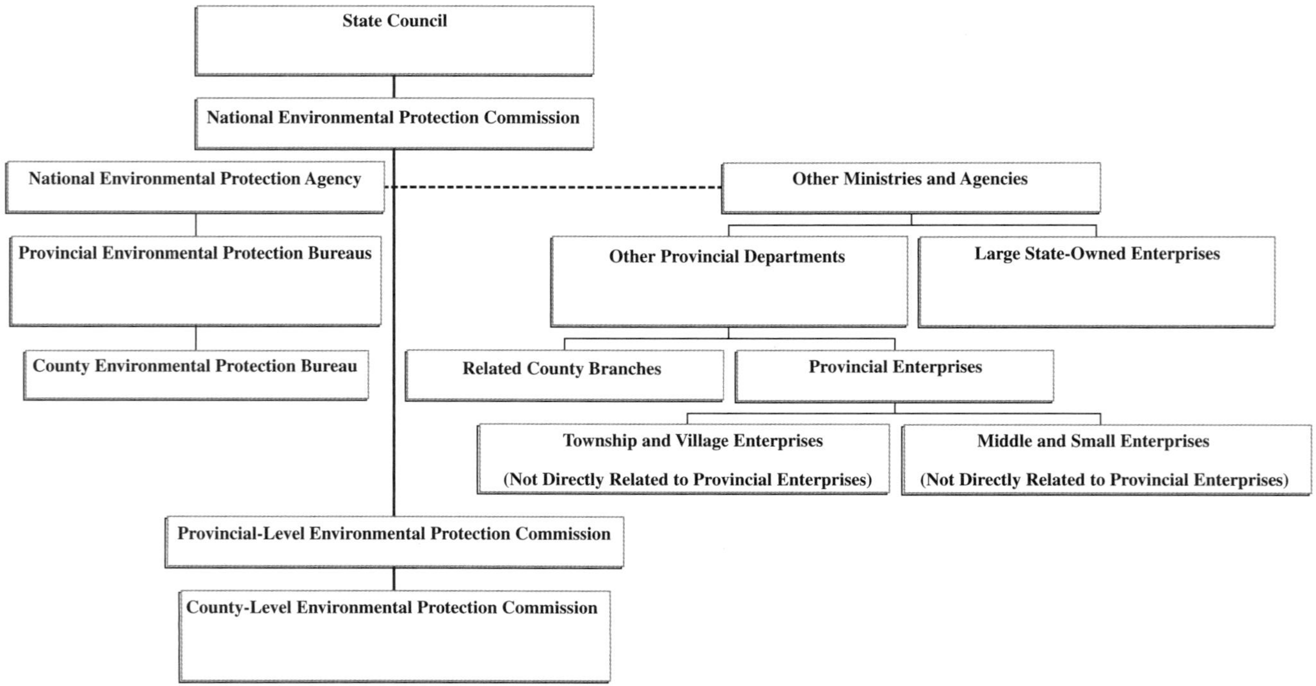

Figure 5.1 Chinese environmental management system

Research Centre for Contemporary Environmental and Economic Policies (NEPA 1994). A sound organisational structure for environmental protection proved conducive to the formulation of related laws and regulations. Since the early 1980s, China has passed four main pieces of legislation, plus 20 environmental protection regulations and more than 320 environmental standards, apart from local regulations. Despite the plethora of regulations, the coverage of the laws is still far from adequate (*The China Daily*, 17 February 1995:4) and the implementation has been difficult. Courts have been reluctant to impose severe penalties on offenders and few take environmental well-being to heart (Walker 1996). Interviews with high-ranked officials in NEPA revealed problems of several dimensions surrounding environmental protection.

Present challenges – China

Conflicting order of law. The Chinese government has rightly advocated an integrated approach to environmental protection. The current state of regulation formulation severely restricts the efficiency of its implementation and Figure 5.1 provides a glimpse into the nature of the problem. Under the traditional system, each national agency and municipality reserves the right to draft its own environmental regulations and standards, and this endeavour is often performed without close consultation with each other or NEPA. At the central level, many policies were independently formulated by distinctive national entities, such as Agricultural, Forestry, Urban Planning and Construction, with their own agenda in mind, and often bore no consideration of the broader picture (Wu and Flynn 1995, Wan 1994). A typical example is the Ministry of Chemical Industry's emission standards for industrial chemical pollutants and the '37 technical-economic policies'. All of these regulations were implemented to 'strengthen the management of chemical industries and instruct in a microscopic manner the local industrial chemical department and enterprises to control effectively new pollution and existing pollution' (PRC National Environmental Protection Agency and State Planning Commission 1994:118).

A duplication of effort is thus evident at the provincial, municipal and county levels with a separate network of Environmental Protection Bureaus (EPBs) as the law-enforcing departments. The People's Congress operates yet another level of environmental protection initiatives.[44] The chain of command is interweaving and a major source of complaint for foreign investors, who are often subjected to the disputes between the State and the local authorities. The political struggle between central and local government frequently spilled onto, among others (investment incentives, tax discounts, etc), environmental policy-making and law enforcement. This further complicates the highly complex and confusing issue of legal jurisdiction. Each local government retains sovereignty over policy enforcement and formulation irrespective of the national mandates.

Corruption at the local level induced self-interest serving law interpretation and distortion. In addition, the local authorities may not honour what the State has conceded (Faure 1994). For example, wealthy coastal provinces have been known to ignore the central government's mandates in favour of enforcing their own. Cases of local 'needs', generally pro-development and at the expense of environmental quality, being given precedence over the national environmental regulations are not unheard of. The steady decentralisation of economic initiatives to provincial, municipal and county levels, each having their own goals for the economy, gives rise to 'multiple power centres with which enterprises have to deal, depending on their scale, legal status, and sector' (Boisot and Child 1996:619). Duplication of effort and conflicting standards, both at the central and local levels, are therefore difficult to avoid.

Haphazard adoption of regulations and standards. China has some of the most stringent environmental standards in the world and yet regulations governing the handling of radioactive and solid (hazardous) wastes are non-existent. Certain laws even exhibit negligence of environmental utility and are abstract in nature, hence poor on operational details. The procedural components of environmental laws lack essential administrative features and thus present an obvious obstacle in implementation and enforcement (Wan 1994). At both the central and local levels, policy makers are more than eager to absorb the 'state-of-the-art' foreign legislation, and devote much time to assessing the feasibility for adoption. The US Resource Conservation and Recovery Act (RCRA), British Standard 7750 and European Environmental Management Audit System (EMAS) are under serious consideration by the NEPA. The US Toxic Substance Control Act (TOSCA) has been adopted partially (the section on toxic substance inventory) and implemented on trial. Local governments look to the Northern European countries for air and water quality standards.

A given regulation, particularly at the local level, can be passed in a relatively short time-frame without due regard to the means for implementation. For a developing country, the policy-making research budget is understandably insufficient. For instance, the environmental protection budget was estimated to be a mediocre 0.85% of GDP in the 1990s (Wang 1994). Copying foreign policy models might be an easy solution and such practice is prevalent among developing nations. The virtue of such action, especially in the condition of disregarding local and national characteristics, remains debatable.

Shortage of trained personnel. Compared to a population of 1.1 billion at an annual growth rate of 17 million (Qu 1994), the mere 75 000 active environmental professionals in China fades into insignificance. The 300-member strong NEPA is embarrassingly under-staffed. The 10 departments and 42 divisions (NEPA 1994) each average no more than 8 employees. The shortage signifies over-burdened staff with never-ending tasks. In the legislation department, the chief who possesses an impressive collection of environmental policies and regulations from various nations, relies largely on himself to peruse the documents with the aid of dictionaries. NEPA and the State Planning Commission (1994:48) openly admitted that 'the present (State) organisation cannot meet the work demand' and 'the local organisations (province, city, county and township) are rather weak and unable to carry out their environmental protection functions (supervision and enforcement of environmental protection laws)'.

Most of the leaders in the civil service underwent the hardship of the Cultural Revolution and their professional sophistication, limited by this unfortunate past, cannot be regarded as being on a par with their Western counterparts. Few boast advanced academic qualifications, and many are in need of refresher courses in their respective fields. The rapid economic growth of China spells new opportunities for university graduates and an overwhelming percentage of them favour employment with major multinational corporations, while the cream look to further their education in Western countries. The infusion of new blood thus becomes a challenge. The shortage in trained personnel gravely hinders the Chinese environmental protection effort. A high-ranked official in the NEPA admitted to not filing an application for World Bank and Asian Development Bank grants because of the inability to meet the Bank's tough proposal guidelines and the difficulty with translating professional documents into English.

Disconnection with industry. Economic reform in China is having a tremendous impact on its industrial structure. The mushrooming of township and village enterprises and the gradual demise of state-owned enterprises are testimonies to this. State-owned enterprise, as the name suggests, comes under the jurisdiction of various ministries, bureaus and departments. The potential conflicts of interest between the environmental authority and its governmental 'comrades' should in any case be minimised to achieve harmony in the central administration. As such, the mission of environmental protection is a difficult one to accomplish. Under the current policy of prioritising deadlines to meet environmental targets, state-owned enterprises retain the luxury of 'delayed' timetables. This is understandable due to the antiquated State of the operational equipment. NEPA has also ear-marked several enterprises within a given industrial sector for regular audits of progress.

Despite the concessions and the drastic measures used to force compliance, environmental protection in the chemical industry, the target industry of this research, is 'still lagging behind the demand of development in chemical industries and the requirement of the State' (PRC National Environmental Protection Agency and State Planning Commission 1994:104). Perhaps because of the comfort level in dealing with only the state-owned enterprises in the past, whereby regulations are conceived and enforced through multiple channels, the Chinese environmental authority is ill-prepared to deal with foreign investors and the unruly behaviour of the the most notorious polluters, township and village enterprises. Policies and regulations have been implemented and enforced without a thorough assessment of the impact on their industry. Ignorance of industrial needs and responses leads to the miscalculation of penalty levels, and encourages defiance or avoidance behaviour from the industry. In China, there is rather little discussion of policy between the regulatory and the regulated organisations. 'Ordinary citizens and economic enterprises also influence the policy process, although the extent of their participation is limited by the ideology of the dominant faction and the overall structure of the system' (Ross 1988). With the intention of arousing attention from the regulatory community, a group of outraged multinational corporations jointly organised a lobby against the NEPA's 'sudden' levy of chemical taxes in 1995. Township and village enterprises and a selected number of foreign investors (NEPA identified Taiwan and Hong Kong as the major culprits) routinely chose to neglect environmental regulations in pursuit of high economic returns on investment, and then relocate, bribe or declare bankruptcy when caught red-handed.

Chinese environmental protection has a long road to travel but its steady progress relies heavily on economic prosperity and a stable political climate. The single largest challenge is considered to be the vast population. This was summed up by one senior NEPA official: 'We cannot be advocating environmental protection when over two-thirds of our people are under the poverty line. Food and better economic conditions are what they need, not a clean environment . . .'.

5.2 The Taiwanese environmental management system

Historical perspectives – Taiwan

The story in Taiwan is very different from China. Since 1972, when Taiwan lost its membership of the United Nations, this island, with 20 million inhabitants, has been somewhat out of the international arena. China's environmental movement, to a certain extent, was a mere response to UNEP's campaign. Such international coercion does not reach Taiwan and the island 'province' existed relatively unnoticed until its recent miraculous performance in economic terms and China's missile threat in 1996. According to an official source (TEPA 1995:638–639), the development of the Taiwanese environmental management system can be broadly divided into four periods. Before 1971, the environmental protection effort was carried out in different government divisions, including the Health Division (reporting to the Ministry of Internal Affairs), the Industrial Bureau (reporting to the Ministry of Economics), and the Health Department of the Taiwan Provincial Government. The Health Division was in charge of infectious disease control and general hygiene-related issues, while the Industrial Bureau was responsible for public hazard and environmental pollution prevention. These two official entities came under the control of the central government.

The two lines of governments–central and provincial–amply reflect this stance. The duty of the Provincial Health Department therefore displayed a certain degree of overlap with the two central government units. The second period began in 1971 and ended in 1982. The Executive Yuan established a new Health Administration under its political wing in 1971. The role of the Health Administration was greatly enlarged to supervise air, water and noise pollution prevention (research initiatives and control measures) and manage municipal waste, including pesticides. The Health Administration also maintains a network of local health bureaus. The Ministry of Economics instituted a Water Resource Management Committee to direct water pollution prevention effort. Besides its Health Department, the Provincial Government added a Water Pollution Control Institute under its Department of Construction to oversee planning, permitting and training activities. The city of Kaohsiung, one of the two Yuan administered cities (the status is similar to a province), set up an Environmental Management Division to handle public hazard and local hygiene issues.

The third period, 1982 to 1987, witnessed rapid economic and population growth in the cities, accompanied by an increasing degree of environmental degradation. The Executive Yuan, which engineered the influential Environmental Protection Proposal for Taiwan Area in 1979, stimulated the birth of the Environmental Protection Agency in 1982. Environmentally associated responsibilities (air, water and noise pollution prevention) were thus delegated to this new unit within the Health Administration and supervisory duties such as the implementing of environmental impact assessment and toxic substance control were appended. The Yuan-directed cities of Kaohsiung and Taipei amalgamated their divisions of environmental hygiene and environmental management to form a single City Environmental Protection Bureau.[45]

The Provincial Government joined its Water Pollution Control Institute with the Environmental Hygiene Experimental Institute to found an Environmental Protection Bureau reporting directly to the Provincial Health Department. Recognising the importance of better co-ordinating the environmental protection effort in various government departments, and with a desire to streamline environmental protection policy making and implementation, the Executive Yuan appointed senior officials to head an Environmental Protection Team in 1986. The fourth period, post-1987, responding to government's mandates of pursuing economic development in conjunction with environmental protection, the Executive Yuan elevated the status of Environmental Protection Agency to a separate Administration (Figure 5.2), in parallel with the existing Health Administration.

The Provincial Government undertook an identical strategy. In moving from confusion (the second period) to normalisation (the fourth period), Taiwan has laid down a clear line of command. The first ever Taiwanese environmental law was adopted in 1992. Even though it had a relatively late start compared to China, the law- and policy-making principles are much more transparent, and conflict between different regulatory bodies is a rare phenomenon. The government acknowledged the distinct nature of environmental problems and formulated regulations based on the principles that polluters pay and polluters remediate, stressing preventive measures, straighten technological control, encouraging consultation and participation, and ensuring public access to relevant information. The content follows the models of direct government involvement (investing in pollution-control projects), command and control, and economic means (taxes, charges, permits and incentives). The laws and policies can be grouped into five categories: basic, administrative, control, preventive and remediative.

Although the draft basic laws are still under discussion at the Legislative Yuan, the rest have been implemented successfully. This late

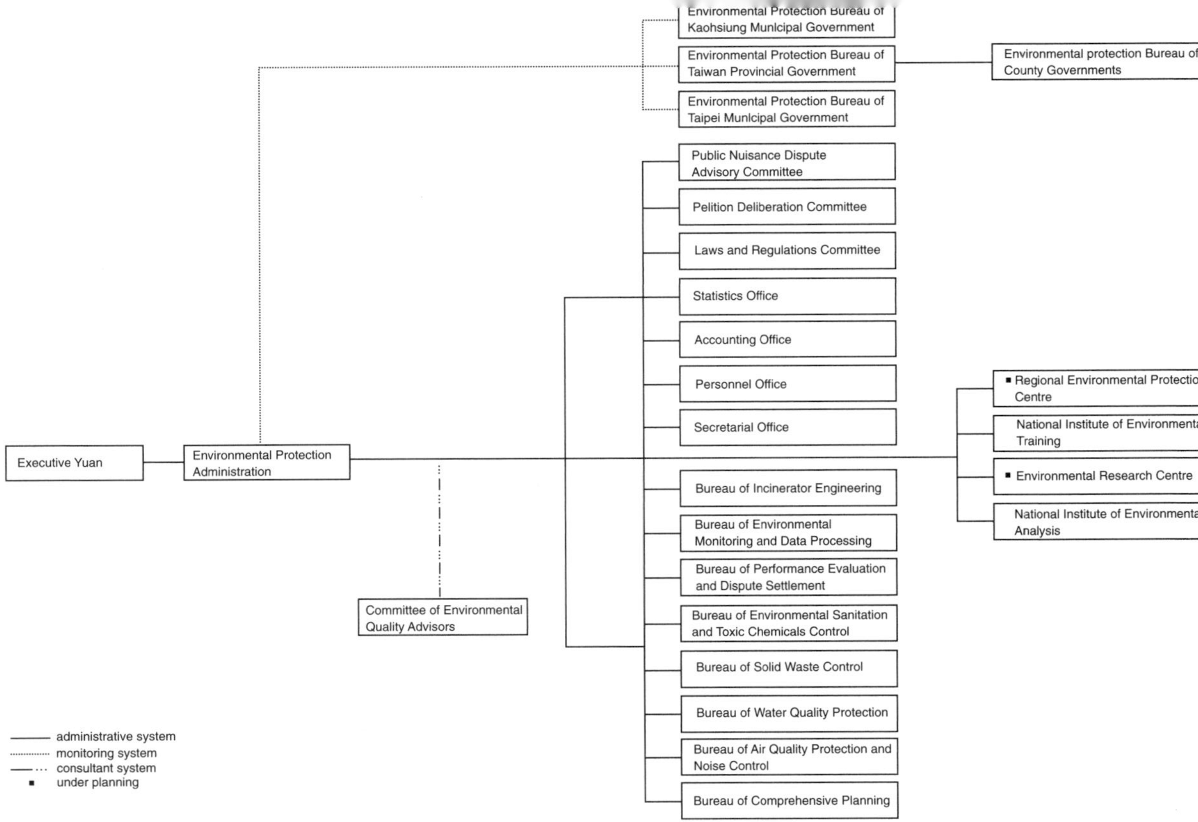

Source: Environment Protection Administration, Taiwan

Figure 5.2 The environment protection organisation in the ROC government

start also has a bearing on the number of laws and regulations in effect. Besides the basic laws, vibration control, management of chemicals for environmental use, soil pollution prevention, drinking water management and toxic substance control acts are buried somewhere in the Legislative Yuan (TEPA 1995:646–647). Interviews with a senior executive of Pilkington Plc., who negotiated for joint venture arrangements in both Taiwan and Poland, yielded criticism of Taiwan's less 'encompassing' environmental legislation. 'I didn't encounter any difficulty in Taiwan, but in Poland, the environmental officials were far more demanding on our environmental protection effort' he concluded.

Present challenges – Taiwan

Contrary to China, Taiwan has more than its share of highly trained professionals. Virtually all section heads in the TEPA, Taiwan Provincial Environmental Protection Department, and the Taipei and Kaohsiung City Environmental Protection Bureaus possess advanced degrees in appropriate fields. Most are foreign educated, often in well-established academic institutions. There is no doubt about the competency of personnel. The problem arises, however, from the free economy and the freedom of choice. Talents are concentrated in large cities and the rural counties cannot help but be confronted with the awkward situation of not being able to recruit the best. In fact, corporations in the industrial parks outside of the metropolises regularly complain about the quality of their local environmental officers. Retention of personnel is a perennial headache. The private sector is more than eager to offer attractive packages to lure experienced officials. To this end, the Taiwanese government has recently implemented laws forbidding 'job hopping' of this nature to curb inside dealings for open tender offers. The Administrator of TEPA, because of the high media exposure and the access to the Executive Yuan, has become one of the more popular posts among budding politicians and, once appointed, the incumbent is enthusiastic to make an impression on the public. Unfortunately, the duration of service is limited by the fixed-term election, and the push for certain policies, because of the personnel turnover and change in vision and perceived priority, loses its continuity.

TEPA has also been criticised for failing to solicit advice from industry before implementing regulations and standards. As far as TEPA is concerned, it obeys the mandates to make public all relevant information including draft regulations and adheres faithfully to the public comment allowance within a fixed published period. TEPA claimed to receive minimum industrial participation in this regard and resented answering complaints after the implementation of laws. Perhaps, the channels of notice distribution were to be blamed. The existing practice is distribution via trade associations and targeted industrial leaders. Trade associations then identify interested parties from whom to invite comments. The operation strongly favours huge, influential local corporations, as they are invariably well-tapped into the network. Multinational corporations (MNCs), because of the scale of their investments, which is small compared to local giants such as China Petroleum and China Petrochemical, are often excluded from the invitation list. A few local corporations have surpassed the mentality of passive compliance and found themselves at odds with the extra burden of policy analysis. MNCs, with their wealth of home experience, are denied their rights to contribute. Whether this is unintentional or not is disputable. Strategists know too well the competitive advantage of being proactive. The MNCs have certainly developed a sentiment of being collectively curtailed.

The prosperity of the Taiwanese economy largely depends on its relationship with China. Realising that integration into world trade will help insulate it from China's aggression, Taiwan is making ambitious plans to attract MNCs, and is lobbying hard to join the World Trade Organization (Crossborder Monitor 1996). Going international means greater exposure to the current world-wide trend of the greening of industry. The fear of the potential impact of ISO 14000 on Taiwanese products has already created business opportunities for the Arizona Environmental Technology Industry Cluster, an enterprising US commercial consortium (Jones 1996). As the internationalisation process speeds up, Taiwan has no choice but to subscribe to the global mandates.

5.3 China and Taiwan – into the 21st century

China and Taiwan, more than ever, are being linked together in the international arena. Taiwan's bid to join the WTO is contingent upon China's gaining entry. In the commercial world, China and Taiwan are dependent on each other. According to Kao and Lin (1994), Taiwanese investment in mainland China has provided hundreds of thousands of jobs, supplied foreign reserves, improved product quality, modernised production technology, and contributed substantially to the overall GDP. China's open position to Taiwanese investment can also be seen as politically motivated in order to forge economic interdependence as a basis for reunification. For example, the latest round of economic structural transformation in Taiwan has induced a large outflow of investment to China. If the trend continues, Taiwan will grow to depend on China for its survival. Is China on the winning side? One cannot readily reach an answer. Despite Taiwan's financial and technological contribution to China, there is an increasingly large trade deficit in favour of Taiwan, coupled with the less than desirable side effects of the investment such as environmental pollution (Wu 1994, Clark 1994). Perhaps the 'abnormalcies', as cited by Wu (1994), really have their roots in political motivation. Faced with its dirty cities, rivers and polluted air, the Chinese authorities may soon lose their patience. Even though NEPA officials had repeatedly expressed a desire to meet with their TEPA counterparts, given the warning issued by the Chairman of the Chinese Communist Party at the Hong Kong hand-over ceremony on 1 July 1997 and the official statement against President Chen of Taiwan, the meeting is unlikely to materialise in the near future.

Both China and Taiwan are actively considering means for collaboration without a substantial involvement of high-ranked government officials. The allowance for three direct links between China and Kinmen, Taiwan, for the first time in 48 years in an excellent example of this much desired change in the making (*The Economist*, 1 July 2001). To discourage unethical investment in any form, the banking sector can attach conditions to its approval of commercial loans (Nitsche 1997). The Bank of China, since 1995, has stipulated environmental protection conditions on its evaluation of loan applications. Moreover, the State plans to establish environmental protection funds, and the departments concerned will issue interest discount compensation for bank loans earmarked for environmental protection.[46] In the pollution-intensive industrial sector, the environmental-protection-leading group of the Ministry of Chemical Industry has developed an ambitious plan for the eighth Five-Year period to integrate industrial chemical production and construction with development in environmental protection. The plan stressed the simultaneous realisation of economic, social and environmental benefits (PRC National Environmental Protection Agency and State Planning Commission 1994:46,108).

China can now afford to exercise tougher guidelines to assess foreign investment proposals. This is particularly true in the popular coastal zones, but tends to be less so in inland provinces. For poor inland provinces, the government can channel large-scale foreign investment or clusters of foreign investments, and assist in the construction of essential infrastructure. Proper planning is crucial and can lead to upgrading the economic climate of a given region. The possibilities are numerous, but the Chinese government should earnestly examine the problem of corruption. Foreign investors have reported stories of needing to bribe a power station operator to ensure stable power supply, for example. Even a large state-owned enterprise complained about 'paying off' over-zealous environmental officers for a brief instance of exceeding air emission standards, regardless of a legally sound time-weighted average.

The essence of doing business in China is best summarised by Child and Boisot (1996:612): 'many business transactions in China appear to be settled through negotiation within a system of networked relations based on interpersonal reciprocal obligations (*guanxi*), with local government being a major player as resource provider, facilitator, and tax collector'. There appears to be no exception in environmental protection, and in many cases, excellent *guanxi* can be exchanged for the payment of a personal or financial favour (an unofficial 'environmental protection fee'). This is hardly a surprise, as Biggart and Hamilton (1992:472) observed, 'Asian economies are organised through networks of economic actors that are believed to be natural and appropriate to economic development'. Scott (1995:44) further commented, 'relations among persons or firms that the West views as collusion, the East sees as normal, inevitable, and beneficial'.

The picture is not as bleak as it may seem. The environmental protection effort is progressing in China, albeit slowly, and the pollution transfer can gradually be dealt with. It is argued that in this somewhat chaotic moment, large reputable MNCs can fulfil a particular mission by acting as intermediaries between two governments technically 'at war' with each other. Large MNCs are resourceful, sophisticated and capable of contributing to environmental policy making. In many aspects, the resemblance between a large MNC and a country is striking. Large MNCs with subsidiaries in both China and Taiwan are in a good position to shape environmental policy development, as the host countries are eager to learn. Dow Chemicals, ICI, Du Pont and several other MNCs are, in fact, pushing for the adoption of Responsible Care in Taiwan, and China is anxiously awaiting their help in administering Cleaner Production programmes.

A careful study of MNCs' response patterns to various environmental regulations in their home countries can aid in predicting the impact of regulations in formulation, and can facilitate in modification. MNCs' wide and varied experience in complying with the regulatory demands, for example, from their plants in the US and Mexico, can assist in pollution transfer control. MNCs can also play a significant role in transferring technological know-how and introducing green technologies. The governments in China and Taiwan should therefore allow more avenues for consultation. Representatives (i.e. the MNCs) from the American Chamber of Commerce in Taiwan, have been meeting with TEPA on a periodic basis and their consultants are in close contacts with the senior officials. The EPA and several EU environmental ministers have visited China and Taiwan to promote green technologies and introduce innovative policy tools for pollution abatement. The fast pace of internationalisation by China and Taiwan will enhance their general publics' awareness of environmental protection as a global issue, and lead to an increase in international co-operation.

5.4 Summary – country profiles

China and Taiwan are two rival siblings experiencing unprecedented economic growth. Despite its recent economic achievements, China is still considered a developing country. Taiwan, through the past four decades of laborious struggle, has brought itself into the rank of newly industrialised country. Rapid economic growth invariably damages the natural environment and neither China nor Taiwan is well-prepared to tackle the adverse effects of industrialisation. The concept of sustainable development has recently been introduced to the Greater China area, and under international mandates both China and Taiwan are actively pursuing measures to improve their records in SHE protection. Their respective limitations in fulfilling their greening roles are summarised in Table 5.2.

II. Company profiles

In the second part of this chapter, while observing the confidentiality agreement, I have developed short profiles of the companies studied. The aim is to render an impression of the official corporate SHE commitment, and the size, as well as the types, of the commercial and manufacturing operations. All names are fictitious; historical, personal and operational details have been omitted to protect the rights of the informants.

5.5 Profile of an MNC – Niesler Chemicals

Niesler, a UK-based MNC, contains a coherent group of international businesses (five major businesses with eight sub-business units and five regional businesses) and ranks among the largest chemical manufacturers in the world. Its products cover virtually the entire spectrum of daily living, and enjoy world-wide market dominance in selected speciality chemical sectors. The development of the Group is largely supported by integrated manufacturing chains drawing on inter-business supplies of key raw materials and intermediates. The operations have in recent years benefited from increased sharing of skills across related businesses, including expertise in operating complex chemical

Table 5.2 Comparison of Chinese and Taiwanese environmental management

	China	*Taiwan*
Country status	Developing, socialist	Newly-industrialised, pseudo-capitalist
Comprehensiveness of SHE laws and regulations	Inadequate	Inadequate
Conflicting SHE laws/regulations	Yes	No
SHE law formulation and enforcement mechanism	Decentralised	Relatively centralised
Deployment of market-based instrument	Yes, permits payment of an environmental charge in lieu of SHE protection	Yes
Use of cost-benefit analysis in SHE law-making	No	No
Allowance for public participation/comment in SHE law-Making	No	Yes
Transparency of legislative chain of command	Ambiguous	Clear
Professional knowledge level of law-enforcing staff	Low	Generally high, though standards somewhat vary in the provincial/ county environmental protection bureaus
Connectiveness to industry	Low	Moderate
Phase of SHE protection	Infancy	Adolescence
Commitment of national leaders in SHE protection	Low	Moderate
Presence of SHE NGOs	No	Yes
Public awareness	Low	High
Public action (voluntary SHE protection initiatives)	Low, almost non-existent	Moderate
Media coverage of SHE protection initiatives	High, though politically motivated	High

plants requiring sophisticated process technology and engineering. Niesler, relative to its principal competitors, has an extremely focused research and technology (R&T) programme.

The CEOs of the operating businesses are fully accountable for the performance, including SHE, of their businesses and are also members of an Executive Group led by the Group Chief Executive who oversees the development of the company as a whole and is appointed by the Niesler Board. An Executive Director, again appointed by the Board, has a specific responsibility for overseeing SHE matters across the Niesler Group. The Board of each Niesler subsidiary is responsible for establishing, implementing and monitoring SHE policies and standards, which are consistent with the local laws and the Niesler Group policy, standards and guidelines, and as supplemented by the implementation strategy of the CEOs of their sponsoring business. Each operating site within the Niesler Group is required to establish and maintain an annual improvement plan, which incorporates measures to meet Group SHE performance targets. The CEOs are required regularly to review overall SHE performance of their business with the Executive Directors of the Board. The Group SHE Manager is responsible for promoting SHE matters and for regular reporting to the Board.

The emphasis on sustaining its status as a leading global player has led Niesler to devote a substantial amount of capital on SHE protection; the total expenditure on SHE for the year of 1996 was in excess of US$0.8 billion. SHE protection occupies a separate and large section in Niesler's annual reports. In addition, the Group has produced environmental performance reports on a yearly basis since 1991. The content encompasses items such as hazardous and non-hazardous waste reduction statistics, substance emission data, compliance with regulatory standards, prosecutions and penalties, complaints by the public, and awards. In the special issue, 1990 to 1995, Niesler reviewed its five-year environmental improvement objectives set in 1990, and outlined its SHE challenges for the next five years. In developing the objectives, Niesler adopted an approach of directing expenditure to the biggest problems for which solutions would bring the most benefit. As a result, the emissions of hazardous wastes were reduced by more than 50% at a time of increased production, and the compliance with environmental consents improved from 90% in 1990 to almost 100% in 1995. Niesler recognised, through its world-wide operations, that environmental laws around the world are becoming stricter, as a reflection of the increased concern for the environment, and meeting these standards can be challenging in countries that have cultures, standards, attitudes and laws that are drastically different from those in the EU or

North America. Despite this fact, in streamlining its SHE compliance effort, Niesler requires all its new plants to be built to standards that will meet the regulations it can reasonably anticipate in the most environmentally demanding country in which it operates that process. Each business operates a Design and Technology Centre to ensure the appropriate adoption of technologies and supply expert advice on the schematic design of a plant. This normally demands the use of best environmental practice within the industry. In recycling, Niesler introduced a product stewardship programme extending its responsibilities from the 'cradle to grave' (life-cycle). In all of Niesler's SHE endeavour, the corporate headquarters conduct routine formal audits and assessments on its operations and contractors. The world-wide activities are operated in accordance with the Niesler Group Safety, Health and Environmental Policy, which is determined by the Board, and Niesler strives to ensure that the health of all its employees, its customers and the public are protected. In its international operations, Niesler added that its environmental performance will meet contemporary requirements, and its operations will run in a manner acceptable to the local communities.

The implementation of the Policy across all the diverse range of Niesler's world-wide activities is through the Group SHE Management System. The key elements of the System are the Policy, Standards, Guidelines, Local Procedures, Auditing and Letters of Assurance. The Policy, Standards and Guidelines augment, but do not replace, legislation that applies to Niesler's activities. The Niesler Group SHE Standards are set by the Board in consultation with the Chief Executive Officers of the international businesses. These Standards are the basic management requirements, applicable to all of the activities in which Niesler Group participates. The Niesler Group Guidelines provide each manager with details of key principles which should be incorporated into workable local procedures. They also provide advice as to how principles should be applied, and give reference to other useful internal documents. The Guidelines are based upon the experience of SHE professionals and managers from Niesler's businesses, territories and corporate functions. Niesler is a proponent of the International Chamber of Commerce (ICC)'s *Business Charter for Sustainable Development* and a supporter of the chemical industries 'Responsible Care' initiatives.

Niesler has several business operations in Taiwan and can trace its association with the Taiwanese community back to the 1950s, shortly after the Second World War. The Asia-Pacific regional SHE Manager as well as the Managing Director for Niesler Taiwan, who also participates in business policy formation in the Asia-Pacific Region, are based in the Taiwan office. Hong Kong is another strategic location for the

Asia-Pacific region, with a concentration of key managers/personnel in various group businesses. The business operation studied in Taiwan (in specialised industrial chemicals) is a joint venture formed approximately 20 years ago with a large local chemical manufacturer, which was formerly state-owned. Niesler holds the majority of the equity shares as well as the control of the management functions. The plant occupies a portion of an active manufacturing compound owned by the joint venture partner and both parties share the maintenance of major utility lines, but each retained 'autonomy' within its own boundary of operation. The compound is located in one of the busiest petrochemical complexes in Taiwan with no fewer than 11 different companies as neighbours. The proximity of the complex to a residential neighbourhood, due to poor government land-use planning and the acute space shortage problem in general, was a matter of much complaint and resentment. Niesler was confronted with a critical event – a large scale protest from the public – a few years ago and that had a significant impact on the Group Policy, Standards and Guidelines *vis-à-vis* contractors. As the frequency of protests increased and the need for hard evidence to establish a fair legal case surfaced, the government and industry co-operated in situating a pollution monitoring centre for the entire complex, and Niesler has 91 emission detectors linked to the centre which operate 24 hours a day.

Niesler engaged in fewer business ventures in China, partly as a result of the country's relatively late 'open door' policy and the setback of the Tiananmen incident. The business operation studied (in household chemicals) is one of Niesler's pioneering projects in China and assumed the form of joint venture with an influential British trading house and a Chinese local enterprise. Niesler owns a majority of the equity shares and undertakes day-to-day management roles of the joint venture. The plant is located in a new industrial complex catering for foreign investors and far away from the city and residential property. The city is one of the first to 'open' and is commercially progressive in Chinese terms. The quality of the infrastructure and the business mentality can be ranked far above the Chinese average. The city attracts a large number of foreign investors and the government authority exercises stringent criteria in approving an investment proposal. Tough SHE standards were imposed from the beginning on Niesler, to the extent of specifying landscaping requirements. The plant was hence built to the most strict Niesler/PRC specifications with pre-construction ground analysis and sampling, above ground pipelines, isolation and alarm systems, catchment area, and no underground storage tanks. More than

25% of the area was not built upon to allow for easy emergency dispersion. The plant employs a Chinese physician as a SHE Manager and he maintains a dual reporting relationship with the General Manager, who reports to his respective Asia-Pacific Business Director, and the Regional SHE Manager in Taiwan, who visits the plant on a routine basis for auditing and training purposes. Only licensed contractors are allowed onsite and the plant offers them additional SHE training prior to starting jobs. The plant operates an innovative recycling programme to supply food waste from the canteen to local pig farmers.

5.6 Profile of an MNC – Eghbalian Chemicals

Eghbalian Chemicals is huge, measured by both its income, in multiple billions of US dollars and the number of its products, in excess of 2000. Larger than the Niesler Group, Eghbalian is, in fact, among the top in the Global 500 listing and operates more than 150 manufacturing sites in more than 30 countries. Its headquarters in the US are a synonym for a medium-sized city. Eghbalian's largest divisions – Plastics and Chemicals – went through major restructuring, and 30 businesses groups were arranged into three global business units to facilitate faster decision making and to eliminate duplicated efforts. The division of Consumer Speciality Products, which comprises three businesses and is primarily operated by Eghbalian subsidiaries, has yet to witness organisational change. Eghbalian is recognised for its leadership in environmental protection, and its strength in environmental research and development has generated much income for its commercial application. Eghbalian's health and environmental science expertise not only provides services for managing company activities relating to the protection of human health and the environment, but also offers a basis for advocating the consideration of sound scientific principles and effective technological alternatives in statutory proposals. Consequently, Eghbalian's remediation technologies are much in demand by other companies, sometimes even its arch-rivals, concerned with meeting the fast-evolving regulatory standards world-wide. 'We know that the winners of tomorrow will be those companies that integrate environmental issues into all of their business policies, and our experience is proving it', proclaimed the vice president of Environment, Health & Safety and Public Affairs.

SHE enjoys a high profile in Eghbalian's Board of Directors. The Vice President is concurrently the Corporate Director of Environment, Health & Safety and Public Affairs. A Committee of the Board of Directors is dedicated exclusively to SHE-related issues. Eghbalian has defined as one of its core values the appreciation of conduct that demonstrates deep concern for ethics, citizenship, safety, health and the environment. The rigour and the involvement of the highest management level in the SHE Policy, Standards, and Guidelines formulation is similar to that of the Niesler Group, but minor differences in wording can be detected. Eghbalian declares that protecting people and the environment is of paramount importance in its business strategy formation and operations. The company therefore aims to eliminate all injuries, prevent adverse environmental and health impacts, reduce waste and emissions, promote resource conservation at every stage of the life cycle of its products, meet the applicable government or its own standards, whichever is more stringent, and will report its progress and be responsive to the public. The Policy, Standard and Guidelines are implemented, again much like the Niesler Group, via an Environmental Management System (see Figure 5.3).

The system, which is more explicit than the other MNCs, calls for using cost/benefit analysis in evaluating appropriate technology to comply with the contents of environmental protection requirements.[47] The delegation of responsibilities to the different corporate levels is analogous to Niesler. Clear accountability and reporting requirements at all levels (corporate, areas, country/site) are specified and each business, area and country/site, including the joint venture sites, is expected to compile emission inventories and fix its own emission reduction goals annually. Eghbalian Technology Centres are consulted in all phases of SHE protection to consolidate the effort and ascertain proper application of the technologies. Internal and external audits (also on the contractors and non-Eghbalian waste management facilities) are performed to enforce adherence to the Eghbalian Policy, Standards, and Guidelines; the procedures are identical to the those of the Niesler Group. Published SHE reporting, in the form of annual SHE reports, is reasonably comprehensive and contains all the vital statistics. Like Niesler, Eghbalian is a strong advocate for an industry-wide adoption of the 'Responsible Care' programme and an early subscriber to the ICC Business Charter. Eghbalian has received numerous commendations on its SHE protection effort, and its waste minimisation programme is highly acclaimed.

Eghbalian maintains a comparatively humble presence in Taiwan, in spite of the presence of a District office. Most of the business policy implementation is executed through its Hong Kong office. The Pacific Area President, Vice President for Operations, and SHE and Public and Community Affairs Director are based in Hong Kong, while the Greater China SHE Manager is based in Taiwan and commutes frequently to

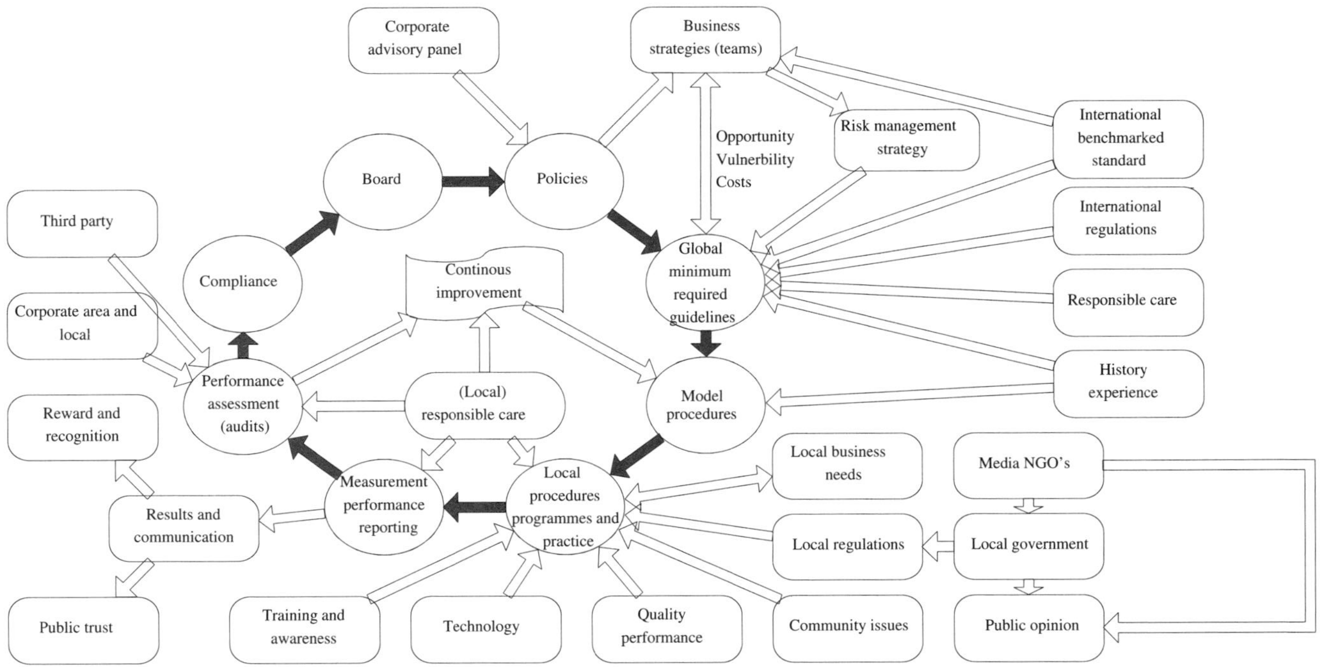

Source: Adapted from a Company Internal Document, Eghbalian Chemicals

Figure 5.3 Eghbalian environmental management system

China. The operations in Taiwan are predominantly sales-orientated, and manufacturing activities, numbered three, are recent phenomena. The business operation studied is a new, wholly owned chemical production plant. The site is located in an industrial complex. Perhaps because of the small scale of manufacturing, this investment project did not arouse much protest from the public, though it encountered opposition in its initial choice of site. The government, which was eager to attract large, reputable MNCs, granted Eghbalian the existing, less controversial site. The SHE protection effort is spearheaded by the Greater China SHE Manager, who happens to reside with the business operation studied. Contrary to Eghbalian's moderately uneventful experience in Taiwan, the business operation studied in China encountered much trouble since commissioning. The Chinese operation is a joint venture with a local upstream chemical manufacturer. The union was somewhat directed by the Chinese government and obeyed the old quota rules of joint venture partner selection, by which an investor had no choice but to enter into agreement with a partner in the same line of business at the chosen site location. The joint venture partner had a separate agenda from the start. Lacking a helpful joint venture partner translated into ineffective dealing with the local power authority and resulted in unstable electricity supply, which often upset the sensitive chemical reactions. Although the plant was built to the state-of-the-art Eghbalian/PRC specifications in satisfying the government's desire for technology transfer, finding experienced Chinese maintenance workers had proved to be impossible. Despite the unpleasant experience, Eghbalian conducted itself responsively to the SHE demands. Unlike many other MNCs, which search for equivalent SHE standards and guidelines when venturing into a developing country, Eghbalian incorporated a vent and liquid waste incinerator and a water treatment plant in its plant design. The capital investment was enormous and represented a bold and costly move to defy 'peer' pressure of relying on contractors for waste disposal.

5.7 Profile of an MNC – Romanowski Chemicals

Romanowski is another big American chemical giant and a long-time business companion of Eghbalian. The two have managed to coexist without much invasion of each other's sacred territories and, together with a number of large chemical manufacturers, have successfully barred new domestic entrants to the American chemical market for decades. Whether this was done as a deliberate business strategy of collusion or as a natural consequence of the government's early protectionist policy remains a good question. It is, however, a known fact that

Eghbalian and Romanowski are well-established in the global chemical scene and are forever expanding. Romanowski is ranked within the top 100 MNCs of the UNCTAD listing and operates more than 200 sites in 35 countries. Romanowski consists of five broadly defined businesses, and recent organisational restructuring eliminated large business sectors in favour of smaller, strategic business units (SBUs). On another axis, the company is organised by region (Europe, Asia-Pacific, South America, etc) and followed by area (Japan, China, Brazil, Mexico, etc). SHE is deemed to be a key strategic issue and a former senior officer of the US EPA is a member of the Board. An Environmental Policy Committee, alongside the Strategic Direction Committee, is an integral part of the Board. The Environmental Leadership Council, composed of senior officers of the company, approves business/policy proposals and oversees performance monthly. The Safety, Health and Environmental Excellence Centre assists Romanowski businesses to assure progress towards corporate SHE goals. In responding to the challenge of environmental policy-making, Romanowski has devised a corporate-wide information-gathering and resource-allocation global planning tool entitled Corporate Environmental Plan to integrate environmental with business thinking. It warrants the most effective use of corporate resources by imposing a common world-wide framework to:

- ensure compliance with existing and future regulatory requirements
- implement overall corporate environmental policies
- develop and achieve specific waste and emissions reduction goals
- improve the prioritisation of environmental initiatives, and
- collect information to aid in formulating environmental strategies.

The Chairman and CEO of Romanowski, who is also named Chief Environmental Officer, has been actively promoting the concept of environmental stewardship in his countless lecture and seminar engagements.

The SHE Policy, Standards and Guidelines formulation and implementation are mirror images of Niesler and Eghbalian's enterprising effort. SHE public reporting and internal reporting requirements also resemble the procedures in place at these two MNCs. One may argue that the US Community Right-To-Know Act, as manifested in SARA Title III, has a part in it, but interviews with a senior officer at Niesler and Eghbalian disclosed that the increased reliance on the same external consultants had a significant bearing on the corporate policy. The name A. D. Little[48] was mentioned repeatedly, as were the names of several noted academic-consultants. The senior SHE officers of the major MNCs meet regularly, either through their common subscription to the US Chemical Manufacturers' Association's (CMA) Responsible Care programme and the ICC Business Charter for Sustainable Development, or via attending conferences. The frequency of their meetings exhibited an increase with new market entry, especially in an foreign environment. The personnel 'exchange', as new business ventures of a MNC promise promotion to the senior officer who has reached a career ceiling in the employing MNC, further contributed to the trend of the industry's standardisation of SHE practices.

Romanowski is especially noted for its safety record and the knowledge behind its success is being transferred to its closest allies. An excellent SHE reputation forms an effective tool in market-entry negotiation in developing countries, in the light of increased global environmental awareness and the host countries' desire to learn from the MNCs experiences. The company policy statement, which stipulates adherence to the highest standards for the safe operation of facilities and the protection of the environment, the employees, the customers and the people of the immediate communities and urges continuous improvement accounting for the advances in technology and new understanding in safety, health and environmental science, is much welcome by the host governments and the general public alike. Romanowski, like Niesler and Eghbalian, had been invited to organise training classes for the host country SHE officers. Romanowski's SHE record, as demonstrated by its meeting in the United States of the EPA's 33/50 interim emission reduction goals of its 17 large-volume toxic materials and the constant upward percentage reduction in its emission of air toxics and airborne carcinogens, is concrete evidence of its commitment to make consistent, measurable progress throughout its world-wide operations.

Romanowski Taiwan and Romanowski China are similar in function. Both are sales and distribution offices that facilitate communication among different SBU manufacturing sites. A corporate site was recently founded in China to provide technical service and training for its personnel. The power to authorise business policy change lies with the heads of the SBUs, who direct the world-wide operations. The SHE protection effort comes under the duties of two managers located in Taiwan and Hong Kong (for Romanowski China). Each SBU manufacturing site employs its own SHE co-ordinator, and reports to both the SBU and the country SHE manager. The Asia-Pacific SHE Manager superintends from the Singapore office.

The business operation studied in Taiwan was established in the 1970s and is wholly owned. The operation is small in scale, low in profile and situated in an industrial complex. The electronic component products generate high demands from the nearby Industrial and Science Park, and is expanding in response to the boom in the electronics industry. Romanowski attracted much attention during the awakening of Taiwanese environmental awareness for its bleaching chemical investment proposal. The academic community and the NGOs launched a large-scale investigation of Romanowski's world-wide SHE records and staged protests against the government for introducing pollution-intensive operations. The first choice site was rejected due to an overwhelmingly 'sentimental and passionate' protest from the local residents. It was here Romanowski re-learned its lessons on community and public relations within a different cultural and regulatory context. The costly exercise exerted impacts on Romanowski's world-wide practices and stimulated the company to aggressively publicise its SHE programmes. Romanowski has since instituted funds to improve the quality of life for the local communities and has been cautious in proceeding with its new world-wide business ventures.

The business operation studied in China is a joint venture with a Chinese chemical company, which was elected from a list drawn up by the government. The negotiation started in the 1980s and was halted by the Tiananmen incident, but resumed very shortly after. The 'goodwill' earned Romanowski great bargaining power in site selection and the plant was commissioned in the early 1990s. In this project, Romanowski enjoyed the majority of equity share and management control but was met with the problem of intellectual property protection. Chinese laws grant patents to the products but not to the manufacturing process. If the process could be duplicated easily and inexpensively, the company would encounter a high risk of making a loss. A case for transferring the most up-to-date and sophisticated manufacturing process (one of the Romanowski's most valued proprietary technologies) was made, but with a cost. The company had to afford the capital investment for offsetting the inadequacy of infrastructural and technical support, in addition to the capital investment associated with SHE protection to fulfil the objectives set forth in the Corporate Environmental Plan. This type of dilemma, involving high initial set-up costs, is not an atypical occurrence in China, and an optimal solution is hard to derive without an acute ethical business vision. Perhaps large, reputable MNCs deserve to be commended for their long-term strategic planning and global environmental stewardship.

5.8 Profile of a Chinese state-owned enterprise – Lin Chemicals

Lin Chemicals is one of the largest members under the umbrella organisation of the China Petrochemical General Corporation (SINOPEC).

The management power rests with several parties – the CEOs of SINOPEC, the President of Lin and the Chinese government (chiefly the State Council and the State Planning Commission). Lin is based in an exceedingly large complex, occupying an entire city in the north of China and employing close to 50000 people. Lin ranks in the top 10 of the 500 large Chinese industrial enterprises in terms of sales income and turned-in taxes and profits, and within the top 5 in the chemical sector based on comprehensive economic efficiency. Lin operates its own scientific research and design institutes, and boasts a construction arm catering for its own needs. Lin's products, totalling six main lines, are marketed to more than 30 countries and regions throughout the world. As a state-owned enterprise, Lin's development is closely linked to and affected by the national development agenda, and its SHE objectives reflect what the State desires to achieve in view of the economic growth rate and international pressure. Lin has been ear-marked as the 'target' petrochemical corporation for demonstrating SHE protection initiatives. A Safety Committee in Production was firmly incorporated under the control of the President of the company.

By Western standards, SHE protection at Lin is still in a rudimentary stage. Besides the national directives, the company lacks a corporate SHE policy and comprehensive standards and guidelines are non-existent. The national 'Eighth Five-Year Plan'[49] has greatly improved Lin's SHE protection effort. Strict national emission standards were applied and penalties for violation were levied. The turning point for the corporate SHE protection mentality arrived in the 1980s when industrial waste water discharge aroused huge protest and mass demonstration from the farmers downstream from the discharge. Blockades were formed on the access road and discharge pipelines were sealed. Since public assembly of such nature is against the constitution of the country, the local police force and the People's Liberation Army were mobilised to rectify the situation and Lin was under strong government mandate to 'clean up'. Lin has since learned the lessons and is slowly progressing along the route of greening.

5.9 Profile of a Taiwanese firm – Wang Chemicals

Wang is a 'legendary' private corporation, as cited by the popular media in Taiwan. Its size is far from comparable to the three MNCs studied, but it enjoys global market dominance in one of the key ingredient for the high performance plastics. Wang's success may be attributed to its fast and informal decision making. Business proposal submission is rare within the company and the President can authorise a verbal proposal in the company canteen subjected to a short feasibility study (or cost/benefit analysis). Wang has fully implemented ISO 9002 and is seeking certification for ISO 14000. Its SHE arm is under the management of a Vice-President, and the President is a defender of ethical business conduct and manages with style. All the profits are fully vested in the employees, and Wang is a noted patron of cultural activities and contributed munificently to the local communities. Wang believes in SHE budget 'without cap' and the company has consistently won environmental improvement medals from the TEPA and its waste water treatment plant is visited frequently by university engineering students for exemplary design. The informal atmosphere within Wang has a bearing on its insistence of not imposing excessive formal procedures on its employees. The Chinese humanistic management style reigns high and the company deliberately shies away from rule-making, individualistic, newly minted MBA graduates. Official SHE Policy, Standards, and Guidelines are nowhere to be found, and SHE issues cover only a small section (violations, penalties and expenditure) of the company annual report. However, the company was able to produce more than satisfactory SHE records. The implication is certainly reflective for those companies which condone rules, procedures, rationality and tight control.

Wang was victimised by the wave of irrational environmental protests in Taiwan, mainly because of its high visibility. Protests were held in the industrial complex in which Wang is a major tenant. Financial compensation was demanded for the adverse health effects resulting from the alleged pollution episodes, and the local government failed to serve as an effective intermediary due to the absence of longitudinal data from either side to clearly delineate responsibilities. Throughout the unrest, Wang was a subject of sympathy from its peers.

5.10 Summary – company profiles

The description of three MNCs, a Chinese SOE, and a Taiwanese private enterprise allows an understanding of their respective organisational structure and chains of commands. The three MNCs are large, diversified, and sophisticated in their handling of SHE-related matters. The Chinese SOE, as would be expected, maintains a close relationship with the state and has been selected as a 'target' corporation for SHE protection. The Taiwanese enterprise has achieved success in the global market place, and can now afford to place an emphasis on SHE protection. The diverse nature of these companies promises interesting observations in the study of greening strategic change.

6
Context – is it Important?

> Now you have got what is described as Chief Executive strategies where Chief Executives around the world are saying 'we must be in China', and there is almost a reckless dash to get involved in China. People feel that they have to be there because of the development that is going on. Back in 1987/8, there was less enthusiasm and there was more concern about the potential risks, because what had happened was that in the early eighties when China first started out, there was a lot of euphoria. People came in and took a very naive view of doing business in China. They saw this vast market and were bemused by the size of the population and the size of the opportunity, and a lot of people made bad investment decisions and partnerships and many of the early joint ventures failed disastrously. I think that was in part because people had unrealistic expectations.
>
> China boasts a large market and it's hard to give up. For example, the Taiwanese market for NR-01 staggers around 400 tons, while in China, the number is 1 M tons. It really depends on if you want to gamble. Then, why didn't we wait until the situation cleared up? One must understand that besides regulations, one needs to pay attention to other factors . . . We are looking at the longer term.
>
> General Manager, China case business operation, and Asia-Pacific SHE Manager, Niesler Group

The question to what extent MNCs engage in pollution-transfer and invest selectively in countries with lax environmental regulations demands a carefully constructed answer. Investment in a developing country by a well-established MNC is often framed as an essential component of its globalisation strategy. The models of multi-domestic and multi-national strategy formation have aroused contention in recent years. Indeed, business policy formation for MNCs is exceptionally complicated and involves multiple groups of stakeholders competing for dominance. The motivating factors for the competition are undoubtedly linked to past experiences, convoluted networks of relations and new strategic objectives. Pettigrew (1987), in his strategic change perspective, referred to such background issues as 'context' and argued for its proper treatment in management research. Definitions for contextual factors are inexorably problematic due to the influence of different schools of thought and a categorisation scheme for them would unquestionably incite comments and debates. An indisputable claim is that contextual factors vary with the *dimension of time*. A business strategy formation with a longer-term strategic intent will involve a more disparate set of contextual factors than will a shorter-term one. A MNC's vision of becoming a true global player has much influence on its business policy formation. The deliberation is predominantly longer-term but a well-defined rationality may not necessarily accompany it, as evident in the case of 'chief executive strategies', as in the case of a firm 'following the herd'.

This structure of this chapter, based on the two broad classification of contextual factors (Pettigrew 1987): inner (self-interest driven) and outer (environmentally constrained). I place economic/market and ethical factors into the former category and institutional factors into the latter.

6.1 Inner context

Economic factors

In the case of this research, the decisions to invest in China and Taiwan by MNCs, were largely inspired by a desire to gain a foothold in the Greater China region and an ultimate desire to complete their global business integration strategies. SHE is an indispensable constituent of this consideration but its image diminishes in the background of the 'big corporate picture'. According to an Eghbalian Pacific Regional SHE Manager:

> [SHE regulation] is not part of our decision process. *It really doesn't enter into it because our greater driving force is market, distribution and these are the things that will drive our plant's siting along with potential*

> *environmental impact. Regulation doesn't really drive our plant siting.* We have not built anywhere that I know of because the environmental regulations were too stringent or not stringent enough. That has not been the over-riding factor. I would be part of any site selection team, but they would first look to those that make business sense and then before the final decision is made on a site selection . . . As part of their general site selection criteria, they have environmental criteria that they are expected to look at. Eventually I need to go visit and do an environmental impact assessment and generally there is enough data around to give you the first indication of whether it is going to be a problem or not. You don't want to be next door to houses, separation distances, all that sort of stuff. *But environmental regulations is not one of our site selection criteria.*[50]
>
> Regional SHE Manager, Eghbalian Pacific

The responses of Romanowski's General Manager in China and an SHE Manager in Taiwan followed the same line of reasoning and echoed the sentiment of MNCs' desire to expand their current markets. *Early market entry* in maximising strategic benefits and a conquest for a large market share when the competition is relatively soft had the greatest impact on MNCs' actions.

> Asia remained a weak point. Although there were businesses in Japan and Taiwan, China would be a big market for years to come. China is also a huge agricultural country feeding 1.2 billion people. But consumption of agricultural chemicals is only one-tenth of that of USA. The agricultural chemical market has huge potential. That's why Romanowski singled out agricultural chemicals from its vast range of products for the joint venture project. Romanowski already had a solely owned plant in Guangdong. But its business is mainly processing. This is the first manufacturing project.
>
> General Manager, Romanowski China

> Next, I'd like to present the rationales for setting up the factory. Romanowski has the largest share of bleaching chemicals in the world market. The major development in this market for the 20th and 21st centuries is in the Asia-Pacific region. In 1989 or 1990, we made a Greater China plan. Given the population in mainland China, the favourable situation of Hong Kong, and the skilled human resource in Taiwan, we think this market is well worth developing.
>
> SHE Manager, Romanowski Taiwan

The Greater China region is judged by many to be the Mecca of future business activities, thanks to its vast population and the entrepreneur spirit of Chinese society. The no-nonsense work ethics and the aspiration of achieving a better living standard are some of the many factors propelling the country to move rapidly forward and form the foundation of a dynamic market. If the market and the potential earning figures induced the MNCs to invest in the Greater China region, the predicted amount of profit should be quite respectable. At least, theoretically, MNCs, which enjoy various forms of tax concession and incentive, should be on the track to recover their initial set-up costs after several years of operations in the region. However, the reality is not comforting. Except for a small number of well-established subsidiaries in Taiwan, all the MNCs studied were making losses. The following statement of an Eghbalian Plant Manager in China epitomised the frustration among the case MNC senior executives:

> So with all these bad things, you know, you come right back around a full circle and you say 'why did you come here?' I mean there must be a reason . . . Philosophers say that there are three major driving forces in the whole wide world. And everything can be put into those three categories. People do what they do either for power, money or sex. Now there may be some more but let's say, let you and I agree that the vast majority of things that happen are driven by those three items. Okay so now let's see. What is the one that's driving in China? I don't think it's sex because the culture here is such that with the one child syndrome, which is pretty strictly enforced; I mean the mind set here, say a couple is in their mid thirties and they have one child who is five years old, their mind set is okay I love my wife but you know sex is dangerous so it's not necessarily true that they are going to have a lot of sex. There's not a lot of drive there. Power – there's three circles of power in China that I've discovered. There's the family circle. There's the company that you work for circle and then there's the country. Unfortunately, Eghbalian lies in the fourth circle. Very interesting. We're trying to drive it down to an inner circle. Another thing I've learnt is that inside that circle you will do anything for those people. For people outside that circle it's okay to lie, steal, cheat whatever because you're really protecting this inner circle. That's against my teachings. I've even questioned if my teachings are right. I still think they are. No matter what God you worship or no God at all. So let's go back here. It's not sex, it's probably power and money. So I mean we're not here

for the short-term money; it's simply not there. It's not sex, it's not power, looks like we're misfit. Maybe it's the luring market or maybe it's the long term 25% of the people on the face of this earth live in China?

Plant General Manager, Eghbalian

Regardless of these disappointments, there is evidence that *market considerations* overshadowed the pollution-haven hypothesis. Observation of the three case MNCs did not demonstrate any correlation between planned pollution transfer and the expansion into the developing countries. In many instances, MNCs' pollution-intensive manufacturing operations are central to their businesses and regardless where they site their plants, these operations would remain the same. Based on my archival and field studies, I could not unearth evidence to suggest that MNCs are concentrating their manufacturing activities in the countries with little or no 'SHE costs'. The question, therefore, might be better rephrased as 'should MNCs engage in pollution-intensive manufacturing activities' rather than 'if MNCs are exporting pollution'.

As curbing the cross-nation diffusion of pollution-intensive activities proves unfeasible, one should perhaps examine the containment and abatement of the associated pollution. One could further dispute that financial loss often lead to cost-saving measures and MNCs might consider sacrificing costly SHE protection for immediate financial relief. One of the case MNCs admitted to delaying a SHE capital improvement project due to the financial pressure. Its SHE Manager readily suggested that such delay did not lower the corporate or legal standards, but imposed a tight demand for the managers and employees to evaluate the existing SHE practices during the interim period. Although the unscheduled SHE audits yielded satisfactory results, it might not be an accurate representation of normal behaviour. On that account, the three case MNCs' commitment to SHE was verified against their official records and the results demonstrated good performance, i.e. over 95% compliance across a fairly comprehensive checklist,[51] but there remained room for improvement. The responses of the informants were of an uncompromising tone even in a situation of less than optimal earning performance:

Question: What would you do if SHE expenditure cuts into the profit margin of a given year?

Answer: Well, once more it comes back to that minimum. They can cut costs but cannot do anything that will move us below that minimum. If there is an approved plan, if they are going to change that plan, then it is a negotiation between the function, business and the geography. That's three parts of our matrix. It definitely does affect our business but the issue with the environment that we have to keep selling to our business people, is that *environment, health and safety management is the long-term cost and ownership is interested in short-term costs. And that is the hard sell.* When you have a competitor down the road that mixes things in open vents, builds a plant for five million dollars and our's costs ten, but we know in the long run that we will be more cost-effective than someone who doesn't put that expenditure upfront. We get challenged sometimes but it has never been a problem. I have never had to take anything to a higher authority to get it done because our business guys are general. An example of this was we built, as part of our site in Thailand, we put an incinerator on that site. It cost one million dollars, plus capital, plus operating expenses. We were challenged and went through the process and it was approved. Did it help to make that site less profitable? Absolutely, in the short term.

Regional SHE Manager, Eghbalian Pacific

Onsite audits of the three case MNCs' facilities in China and Taiwan revealed better or equivalent SHE protection standards when compared to their counterparts in the home countries. Modern designs and equipment might have their contribution, but human factors were much more important. Both the expatriate and local staff demonstrated commitment to SHE protection, though the level of commitment varied with the prior exposure to SHE issues. Expatriate staff conversed enthusiastically about being eco-friendly and leaving a green space for the generations to come. Local staff, on the other hand, had to obey the orders faithfully under a strongly enforced penalty system and SHE training programme. There were signs of 'awakening' particularly among the Taiwanese workers but less so among their Chinese comrades, who were in most cases preoccupied with making a decent living. The fulfilment of basic living needs was a pre-requisite for the awareness and appreciation of SHE protection.

Personally, I feel that we have to be engaging in environmental protection. Our company policy is that *we need to protect environment regardless of the cost.* We need to achieve excellence in SHE. SHE is certainly one of our top priorities. You need to implement all measures pertaining to environmental protection. It's no use just reciting the policy statements.

Plant General Manager, Niesler Taiwan

> But, we definitely feel responsible corporate citizens. We've got to lead the way, we have to show the way how it could be done, actually. And I think it's a mind set, maybe you know. The fact that historically we never have a right mind set and therefore we keep on thinking that perhaps how to minimise it because we try to do things differently, we incur a lot of costs. But if we don't say actually that's not quite true, we want to do it this way, that it is not necessary that you need to produce waste. In fact it can be done, waste can be avoided. But with a different mind set then you may not think that would cost or incur you extra cost . . . To comply with safety, health and environment is a licence to operate. *It's a pre-requisite before you can start thinking of anything else, unless you comply with it, you don't have a licence to operate, so what else can you talk about* . . . At the end of the day safety and health and protection of the environment is our number one priority, greater even than profit. That is not just a statement, that is a fact and something we are trying to instil in all our employees, which is not easy.
>
> Plant Operations Manager, Niesler China

> Eghbalian believes very strongly that if we cannot do it right in China from an environmental point of view, we would not make any investments. So the environmental standard that we observe in this plant is every bit as stringent as it is for the Eghbalian plants elsewhere. That was agreed upon upfront and is in the JV contract that this plant will follow the Eghbalian environmental guidelines. The position of Eghbalian Chemicals is, if the joint venture partner cannot agree with that philosophy, then we would not have a joint venture with this partner. I support this 100%.
>
> Plant Operations Manager, Eghbalian China

'Ethical factors'

Trendy and topical it might be, but business ethics is nevertheless imprinting the mindsets of MNCs' top management teams.

> Romanowski has set several core values – among them are safety and environmental protection, along with ethics. These three things cannot be compromised. They are highly valued in Romanowski because they contribute to the company's reputation and success. So, whichever country we are in, we carry out work in these three areas. Ethics starts from every employee. Every employee is made aware of the principle of ethics. They understand that if they have done some-

> thing wrong or against the law, even if it is for the benefit of the company, the company would not appreciate it and they would be punished. As we are a floated company, we must be responsible to all shareholders. If an accountant tries to fiddle about figures at the end of a financial year, he will be penalised even to the extent of being sacked. In terms of safety, as Romanowski started its business on hazardous chemicals, safety has always been a high priority. At Romanowski we value the people more than the equipment. We must be responsible for the lives and safety of our employees. Romanowski's value concept is clear to the public. When a member of the public buys Romanowski's shares, s/he understands that Romanowski is committed to environmental protection and money will be invested in this area. We make every employee and shareholder understand that the money invested in environmental protection is worthwhile and will eventually generate a higher return for the company. Of course, the results may not be tangible. *You can't know exactly how much the company's reputation is worth. When an employee is injured, you can count the loss to the company in terms of insurance paid out, etc. But with some environmental issues, the money is intangible*. Shareholders will understand that.
>
> Greater China SHE Manager, Romanowski China

The responses of employees to such indoctrination again diverged with the maturity and pervasiveness of business ethics movements in their home countries. Taiwanese employees were, in general, more aware of the issues and could discuss passionately about their ethical philosophy versus MNCs somewhat 'foreign' mission statements, policies and guidelines, even though their 'passion' far exceeded their action. Chinese employees, on the other hand, required much persuasion to embrace the ethical concepts and extend them to SHE protection. An SHE Co-ordinator of a case MNC operation in China remarked on the 'hollowness' of the published SHE standards and the 'grandness' of the ethical guidelines. Chinese employees were proficient exam takers and could easily score above 95% on the SHE quizzes and refresher exams, but the knowledge meant nothing more than a licence or a permit to employment. An employee might go through the training for the purpose of procuring a set of expensive personal protective equipment and would resign the next working day after attaining this short-term objective. The SHE co-ordinator recommended that senior managers re-appraise the extant channels of communication and assess the suitability of implementing a programme that was geared toward the situation and characteristics of another culture. 'Western' business ethics might have descended in China at a wrong time when people are more concerned with making a quick buck than listening to ethical preaching.

Business ethics aside, most MNCs demand enumerated proposals and detailed *cost-benefit analyses*, i.e. return-on-investment calculations, etc., in approving an investment. All three case MNCs declared holding no upper limit on the SHE budget, but capital investments on SHE, especially those above certain dollar figure, have to be reviewed by the headquarters and the sponsoring businesses alike. The process can take a year or more, the only exception being the regulatory mandated improvement, which follows a more swift path. A crisis state such as being confronted with massive public demonstration and protest would also expedite the course of action.

> It's the standard practice that we perform calculations, may it be ROI [return on investment], IR [interest rate], or discount discourse. We need to know how much we can get back from our investment. Also, we need figures to convince the board that the investment is worthwhile. Based on our initial calculation, this particular SHE did not make sense at all and we hadn't factored economic depression into consideration. Also, the initial operation of our new plant was not at all smooth. The positive return of the investment is therefore hard to realise. But in light of our long development and survival, we had to undertake the investment. Environmental protection was certainly a factor in our decision making. We have to be constantly engaging in environmental protection efforts in response to the everchanging environmental regulations. In the past three years, we spent close to US$600 million in pollution prevention. Then, in our annual proposal of budgets, we have a expenditure proposal programme. We've controlled our spending quite tightly. However, if the proposal is SHE related, it will be assigned high priority. If I state that the proposal is SHE related and without such expenditure, we won't be able to comply with the SHE standards, the boss can't issue a rejection. This is in fact our global practice. Needless to say, *we don't want to see just SHE expenditure without financial benefits. But still you need to address SHE.*
>
> Plant General Manager, Niesler Taiwan

6.2 Outer context – institutional factors

Stakeholders

Regulatory demands had been a recurring theme in the discussion of SHE issues. SHE protection has been characterised as regulation-led and enforcement dependent. A change in SHE regulations is analogous to a shift in tax policies with immense financial implications on the businesses. An ability to influence the direction of SHE policies and regulations is a definite competitive advantage because of the huge capital involvement and the possibility of generating good publicity for 'advancing' preventive measures. In the industrialised countries, professional lobbyists are hired by various industries to track the development of SHE regulations. The recent EPA investigation into the famed Harvard Six City Study on air quality (internal sources: Harvard School of Public Health) is an excellent elucidation of the lobbyist power, which exerted pressure on behalf of industries in probing the reliability of the data sources for formulating clean air and gaseous emission standards. Regulations could be formal, with a well-established law enforcement mechanism, or informal, such as commonly accepted practices and industrial standards, thus MNCs had, by and large, broadened the definition of the SHE 'regulators'.

> *We feel that environmental protection is a licence for operation.* Our survival relies on maintaining a good image in environmental protection. Especially for a MNC such as Niesler, the failure in SHE in a specific country can impact its world-wide operation. Bhopal is an excellent example. As you can see, we engage in the pharmaceutical, household chemical and CFC manufacturing (used to). In home country, the manager of the household chemical division received boycott threats from customers who care about the issue of ozone depletion. By the same token, the manager of pharmaceutical division received complaints ('we are stopping our prescription of your drugs') from doctors about our production of CFC. To us, this was a life and death situation.
>
> Asia-Pacific SHE Manager, Niesler Group

All stakeholders can be regulators, and as global enterprises, MNCs *cannot afford to tarnish their precious reputation, since the resultant price can be exorbitant.* In the age of instant telecommunications, even the slightest improper conduct in an obscure corner of the earth can have its implications. Romanowski learned an unexpected lesson in its Taiwanese investment project.

> Considering its rather successful business in bleaching chemicals and assuming a reasonable consumer demands, Romanowski proposed to establish a factory in Taiwan. At that time, the environmental awareness in the community was not very strong. Maybe due to the lack

of appropriate communication, the investment plan was rejected by the local community. There were political factors involved and resulted in a well-publicised conflict between the business and the local environmental protection. Romanowski made a struggling but an insolvent effort to reconcile the situation. NGOs, academics, students, and the local residents staged a large-scale protest. *Our worldwide SHE records were scrutinised and all the violations and penalties were cited in the meetings with the concerned citizens*. The investment project almost fell through. I think, the experience we drew from the first choice site had affected our approach in negotiating for a second choice site. Consent of the local community is indeed very important for the manufacturing business. We moved to consult foreign and international environmental laws as well as our peers' past experiences of dealing with the local communities . . . Communication work has to be done first. The local community representatives and the chiefs of local villages originally regarded Romanowski as a 'pollution-transfer' company, because Romanowski's top-selling product is agriculture chemicals, as everybody knows. This made life difficult for us. We then established one-on-one teams, which visited each household to publicise our commitment on safety, hygiene and environmental protection. We also invited them to visit our other SBU factories in Taiwan. They were impressed with our conduct there. We also made a commitment of 'coexistence and co-prosperity' to the local community. The commitment is, we are a world-class company and would conform to the government laws and the high operational standards. We were also willing to provide some funds for the local community work. The effort 'to win them over' is still ongoing. The attitude of the local community changed gradually from negative, to neutral and finally to positive. At the beginning, the percentage of people against Romanowski stood high at over 80%. As time went on, some local people worked as our ambassadors and now over 90% of people support us. We also made some material contribution to the local community. For example, we would buy raw material from the local people even it is not necessarily cheaper. Also, in small projects, we would give the locals the first priority to bid under the condition that they meet the contract requirements. There are about 320 employees in the factory and 67.5% of these are locals. Working in a high-tech chemical factory like this one, you cannot work on the line without proper knowledge and discipline. That translated into having to spend a large sum of money on hiring inexperienced staff and training them.

> We had also donated about 1 million US dollars to the local Culture and Education Foundation. After several years of hard work, the very existence of the bleaching chemical factory has been accepted by a community which was against it in the beginning. This is quite rare among global enterprises.
>
> SHE Manager, Romanowski Taiwan

MNCs' SHE responsibility has in recent years grown to encompass their immediate business relations, including contractors, suppliers, clients, etc. This group poses a real challenge for MNCs in the developing or even the newly industrialised countries, where SHE awareness is in its infancy stage and local politicians are searching for circumstances of high media potential to publicise their policy perspectives. MNCs are conspicuous targets, and in an increasingly litigious and global society, there is no shortage of zealous prosecutors waiting to exercise their authority. The Niesler Taiwan contractor case served as a perfect example.

> The actual disposal was done through a contractor. They purposely built two ships using special alloy for the tanks to handle the operation. Unfortunately, these two ships did not follow government's instruction faithfully to dispose by-product acid (BPA) at the specified locations. The fishermen uncovered such unlawful practices and entered into a large scale protest against Niesler . . . I must say, albeit subjectively, that Taiwan's environmental protection mentality is not 'pure' at all. There is a substantial involvement of politicians in the form of NGOs with their very self-serving objectives. Hence, environmental protection effort in Taiwan is highly political. The politicians often stirred up the local residents and fishermen to seek financial compensation and the amount demanded is usually huge . . . We were under pressure from all directions to settle the matter in a professional and speedy manner. But as the event involved political and financial motivation, it was exceedingly difficult to reach a satisfactory solution. It was a complicated and highly politically charged event . . . The fishermen's protest prompted the TEPA to develop a different guidance. TEPA stated that if the corrosive waste could be concentrated to certain pH value, it was permissible to engage in deep sea disposal. We then proceeded to purchase equipment for the neutralisation process. However, the fishermen refuse to accept such measures as satisfactory. They demanded financial compensation. How could we deal with it then? We had the conditional permission from the government but yet on the other

> hand, we had pressure from the fishermen. Which authority should we submit to? Even when we agreed to compensate, they could not come up with a report certifying that the damages had actually occurred . . . We even compromised by suggesting to establish a moderate emergency fund to help, under the control of the government. Unfortunately, we could not arrive at a mutually agreeable figure. It was very frustrating. It was unreasonable behaviour. We then decided not to proceed with compensation and went on to shut down our manufacturing operations until the crisis was satisfactorily dealt with. If we paid up, there would be follow-up problems. The decision to stop production affected our employees and clients . . . We didn't expect to run into such a major crisis . . . *We need to maintain a long-term perspective. It is not the way to do business if we just focus on the short-term benefits.*
>
> Plant General Manager, Niesler Taiwan

The role of the formal regulators, in this case, was eclipsed by the politicians, NGOs and the concerned public. In a green era, SHE-led mass demonstrations have emerged to be the favourites of the mass media. It is sometimes argued that informal regulators are infinitely more powerful and influential than the formal government bodies. MNCs would not hesitate to agree, as their past experiences coerced them to be extremely cautious and sensitive in their dealings with various groups of stakeholders. Such gestures might be stained by an ulterior motive and could be considered as a public relation gimmick, but they performed wonders in the eyes of a plain individual. A leader of the NGO that represented the fishermen in direct confrontation with the Niesler Group, recounted his first meeting with the MNC.

> By any measure, Niesler is a first-rate company. The CEO sent a chauffeur-driven limo to fetch me from my door step and they were courteous, even to a lowly person such as myself. I haven't received much education but possess a keen sense of people. Niesler managers were sincere and treated me nicely. During the meeting, I asked sharp questions but they responded politely and sensibly. That was different from the Taiwanese local firms. They really cared about the environment.
>
> Chairperson, Environmental Protection NGO, Taiwan

SHE regulations, regulators, enforcement mechanisms

The ability to please the informal regulators may be a key variable in the MNCs success formulae, but first and foremost MNCs are subject to the legal regulatory framework of the host countries and SHE issues are securing unprecedented attention from the host governments. China and Taiwan are both promulgating SHE laws and policies at lightning speed and MNCs are hard pressed to comply with regulations that might have been in discussion for only a short duration and may even contradict the existing laws. In China, the intention of the host government to solicit MNCs participation in SHE policy making may never materialise, due to the multiple levels and overlapping layers of jurisdiction. Moreover, MNCs are under tight time schedules to ensure smooth running of their plants and answer 'unspoken' demands from different directions and authorities.

> Based on my experiences, no one is able to give me a thorough briefing of all the Chinese environmental regulations. This includes even the government environmental protection officials. No one knows the regulations well. The National EPA in Beijing sets up a regulatory framework and then each province and each city can set up their own standards. And then at the industrial park level, the officers in charge are allowed to add more standards. There is really no one who knows the regulations thoroughly. This is our major obstacle in promoting SHE effort in China. The effectiveness of environmental regulations spreads only to the provincial level. Anything beyond that is up for negotiation. I can say that we are in compliance with all the major Chinese environmental regulations as evident in our obtaining of operations permit. However, I am not entirely confident that we have obeyed all the regulations.
>
> Asia-Pacific SHE Manager, Niesler Group

> You are talking about setting up a political action group, you are talking about setting up a normal interaction between companies and EPA where there is a give and take of technologies. We don't have the manpower to do that. Right now I have an environmental local boy who works for me, he is Chinese and goes to local policy meetings, but to try to influence? No. To learn what is going on? Yes, and report back to us. We don't intend to have layers on route, we would deal with the central government and Environmental Protection Agency, its all rules and regulations right now.
>
> Plant General Manager, Eghbalian China

The Chinese and Taiwanese authorities, as reviewed in Chapter 5, are very different in their management of SHE issues. A plausible explanation may be that Taiwan has been *under Western influence for a longer period* of time and it is *wealthy enough to address the cost-sinking environmental problems*. The Regional Operations Manager of Eghbalian Pacific voiced his personal but sobering viewpoints on SHE protection in the Greater China region:

> One of the things that we always have to remember is that in Taiwan, Hong Kong, Australia, Japan, our socio-economic status is that *we are not worried about where our next meal is coming from and a lot of the countries are taking economic growth over environmental protection still have a standard of living where people are concerned about where their next meal is coming from*. We can get holier than thou but we have to understand what their driving force is, and that is putting food in peoples' mouths, having hospitals, medical care, things that we take for granted and are not necessarily there in those countries. You can't stop having someone in Indonesia truly worry about sustainable development when they are basically living in very primitive conditions. Get real. Greenhouse gases, global warming? We sometimes get a little out of our tree. Most of our population does not live the lifestyle of Taiwan, Hong Kong, US, the majority of the population live a very much substandard one compared to that. I guess we are trying to play parent. We learned during our time and that they should not make the same mistakes. But they are saying they have the right to make the same mistakes as us.
>
> Regional Operations Manager, Eghbalian Pacific

A top Chinese NEPA official shared the same sentiment and pleaded for assistance and sympathy from the international organisations and the OECD countries:

> The demands from the World Bank are unreasonable. We've pretty much given up on applying for loans from it. The reduction on coal burning cannot be achieved easily. After all, it's the cheapest form of energy in China. I am pro-environmental protection and hate to see our country becoming a pollution haven but you need to realise that we have over one billion people to feed and there are people on the streets running around hungry and live under miserable conditions. Do they really know our problems? Stop being a hypocrite. If they want us to protect the environment, they should give us funds to do so. We are trying our best, but there is only so much we can do, with such limited financial resources.
>
> Section Chief, NEPA, China

The hunger for 'foreign aid' as a result of an insufficient budget might be the cause for the two separate NEPA schedules for regulation compliance. There was a general consensus among the Chinese policy makers that foreign companies are better equipped to meet the tougher SHE standards and should, by all means, transfer only the best environmentally friendly technologies. Chinese SOEs, on the other hand, complied to more lenient terms, even though a substantial number of them are financially and technologically capable of meeting the more stringent standards. 'Unfair' treatment was a major subject of discontent among the MNCs, for this culminated in 'unfair' competition and contributed minimally towards improving SHE conditions in China.

> Their environmental protection effort is at a very early stage. Some of them take a perfunctory attitude. They don't invest enough money in environmental protection processes and equipment and that's fine based on the current NEPA schedule. Romanowski invested a lot of money in this area not because it is required by the government but because it is our policy to protect the environment. This results in a high cost. Like this installation, a Chinese enterprise would only spend half on a similar installation. Investment cost such as this can not be recovered in a short period. This creates an unfair competition.
>
> Greater China SHE Manager, Romanowski China

However, all three case MNCs proclaimed that the tougher NEPA schedule caused little or no problem for them, because they are committed to SHE protection in any event. They, however, complained about the unreasonable regulations. The introduction of a chemical tax resulted in an uproar:

> It is not similar, it is worse than TOSCA. TOSCA defines things (confidentiality, confidential inventories, what is and isn't required to be reported), none of this has happened in the need for regulations. They have just said we have to register (imported chemical not locally manufactured) and it will cost you \$10000 a time, to be renewed every three years and no-one knew whether every time you make a little change in the molecule, even US under TOSCA is a 2% rule. Here there was no clear definition of that and so the possibility was we could have ten chemicals but just change a little bit on the end. Every one of those would have had to be registered at \$10000 a part

and the amount of data you needed to supply and all this information was totally unclear. I think it is getting to a point where it is going to be unmanageable and I got a message from the US today that said they may even be getting close to accepting the TOSCA inventory, so you don't have to go through making the inventory. If it was on the TOSCA inventory, it would be on the import list and you wouldn't have go through this registration process. I don't know where it is going to end up. They brought it in without any thought of how they would implement it and only imported chemicals. Our question is, why are imported chemicals worse than locally produced?

Regional Operations Manager, Eghbalian Pacific

TOSCA in one form or another, has been adopted in many countries. Toxic waste control is an important issue. Developing countries want to prevent toxic waste dumping by industrialised countries. All counties want to devise variations while adhering to the original as much as possible. It's a tough trade-off. The Philippines and Korea have their own TOSCA in place. Taiwan is seeking means to establish its own toxic waste control system. I do not think China has considered its implementation of TOSCA thoroughly. The chemical tax is unreasonably high and China does not have a window period, unlike the standard practice in the other parts of the world. Chinese government imposes charges on the chemicals which have already been imported and appeared on the inventory list. They also levy an application fee for the same chemicals to be imported. The regulation is very much chemical rather than company oriented. The import duty thus form a trade barrier. The Chinese government does not have the expertise to evaluate all the information to decide if the chemical can be imported. The law is no other than a form of registration rather than a control, as the government permits importing of the chemicals undergoing registration concurrently. This is utterly unreasonable. For MNCs which deals with foreign countries, they must be prepared for this kind of scenario.

Asia-Pacific SHE Manager, Niesler Group

When compared to Taiwan, China is less sophisticated in SHE protection and focuses its effort more on economic objectives, as in the case of chemical taxes, rather than in environmental prevention and education. According to the same manager in the Niesler Group:

In terms of environmental protection, China is behind Taiwan. China still focuses primarily on economic development. Chinese government considers environmental protection to be important, but the officers are in general open for discussion if non-compliance occurs. If the company is willing to pay a charge, either penalty or 'environmental charge', for violating the standards, they can offer the 'concession'... Taiwan is very fast and productive in promulgating regulations. They are, however, deficient in three areas. First, they failed to perform cost-benefit analysis. Second, they were not concerned with the best available technology. Third, they neglect to consider if the infrastructure can support the regulations. Consequently, the environmental laws push the industry to rebel. Take us for example, we are very sensitive with the SHE issues and anytime if there is a violation, we have to report it in our annual report. But in many circumstances, it's simply impossible to meet the regulatory standards. TEPA adopted a series of US environmental laws without considering if we have enough resources or ability to meet them. The waste treatment licensing law was in fact borrowed from the States. The waste treatment company needs to apply for a licence for each chemical they can treat. This law is quite good in the setting of the United States where you can find hundreds of waste treatment companies. In Taiwan, we only have a handful of waste treatment companies and we are facing the problem of not being able to locate a company with a licence to treat a particular chemical in our waste stream. The licence should allow the treatment of associated chemicals which might even be easier to treat. The lack of flexibility is a major problem. Also, the waste is not allowed to be transported from one county to another. Recognising that Taiwan is small country, locating a suitable waste treatment company in a given county can be difficult. I just thought of the fourth deficiency in the Taiwanese environmental laws – the lack of exemption. In US and UK, such provision is in existence. If we can prove that even though we can't meet the regulatory requirements fully, we are not creating additional environmental problems, the regulatory authority will give us exemption to do things differently.

Asia-Pacific SHE Manager, Niesler Group

The 'concession' (or 'consensus level') is non-existent in Taiwan. China seems to be quite flexible with its standards. Several companies pay the 'penalties' and it's becoming an accepted practice in

> China. In Taiwan, it is not acceptable. All companies must meet the standards. Otherwise, they are penalised on a daily basis or face the fate of being shut down. Therefore, in China, as far as our company is concerned, we are on disadvantaged ground.
>
> Asia-Pacific SHE Manager, Niesler Group

Taiwan, in fact, is not too much ahead, based on his opinion and should learn to examine contextual issues before implementing SHE protective measures.

6.3 Summary

Through the interview excerpts, the importance of contextual factors in business policy formation can be deciphered clearly. *Economic consideration, stakeholders and regulations form a neat boundary for manoeuvring with respect to SHE.* Market considerations were cited as the most important, though institutional environments impose constraints on the 'choices' open to MNCs. The 'pollution haven' hypothesis, which assumes that corporations invest in a developing country motivated by lax SHE regulations, is therefore not supported. The findings suggest that the power of stakeholders should not be ignored. MNCs have learned an important lesson in the Greater China region from failing to address the needs of stakeholders fully. SHE regulations and enforcement mechanisms define the rules for the game and are crucial in ensuring the responsible behaviour of the firms.

7
Strategic Response Patterns

> In general, the big corporations have more resources, knowledge expertise, and clear commitment to environmental protection. We are not having an easy time responding to different demands (EPA, public, etc.) and yet we are considered to be resourceful. If I run into problem, I can always consult Thomas and Stefan in Taipei, or else, I can consult Niesler UK. I have no idea how small corporations can cope with all the demands. Thomas is an experienced SHE Manager. He is in charge of both internal and external affairs, including public relations, maintenance and running of systems, data storage and management, audit, collection of samples, feedback and updates. We are quite good at this kind of thing. If it's a small corporation or state-owned enterprise, the promotion of SHE activities can encounter severe difficulty. We have been actively promoting Responsible Care since two years ago. Last year, in our plant, we organised seminars for assistant managers and above to better implement Responsible Care programme, including a transportation safety module. In general, we organise quite a few SHE seminars every year. We send our SHE out to attend classes and increasingly we are also sending our line managers. In this way, we are not disconnected from the state-of-the-art practice and the managers can realise the relative importance of SHE. All these help to improve our internal practice.
>
> Plant General Manager, Niesler Taiwan

In Chapter 6, we witnessed evidence indicating that MNCs are bounded by various contextual factors in their responses to SHE protection demands. The complexity of business policy formation in MNCs were briefly discussed, but their impacts on the strategic benefit of a response is best represented by the interview excerpts presented in this chapter. Based on the modes of motivation, strategic responses of MNCs fall into two broad categories – passive and proactive. Passivity implies little deviation from the institutional demands, while proactivity presumes active choice behaviour. The organisation of this chapter assumes the presence of these two mechanism and adheres to two main lines of presentation – response to structures and response to institutions.

7.1 Context – response interface

The ability to harness strategic benefit does not imply adequate protection for SHE. And the best of strategic intentions to protect the environment can be interpreted, based on the interpreter's objectives, as being 'green' in disguise. The Plant General Manager of Niesler Taiwan, who is the informant in our exposition, commented:

> Wang Chemical is one of our major clients and we know them fairly well. I am also very interested in their management styles. In many instances, I wished we could learn more from them. It's hard to say who is more right at this time, but at present, I consider them to be more successful. The General Manager of Wang once mentioned to me that they need all the time they can get to handle changes, especially in this rapidly changing market.
>
> Wang never publicised its effort. In terms of PR, they are quite low profile. They've done a lot of things and this invited irrational criticism. I really admire Wang Chemical as a company. The chairman is someone with social responsibility. They spent money for good social causes. Wang formed a not-for-profit foundation to manage its charitable activities. When environmental protests occurred, the activists were inquiring into Wang's contribution to the society. *Wang replied with several examples including benefactions to improve local health service facilities. The activists in turn argued that environmental pollution induces various diseases and the facilities were there to benefit from the pollution.* This is complete nonsense and this is indeed the real situation. Wang's approach to environmental protection is very similar to ours. There is no limit to capital expenditure on SHE, if there is a real need. It's the top priority. However, unlike Romanowski, you don't see that many PR-related commercials coming out from Wang. Wang has relatively little media exposure, but its commitment to SHE is no less than Romanowski's, even though the professional standards

may not match that of Romanowski or Niesler. I'm not sure about its implementation. However, I consider having a clear commitment as the essential first step.

Plant General Manager, Niesler Taiwan

In this case, the intention to be proactive was not sufficient to please the environmental activists. The disparate interests of the stakeholders requires more *pragmatic* strategic responses. A successful formula is difficult to derive and a success story is arduous to duplicate. MNCs strategic response to SHE protection demands evolved and matured via painful experiences such as the Union Carbide and Exxon Valdez tragedies. The SHE Manager of the Asia-Pacific Region, Niesler Group articulated the stages of corporate environmental protection:

> There are three stages of environmental protection, according to ADL [Arthur D. Little]. The first stage is to solve immediate problem, such as explosion, etc. Companies care little about people and only are concerned about the basics. The typical work is correction. SHE is an extra cost. The second stage is to meet the regulatory requirements. It's still quite reactive. SHE costs are considered to be necessary. The goal is no other than policing. From stage one to stage two, the company predominantly worries about negative publicity. The third stage is to be proactive and control risk. It's an integrated risk management. The companies seek to identify problems at an early stage and regard SHE as something with a return. The concept was developed in 1986–7. I personally feel that we are in a fourth stage . . . Under many circumstances, the issue is that of the risk and return. However, I also feel that *SHE creates another business opportunity*. For example, X-105 is an environmental threat but also a business opportunity. X-105 is a very mature product and Niesler, Romanowski and Formosa Plastics all were making it. But none of us has the licence to produce it now. The fact is well-established and we are losing a competitive edge in the market place. We at Niesler has decided against producing traditional X-105 due to the environmental concerns. Niesler and Romanowski came up with a new X-105, 'X-106'. Even though X-106 is regarded as over-capacitated now, if we look at it from another angle, this is an obvious business opportunity.
>
> Asia-Pacific Regional SHE Manager, Niesler Group

Provided the statement scrupulously portrayed the current MNC corporate mindset, we can conclude that MNCs have progressed from passivity to proactivity and perhaps even to an active choice behaviour. The integration of SHE considerations into MNCs' strategic planning has received endorsement from the public and shareholders. A successful integration, as in the case of Niesler, could be a competitive advantage in the global marketplace.

7.2 Response to structures

Examination of the organisational structures of the three case MNCs indicated high involvement of the corporate boards in SHE issues (see Chapter 4). It is almost a norm that a senior vice-president oversees the SHE protection effort, alongside the corporate business strategic planning and a high-profiled SHE committee is charged with the responsibility to report directly and discretely to the Board:

> In Eghbalian we have been going through a lot of change as well. The good thing is that we have had some *constancy of purpose in terms of SHE*. We did not have a real corporate structure like this until about five/seven years ago. We had people here but it was not joined together. A lot of things we haven't talked about corporately as well. We now have an SHE sub-committee of the board where we have to report our performance and our senior vice president is a member of that. *We also have a CEAC (Corporate Environment Advisory Committee) with people like the ex-Chairman of the USEPA and the ex-Environment Minister of France and some very high profile people.* Yes, we were the first off the rank. But that's just because of our senior vice president who is responsible for having it. We have always had an SHE sub-committee of the board where every three months they meet and review SHE performance. A couple of times every year, we as an area have to go and review our environmental health and safety performance . . . Our senior vice president has been at the head through all of this change in our organisation that has been going on at a business level. Here in the Pacific, while this is a new position, I have been in this area for ten years, so we have maintained a constancy of purpose. We have not had the turnover that you have experienced with some of the other companies in environment health and safety. We have kept these people here, the environmental guy has been there for a long period of time. We have just had a change of the health services level. There has been a constancy of purpose because you have the constant leadership from a functional standpoint.
>
> Regional SHE Manager, Eghbalian Pacific

The strategic initiatives thus transpire in a top-down manner and across all businesses, whereas strategic responses originate in a bottom-up fashion with the local SHE co-ordinators collecting all the relevant information for business policy formation. This model, as stated, is overly simplistic. Strategic responses vary with organisational structure and the allocation as well as the distribution of power. A powerful and well-respected figure, such as the senior vice president of Eghbalian, can single-handedly authorise a given response irrespective of the cost. On the other hand, a corporation which places trust in its lower-ranked employees may exercise minimal influence in a given strategic response, as long as the individuals involved feel willing to accept the consequences. This usually only occurs in an environment where the MNC relies on the local staff to decipher the local institutional demands. However, Eghbalian seems to be an exception. Evidence suggests that top-down and bottom-up models co-exist in the corporation.

> The reason is the company allows decisions to be made at the lowest level, so unlike a hierarchical management structure: I go to meetings in Australia with people from Niesler who would be twenty years older than I, and I can make decisions and they would have to go back to headquarters to be able to say yes or no. Eghbalian gives you a lot of responsibility very early in your career and you get addicted to that, you like that style and that really I think is a lot of what happens.
>
> Regional SHE Manager, Eghbalian Pacific

The strategy of *co-option* was deployed in Eghbalian and Romanowski's appointments of ex-high-ranked government administrators to their Boards. Even when off active official duties, these former senior bureaucrats can contribute in preparing the MNCs' responses to future policy changes and serve as effective public relations figures in dealing with their successors. University presidents and leaders of major stakeholder groups are also favourite choices for the Board for the reasons of tapping into knowledge-creation networks and appeasing the concerned stakeholders.

7.3 Response to institutions

Passivity versus proactivity

The active choice behaviour and the proactivity patterns among the three case MNCs can be treated as responses to future demands. *Antic-*

ipation causes MNCs to engage in strategic planning and it is consequently difficult, if not impossible, to segregate voluntary from involuntary actions. All MNCs are well-trained law-abiding global citizens, hence *complying* with the regulatory requirements and sets of internal standards are beyond negotiation. Strategic thinking means prospecting and masterminding pre-emptive moves. *An early response maximises strategic benefit* by overtaking unprepared competitors to shape the market structure and define the nature of competition. The absence of head-on competition among the three case MNCs in the Greater China region and a sense of mutual dependency in foreign soil eased the formation of a coalition to promote their common interests.

> Yes, *we do engage in information exchange, cross learning, and share our expertise with others*. But we can definitely do a better job. Currently, the effect is not at all encouraging but doing something is better than doing nothing. *We should engage ourselves in this kind of effort early.* We work together in petrochemical trade association and Am Cham, or even in our own industrial park committee, ROC Environmental Protection Association. There exists channels of different forms. Especially in Am Cham, there is a chemical manufacturer committee. I am a member, so is our Asia Pacific SHE Manager. We have our monthly meetings. SHE is one common topic and of course, there are other topics of discussion such as Taiwan's industrial infrastructure, policies and regulations. The chemical manufacturers committee recently asked Productivity Asia, a consulting company, to push for the adoption of Responsible Care programme. The committee also provides constant updates of the changes in Taiwan SHE regulations.
>
> You mentioned that Romanowski has a good record in safety and Eghbalian boasts similar performance in environmental protection. I agree that Romanowski overall has a good record but in comparison with Japanese companies, Romanowski can still improve. Japanese approach to safety is more down to earth. It's just that the Japanese do not actively publish or publicise their efforts. *Romanowski indeed has a good safety record. Internally, they have a highly effective safety enhancement programme. We used their concept and ran a similar programme here.* Our Asia-Pacific SHE Manager simplified Romanowski's programme to boost the awareness of our employees. It's important to observe the unsafe acts. It's most dangerous if one is in complete darkness. So, we have introduced the simplified version and will continue to implement it. It will be a continuous

process. Japan's attitude towards SHE is that zero safety hazard is essential and to be proud of. Here you can see the difference. *Romanowski devotes much effort to PR, but they really have a good record. We aim to achieve the same record.* Our record is far from reaching Romanowski's. On the other hand, I feel that Romanowski is overdoing its PR. *But there are spin-off benefits, they provide a good model for the local companies*. It's definitely over-selling.

Business Director, Niesler Group

The coalition is conducive to information exchange and facilitates norm-setting. The response of imitating the leader not only improves an organisation's SHE performance but also enhances its survival in the market place, as the regulatory agencies may adopt the model effort as a benchmark.

We want all the MNCs to copy the best of their peers. They have ample resources to do that and if they want a share of Chinese market, they must be prepared to give us their best. They can forget about giving us the second class stuff. *When it comes to SHE protection, we want the best technologies and the best preventive measures and the best practices.*

China NEPA Official

I am aware of Romanowski's safety enhancement programme and it's indeed a good programme. We are advising all the MNCs in Taiwan to work with Romanowski which often conducts safety classes for us, either voluntarily or for a small fee. *I think it's essential for our own local enterprises to adopt the similar programme. They need to improve or face a tough penalty.*

TEPA Official

Being a *trend pointer* has its strategic advantages. The regulatory authorities are more likely to bestow favourable treatment and a good SHE programme is marketable. A pioneering and outstanding effort in SHE protection is believed to embellish a company's image, boost confidence in the stakeholders and elevate employees' morale. The leadership position prompts the company to examine its standing strategies carefully and seek constant improvement to retain its superior status.

The accident in Bhopal, India caused casualties of around three thousand people. This made it really difficult for Union Carbide to carry on with its business. As a result, the 'Product Start-up Programme' was initiated in North America, especially in Canada, to cover the life-cycle of a commodity. We had to look after over 1800 different products. At the same time, the Chemical Manufacturers' Association (CMA) started its 'Product Stewardship Program', again in response to the Bhopal accident. So, Romanowski got involved in these initiatives. CMA later broadened its scope from product stewardship to manufacturing process safety management and environmental protection. About ten years ago, CMA in America started to promote the 'Responsible Care' programme. Romanowski was naturally an active subscriber. Responsible Care is a very important benchmark. Under this umbrella, various regulations and guidelines such as EPA and ISO, as well as Romanowski's own standards and operational procedures, become a measuring yardstick to check where we stand and how we can best improve.

When the plant in Taiwan was established, we devoted more emphasis in this regard. At the moment, I am responsible for the enforcement of the Responsible Care programme in Romanowski Taiwan. Many organisations, both public and private, have come to us for advice . . . In fact, Romanowski has come a long way. We have relatively good resources, not necessarily the best among the companies, to promote Responsible Care in Taiwan and yet we achieve excellent results. We always get invitations for our internal experts. *We are committed to Taiwan, as proven by the number of our operating factories and our SHE undertakings*. Community awareness, started from 1991; Emergency Response, is one of the components. We simulated various scenarios, taking into account risk management in the worst case, such as power cuts, interruption to water supplies, earthquakes, gas leaks due to careless operation, etc. The outcome was quite satisfactory. For example, none of the chemical waste barrels under the Sanyin Bridge was from Romanowski and we adopted a very proactive approach when the story hit the news. We contacted the environmental protection bureau straight away to assess our potential liability. Our system eliminates such possibility in theory . . . I must also add that we place premium importance on employee health and safety.

Apart from our working guidelines, procedures and rules, we try to provide a safe and environmental-friendly working environment . . . This brings us back to the original question of why Romanowski emphasises so much staff safety, while everybody else is busy promoting their business. I don't have the statistics with me, but I can give you an example. Given a worst-case scenario, say a worker has

> his arm broken during an operation, we have to calculate how much we have to pay in compensation since he won't be able to work, if we have to find another person to replace him, whether that person will have the same commitment, and the cost for repairing the machine, and we have to make sure it would be on-line and so on. *The loss would be immense.* An accident like this would reduce productivity and increase costs, which ultimately hurts the business. This is only a minor case. *In a major case like an explosion, the issue would not be only business, it would be a matter of survival. That's why Romanowski takes a completely different approach from other companies.* Here I shall give another example. Sixty-six Asian companies and Romanowski have joint venture agreements. Our first step before the plant was constructed, even before the contract was signed, was to check if their sewage system could handle our sewage. So we conduct audits on the physical environment for operations. Even though management control of the joint venture may lie with our Asian partners, SHE protection was taken over by Romanowski, because this is our core value, and Romanowski has much experiences in these aspects. You can see we hold a different policy from other companies, which I have always thought is the right policy for an old company like Romanowski. And we are strengthening our effort further. As for the goal for our bleaching chemical factory, the accident record since January is zero, no incident at all in safety, health and environmental protection since its commissioning. This is unsurpassed in the Greater China region.
>
> SHE Manager, Romanowski Taiwan

The key ingredients of a successful strategy encompasses the *instinct to act in a timely manner and ahead of the competitors*, the foresight to *co-operate* with, and *accommodate* the subtle demands of the regulatory bodies, an appropriate level of manipulative power to *influence* the course of less optimum impacts, and a determination to *innovate* so as to integrate business and SHE protection goals. Romanowski may not be as 'green' as it professes to be, but its peers and regulatory authorities credited it with an enviable safety record.

Balancing acts

Universalistic guidelines

Eghbalian and Niesler each are recognised for excellence in specific SHE protection initiatives, but there is still much to be done. All three case

MNCs perform feasibility studies before a strategic response can be implemented. The questions of how cost can be best balanced with benefit and how profit can be matched with social responsibilities constantly challenged the managers:

> I have been in constant dialogue with TEPA about the difference in behaviour between the MNCs and Taiwanese firms. *TEPA is pondering over the fact that MNCs are much more willing to invest in SHE. I told them that the issues hinged upon cost-benefit analysis.* The majority of the Taiwanese firms have only one manufacturing plant specialising in only one product. If any of them runs into trouble with its SHE protection, they can simply shut down its operation. For MNCs, a similar violation in one locality will affect their world-wide operations. For a local company, the loss of shutting down a plant may only be NT$1M but for an MNC, if the SHE violations in Taiwan are made known in the States or UK, the loss will be the multiples of NT$1M. A local company can calculate that the SHE investment may cost as high as NT$10M and the penalty is only 10% of the cost. The decision of what to do is quite obvious. For us, the cost of failure to address SHE issues is much higher. Take for example, Formosa Plastics, which is a Taiwanese MNC, facing a strong opposition from the NGOs for the new plant they plan to build in Taiwan. The NGOs assembled all their past records of SHE violations, both locally and internationally, and organised a large-scale protest. By the same token, when Formosa Plastics was applying for operation permits in Texas, the NGOs in Taiwan faxed all their local SHE violations to persuade the Texan government into refusing the permit application. Formosa Plastics hence came to a realisation that the penalty is not just a single penalty, but multiples of penalty. That is no way that we can persuade the majority of local companies not to behave in this way. In fact, it's perfectly logical. *Everything in business in based upon cost-benefit analysis. A clearly good business decision in pure financial-benefit terms may not be a morally correct one.*
>
> Asia-Pacific SHE Manager, Niesler Group

> We have a biological observation unit. The process produces a high volume waste so you need lots of space. Our tri-venture partners could not understand why we wanted to use so much real estate to put in such a treatment facility. But we did anyway, it was not a case where the business basically went along. The same with the thermal oxidiser for burning the waste chlorinated materials which produce

> HCO which we sell, we use most of it and sell what is left. In both those cases, given part of our technology that was never questioned by our business guys as being required. *Even though we were building in China where it would be needed to meet the regulations, no-one's sure what the regulations really are, but we wouldn't build the plant without it. We say, we will build the same plant regardless of where we are building it. Is it exactly the same. No, you have to use little smarts to make sure that what you put in can be serviced. As you were seeing in the plant, we don't have our computer control system that we would normally have, we have one but it is a commercially available one because there were support people available in China to support that where we would have to put in a whole infrastructure. It didn't make economic sense,* but those sorts of decisions are made but it doesn't allow us to compromise on our environment, health and safety standards. We can maintain the same standard of safety with that system as with the other, it just is not as good as far as the overall productivity of the plant is concerned.
>
> Regional SHE Manager, Eghbalian Pacific

The desired balance is often attained through a well-formulated strategy. Niesler Group answered the demands of the regulatory authorities from a different angle and was able to harvest respect and appreciation from senior government officials:

> The Taiwanese government wants us to participate in the development of a Asian Regional Operating Centre (AIR) and we have actively supported this initiative. For a big plan like AIR, the government needs to think of ways to implement it. *We at Niesler have always supported this kind of high-level initiative.* For example, we have plans to build another facility in Taiwan with an investment capital of NT$10 billion. We will use the most up to date technology . . . Thomas, though a Niesler SHE manager, spends much time helping TEPA and the Labour Commission by offering them training courses and assisting in the interpretation of laws and regulations. We take pride in helping others, whether government or our neighbours in the industrial park. We keep no secrets from them in the area of SHE and are always willing to share our SHE expertise. *We even help our clients to solve their safety problems.* We send our people to investigate the situation and recommend appropriate measures. The decision to adopt them lies with our clients. They know their own situation the best, but we can offer them our professional advice.
>
> Business Director, Niesler Group

The special recognition can be subsequently equated with less regulatory compliance cost, since the company is involved in the policy-making process and can be better prepared to handle changes in a cost-effective manner. The strategy of rendering assistance to peers creates sets of industrial standards consistent with Niesler's own and helps to build closer a rapport with clients. This ultimately leads *to greater legitimacy* in the society and more business opportunities. The scenario can thus be termed 'win-win'.

A well-intended strategy can be prevented from its full implementation by specific local conditions. A contingency plan is often necessary and if such fails to serve its purpose, MNCs need to be creative and adaptive in their responses.

> Each industry has its own trade association. There are about 40 to 50 members in the petrochemical trade association and all of them are big. In fact, all the corporations in the industrial park are members. The petrochemical trade association is quite active. When there is a new regulation, regardless if it's environmental or tax/finance related, the association will immediately forward the information (venue and time of public hearing, draft regulations, etc.) to the member corporations. So, the diffusion of information is fairly rapid, through the trade association. Certainly, we need to determine if we should take a more active role in communicating our needs with the trade association and initiate proactive measures. I believe we can do a much better job. In sum, the petrochemical trade association is performing quite a satisfactory job. But given the enormous amount of lengthy new regulations and the absence of executive summaries, it's hard for us to follow through. They should give us something brief, which summarises the difference between the new and old and the first and the second versions of the regulations, to more effectively convey the essentials. *I doubt if many people really fully understand the EPA regulations. It's only when the penalty comes, one gets to understand the regulations*. A summary will also help us to decipher what is relevant to us and prevents us from wasting time to read through the entire document. It's not that there are no regulations. When problems occur, EPA can usually cite the specific date and time when the regulations were passed/changed. If the industry fails to read them, it's its own fault. EPA should change their ways of communication.
>
> Plant General Manager, Niesler Taiwan

> Before any regulations/policies, and I mean any regulations, can be put into effect, by law, the authority needs to hold a public hearing

> but the invitations are normally only sent to different trade associations. The membership for different trade associations is usually large and *they have the tendency to invite only the big ones*, such as Taiwan Power, Formosa Plastics, China Petroleum, to participate in commenting. Niesler, in comparison, is quite small. Before the establishment of our first plant, we were a non-entity and hence, didn't get a chance to participate in anything. We did not know the law formulation procedures well. Obviously, one can only find environmental experts in big corporations as they have more resources. However, the old mentality dies hard. Big corporations such as Taiwan Sugar sent representatives to the meetings but without actually contributing anything significant. They are used to the traditional ways of doing things and are somewhat disconnected with the current needs of the industry. I doubt they can best represent the industry. EPA has already held several public hearings and yet received little feedback. It's only when the regulations become effective, the corporations begin to voice their concerns. Maybe EPA should change their ways of doing things by inviting responsive corporations and not sending invitations through the respective trade associations. They know fully which corporations are willing to contribute.
>
> Plant SHE Manager, Niesler Taiwan

Particularistic guidelines

Local law enforcement authorities may have their own agendas that interfere or even conflict with MNCs' implementation of their strategic responses. The self-serving motives are almost impossible to refute and MNCs quickly learn to evaluate their strategic plan on a constant basis:

> Regional environmental protection offices demand detailed information. For example, we are planning to set up an engineering plastic compounding business in the Special Economic Zone (SEZ). The local environmental protection department demands detailed technical data, such as the temperature of the water bath for extruded strands. *They want to learn as much as possible from foreign companies. They use this method to obtain information from foreign companies. Because if they asked directly they know they wouldn't be able to obtain such information. But if a foreign company wants to obtain approval to set up a project, it has to provide such information in order to get an approval.* Environmental departments are always under-staffed, because they are money-spending rather than profit-making departments. Nowadays,

> many environmental departments set up companies to provide environmental services. For example, our SEZ factory bought a generator but it had a noise problem. SEZ Environmental Department approached us and said their company could provide the service to design a noise insulation system.
>
> *Comment*: This seems to pose a contradiction. Environmental departments are supposed to be law-enforcing organisations but at the same time they are providing services.
>
> *Response*: Yes. This is like an ISO 9000 standard organisation providing services, which is unimaginable in the West. This would present a conflict of interest. Of course they would fail to get your business. This is the same with other departments such as power supply department. *When you submit your engineering drawings for approval they would ask you to let their companies undertake the work. If you don't they will delay the approval process for several months without granting you an approval.* The same is true with fire protection aspect and so on . . .
>
> Greater China Area SHE Manager, Romanowski China

In general, irrespective of their concerted effort to influence SHE policy making, MNCs tend to *comply* with the regulations, both external and internal, with diligence. The problem occurs when it is difficult to obtain a complete picture of regulations and policies, such as in the case of China:

> We relocated the households that were within the enclosure of the plant to be built. We didn't do anything to the households outside this boundary. We guaranteed them a pollution-free environment. There was a dispute at the time. NEPA said this was not within the rules. But Romanowski insisted that this could be achieved. In the end we wrote a report and submitted it to Zhu Rongji. Zhu Rongji pointed out to NEPA that it should consider changing its policy. It is understandable that they did not have complete trust in Romanowski's claim of a pollution-free environment. But, by the same token, they could not prove that Romanowski would not be able to achieve this goal. With the involvement of Zhu Rongji, the way to solve the problem was to write down a 'military pledge' stating the goals to be achieved (e.g. chemical oxygen demand level, etc.). If these goals were achieved, then the business would be allowed to carry on. This shows that a flexible approach was adopted

> in respect to this joint venture. Without this flexibility, this joint venture wouldn't have got where it is now. Romanowski has a very clear view on the safety and environmental issue. *We implement environmental protection measures not because we are under the pressure from the government's regulations but because we want to be responsible for the society and the public. We do these things on our own initiative.* That's why we are nationally renowned for our excellent environmental protection work. The work starts at the very beginning. For example, even before the commencement of construction work, we had already started environmental work by drilling some deep wells to survey the ground water. We also carried out work on other environmental items such as soil, plant, vegetation, etc . . . *Although the methods used were Romanowski's own, the implementation of such work was usually entrusted to an independent local organisation, i.e. a third party. This could ensure and prove that Romanowski's environmental promises were not all talk but they were really up to standard.*
>
> Plant General Manager, Romanowski China

The overlapping jurisdiction of laws and the ambiguous law enforcement structure in China nullified the endeavour to locate the change agent for exerting inputs on policy making. The introduction of a chemical tax, as discussed in the previous chapters, triggered a series of *defiant* behaviours and ended with bargaining for a lower rate of charges. It is obvious that reasonable regulations are necessary to ensure voluntary compliance by the MNCs. Most of the time, MNCs would consider whether the compliance cost is likely to produce optimal impact and the regulations are easy to follow. They then must be convinced that certain types of monetary-induced favouritism are absent in law enforcement. Most reputable MNCs are ill-prepared to deal with corruption and would not consider bribery as a viable strategic response in the first instance. In country settings such as China and Taiwan where *guanxi* flourishes, *MNCs are rooted in a disadvantaged ground for upholding their corporate principles.* Moreover, MNCs are visible targets and a defiant response will undoubtedly attract closer scrutiny on their performance in other areas. Even without the adversarial reaction, MNCs face tight scrutiny from the host governments.

> Based on my personal experience, if their visit is to promote and ensure smooth adoption of new regulations and policies, EPA will tell us in advance. Also, if they receive complaints from the local

> residents regarding odour and dark-coloured stack emission, they will inform us before taking the issue further. Otherwise, the inspection is non-routine and they've never informed us. You have to understand that southern Taiwan has the highest concentration of industrial facilities in the country, just take a look at the number of industrial parks around our plant. Our county EPA may be the busiest in the country. Here we are talking about the biggies. There are small facilities around. *It's easier for EPA to focus on the biggies and expect them to be in full compliance before shifting their attention to the small ones*. Regarding the standards of EPA personnel, it's true that they are far from uniform. There are even people without proper college degrees. It can't be compared with Taiwan EPA.
>
> Plant SHE Manager, Niesler Taiwan

All the three MNCs behaved *similarly* in the Greater China region, possibly due to their frequent exchange of information and their cross-learning from each other. It would be an exaggeration to state that the MNCs studied are becoming identical, since each still maintains its unique corporate structure and recognises the others' strengths and weakness.

> I think we have a better management system in place (compared to Romanowski) and we have had a different approach over a long period of time to the environment. We have a lot to learn from them in safety and they can learn from us in the environmental area. I am trying to work with Tom, who is their SHE guy out in Singapore and develop a relationship where we can use one another's strengths and weaknesses and improve one another. It is easier to work with Romanowski probably because, while their organisational structure is very different, their philosophies are very similar. When you get to Niesler they have a very different philosophy, a very different management structure. Romanowski and Eghbalian are very flat, we don't have a hierarchical management structure. Niesler has a much more hierarchical management structure in what is a typical British company versus an American company. So someone like Romanowski and Eghbalian have more philosophically the same approach than probably Niesler would have. I used to have a lot to do with Niesler when I was in Australia, but they don't have people in Hong Kong so I don't interface with them very much anymore. I interface more with Amoco, ARCO and a few other companies rather than Niesler. For example in Eghbalian, one of the differences

between Niesler and Eghbalian is that Niesler have been trying to change their philosophy on SHE because they realised their performance was falling well behind industry averages and they have made a very big effort over the last five years to make some significant changes but in Eghbalian, it is absolutely and utterly clear that the Line Manager is responsible for environmental health and safety performance, and I am there to help. I am their technology resource, I am the conscience of the company and all those sorts of things related to ethical issues. You are responsible for safety, the Site Manager, he is responsible for environment health and safety. It is in his job description. It does not mean it is not shared. I share responsibility but he has the primary responsibility. At Niesler it was not that clear. They used to have Safety Officers. We don't have Safety Officers that act like policemen. That is not our role. That is similar with Romanowski, Amoco and these other people . . . Amoco and Eghbalian are probably the two companies with regional SHE director here in Hong Kong. ARCO is in Taiwan, Romanowski is in Singapore, some people have them in Japan or Australia but I tend to interact more with the companies that have like organisational structures.

Regional SHE Manager, Eghbalian Pacific

Towards learning

The strategic response patterns of the case MNCs, however, demonstrated a certain degree of convergence. The critical incidents experienced by Niesler and Romanowski formed a lesson for their peers and their responses were analysed meticulously in constructing a model strategic response model for specific situations.

We hope to reduce non-compliance and injuries but we want to increase the number of learning events. This serves as a reflection of our employees paying close attention to SHE. *So far, most of the learning events were reported by the managers. We want to encourage our base workers to actively participate, perhaps through offering incentives. We hope to have bottom-up rather than top-down reporting. This is very difficult given the climate in Taiwan.* We had a re-roofing case which illustrated the difficulty in dealing with Taiwanese contractors. We considered the roof as an unsafe place, due to its height, to conduct work. Therefore, we demanded our contractors to come equipped with life lines. This policy turned off most of the local contractors.

They claimed that they could not function effectively with a life line in their way. It's tough for us to enforce our SHE policies. That's why we need to implement the penalty system.

Comment: Surely, if the contractors have enough contracts to keep them busy, they will turn down jobs which involve much hassle.

Response: *Well, the contractors need to maintain their reputation. It's bad to lose an account. Their peers will be talking. It's a combination of losing our account and having to pay the penalty. It doesn't look good if they have this kind of record . . . There is quite a bit of learning.* With respect to waste disposal, originally we had a contractor to handle the case. Because of its misconduct, we suffered directly. This taught us a good lesson that we need to ensure our contractors follow our standards. It should not be the case that once we turn the case over to contractors, we are no longer responsible. The key lesson from this incident was that we need to audit our contractors carefully. For example, we routinely engage in regular maintenance of our facility and need to hire contractors for this purpose. They are not our regular employees. We stop our production completely during annual maintenance (shut down). This implies that everything needs to be completed in a timely fashion. We devised detailed plans to make sure that each task is performed according to a fixed time schedule. It's quite a tiring experience for us and therefore we need to pay particular attention to SHE. We are usually quite disappointed with our contractors' SHE behaviour. A few even use under-age workers. *Therefore, we decided to offer safety training to our contractors.* After the training, we affix a sticker onto the safety helmet of the contractors for our own routine check-up. After they enter the facility, we perform spot checks. The contractors couldn't be bothered. Most complained about having to be equipped with safety shoes and helmets and commented that no other place imposed such demands. After a few years, they learned that if they want a job from us, they have to comply with our SHE regulations. It must be noted it's indeed difficult for contractors to manage workers with a very high turnover rate. *We copied the Formosa Plastics' solution with attaching penalty clauses in the contract.* We would impose various levels of charges on various forms of SHE violation. It not our intention to derive more income from their action, but we are interested to see if penalty will serve as a motivating factor to change contractors' SHE behaviour. And the results proved our points. Penalties helped to improve contractors' SHE behaviour. The effect was much more than satisfactory. We no longer had to nag. Penalty was one thing but the underlying reason was that no one wanted a poor record. *Let's get back to learning. I felt that an investor should know the local environmental regulations well and then pay particular attention to them. One shouldn't violate any law.*

Plant General Manager, Niesler Taiwan

Comment: In Taiwan, you have the choice but, in China, you are often stuck with the officially appointed contractor.

Response: Yes. But if we give up our effort to manage contractors in China, it's no other than admitting to defeat. We require our contractors (and onsite workers) to attend a mandatory SHE training and then we follow them around the plant to remind them of the best SHE practices. *Our control even extended to the living quarters* and for this, we ran into heated debates with our engineering consultants. They felt that we should place the living quarters outside the plant boundary. Only when the workers enter the site, we enforce our standards. It's a new experience for us. In our Taiwan plant, they started with giving the contractors SHE training and then progressed to offering incentives. Niesler Taiwan's SHE performance showed a corresponding improvement. What I am saying is that initially there certainly will be resistance but the resistance level will decrease as time goes on. *May I emphasise that culture-induced behaviour takes time to change*. I often advised our expatriate managers to look at the SHE problems in China and Taiwan with a different perspective. After all, safety regulations in UK came into effect 100 years ago and in Taiwan, the similar regulations did not come about until 15 years ago. If we compare the beginning stages in both countries, Taiwan may come out okay. Over the years, through my periodic inspection of our plants, I can detect improvements at our plant level. I frequently volunteer my time to give training sessions at TEPA and the Labour Commission. To other firms, this effort is totally unproductive but our GM supports me. We feel that we should strive for the first in whatever things we endeavour. My active participation in the greater SHE community will also instil a sense of pride in our employees. Chinese place great emphasis on *manzi* (face). A little effort goes a long way.

Asia-Pacific SHE Manager, Niesler Group

MNCs' response and treatment of contractors have gained wide-spread notice after several large-scale protests in Taiwan. Current practices unite the contractors with the MNC employees. The strategy is an integrative and internalising one which stimulates MNCs' involvement in educating the local communities and forms an effective benchmark in SHE protection.

> *Taiwanese contractors aren't sophisticated enough to realise the importance of SHE. This is probably due to their lack of specialised knowledge and low education level.* All the corporations in the industrial park impose SHE demands on the contractors but it's generally hard to enforce them. We spend a lot of effort trying to force them to comply with our own standards. We educate them, cause we regard them as our front line people. We shouldn't ignore them. When they come onsite, we give them an introduction to our processes and the potential hazards. We also specify the types of personal protective equipment they should come equipped with. They also have to come for lessons and we welcome their feedback. They have to sign their names after completing the classes. We then issue a green sticker marked with their SHE lesson completion dates to be affix onto their safety helmet. In that way, their colleagues and the Niesler employees can easily tell if they've completed the classes. The duration for exemption from attending such classes is six months. When they come onsite again after six months, they have to attend refreshers. After completion of classes, we require that they at least wear safety helmets, glasses and boots. We require all our contractors, not limited to those handling piping and including those in scaffold-building and truck-driving, to comply with this education requirement. Of course, the contractors complain a lot and sometimes they ignore the rules when there is no one watching. So, starting this year, we imposed charges on non-compliance. We, in fact, devise a penalty table with specific amount of fines for specific offences. This proved to be very effective, as everyone cares a great deal about how much they are making at the end of the day. The penalty can also be viewed as an effective means for transferring SHE responsibility to the leaders of the contractors. This November, we witnessed a substantial improvement in our contractors' effort to comply with our SHE requirements. Local contractors, no matter how technically superior they are, often lag behind in SHE. We are glad to see the improvements and our contribution to raise the local standards. Besides offering training classes to our contractors, we also carry out audits. *We audit their SHE procedures in*

> *their own offices. We imposed penalty system on the contractors not to earn extra income. We are more concerned with their SHE awareness.* This system is extremely effective. During our shut-down phase, we organised safety tours for our managers to visit specific zones within the plant. This the dual purpose of supervising our contractors and identifying potential SHE problems. We do not punish our employees after each learning event. Instead, we help them to improve their working habits.
>
> Plant General Manager, Niesler Taiwan

The response of Niesler was a net outcome of its painful experience of dealing with the contractors. Other MNCs may not engage themselves on such an extensive scale. The response is more legalistic and the overriding concern is on self-protection:

> *Question*: With regards to distribution operations, local contractors may be used. If their practices are not acceptable to your standard, how do you go about to demanding an improvement?
>
> *Answer*: That's the reason we never use cowboy contractors. Instead, we use long-term contractors and if they want to continue business with us, they have to let us audit them and comply with our requirements.
>
> *Question*: So far have you met any difficulties with the system?
>
> *Answer*: Not from the high-up level. The high-level officials pass the responsibility to the lower levels, i.e. the contractors. Sometimes we find they don't always carry through our requirements and instructions. That's why we have a transport emergency team. In case of any mishaps, we have a system to deal with the situation with 24-hour phone call response.
>
> *Question*: Niesler adopts extreme measures. If a contractor fails to meet requirements, he will be penalised and fined a certain amount of money.
>
> *Answer*: We don't have this kind of system in our Chinese plant. The responsibility may not lie on the contractor alone. Other transport organisations may be involved. The contractor can always blame others. *Things are very different in China. In case of an accident, we have to deal with the aftermath ourselves. That's why it is not as cheap to set up production business in China as many may think. Although the labour*

> *cost is low, the operating cost is very high.* The total cost may be higher in China than setting up a factory in the USA.
>
> Greater China Area SHE Manager, Romanowski China

In accordance with the principles and guidelines of the Responsible Care programme, all MNCs extend their SHE practices to cover their suppliers and the immediate stakeholders.

> Not really, but our new acetone supplier has to provide us with MSDSs [Material Safety Data Sheets]. We are registered with ISO 9002 for our quality assurance. We require our suppliers to be consistent with our quality, specification and acceptance demands. We also send our people over to conduct audits on an erratic basis.
>
> Plant General Manager, Niesler Taiwan

7.4 Summary

There is an emerging pattern of MNCs' strategic responses in China and Taiwan, and it is context-dependent. Several factors noted in this chapter, for example top-level commitment and coercion by institutions have contributed to this phenomenon. MNCs, like all other businesses, are sensitive to cost. Balancing self-interest with institutional constraints in producing viable responses requires well-formulated strategies. In responding to different demands, MNCs recognise the importance of accounting for specific local conditions. In Chapter 8, I shall discuss issues pertaining to globalisation and localisation, assessing how MNCs manage their environmental policies globally.

8
Globalisation versus Localisation

> I understand that MNCs follow a set of global standards wherever they go. Some of those standards are more stringent than our national standards. As far as I am aware, Eghbalian, Niesler and Romanowski conduct themselves in a respectable manner in terms of SHE protection. We never have any problem with them and I am truly impressed by their standards of operation. I hope they will contribute much, in technology transfer and funds, to alleviate our current environmental stress. We can certainly use some foreign expertise.
>
> Senior Official, NEPA, China

> We require the submission of environmental impact assessments (EIAs) before an investment project can be approved and through this process, I became familiar with MNCs' global standards. Those standards are more attuned to their home country operating conditions. I am not saying that MNCs are lagging behind in SHE protection . . . MNCs must take local conditions into consideration when siting their plants in a country which is culturally different to what they are used. Romanowski paid a costly price in Taiwan and I would recommend all MNCs to be extremely cautious in applying their global standards world-wide.
>
> Senior Official, Ministry of Economics Taiwan

The basis of MNCs' strategic responses is a set of policies, guidelines and standards, collectively termed 'global standards'. Their implementation and adherence are enforced by the corporate headquarters by various means, for example, periodic and sporadic internal and expert audits.

For safe-guarding and reassurance purposes, a consistent performance in SHE protection is achieved indirectly through engineering codes as well as business management guidance, and directly by corporate SHE standards. The development of such standards is a prodigious undertaking, involving experienced personnel, lengthy research, and consultation with regulatory bodies and industry experts.

Rapid globalisation of businesses challenges the validity and applicability of MNCs' global standards. MNCs' policy research and past experience prepare them well to deal with their home-country scenarios. However, in venturing internationally, MNCs still have much to learn. Each new business venture in an emerging economy commands fresh attention and in-depth examination of specific host-country environmental conditions. Surprises and frustration are inevitable. Expatriate managers, after a period in the host countries, often question the efficacy of the global standards and proceed with proposals for revision. In China and Taiwan, two localities with drastically different cultural contexts from the MNCs' home countries, the conflict is expected to be great. This chapter provided an insight into the core of the controversy, i.e. the needs to balance the conflicting demands of globalisation versus localisation, through an examination of implementing and enforcing the MNC standards of engineering, management, and SHE in China and Taiwan.

8.1 Engineering standards

Control mechanism

Each MNC maintains a working library of engineering codes to standardise its process operations world-wide. It is usual that distinct generations of technology coexist for a given process. It is advantageous for MNCs to use the latest and the cleanest available technologies globally whenever possible for the following reasons. First, the time saving achieved by eliminating paperwork exchange between 'new' and 'old' generation maintenance workers and engineers helps to minimise transaction and operating costs. Second, using the 'state-of-the-art' process design satisfies the governments' desires for advanced technology transfer and could lead to gaining speedy approval from host countries for investment projects.

The adoption of the MNCs' more advanced SHE standards has been insisted on even in joint venture arrangements. This can be treated as a good strategic move. It satisfies both the MNC headquarters' desire for control (via increasing joint venture partner's dependency on MNCs to supply the technological know-how) and reduces the costs of preparing new, site specific plans. As a norm, MNCs would supplement this form of control with technical reviews, audit, and assessment. All the key area managerial staff are obligated to participate from project inception to conclusion in ensuring proper adoption of the corporate standards. These key personnel also act as intermediaries between the corporate headquarters and local subsidiaries. They routinely visit local plants, interview the plant mechanics, engineers, and equipment operators to facilitate the bi-directional flow of essential information.

> The standards are set up here. Let's say we are going to build our plant in China again, I'll take you through the process that we have for that particular plant. *Even though it is a joint venture, we took the Eghbalian standards and incorporated them.* They were translated into specifications for the engineering company. For example in here we have a requirement for grounding to make sure there is no static electricity, and have a minimum grid and need to have a certain resistance so that you dissipate static electricity. This is included in the engineering specs that go to the engineering company who have to design our plant. The technology is Eghbalian's . . . *To some extent you could call that clean technology transfer. This is already stipulated as part of our policy*. At every stage of the project, stage one will be like a preliminary review. There is an environment, health and safety review and what needs to be understood is, where are you going to build, what are the issues associated with the site. *The area people are involved in this process: so myself, Mike, David and these guys, we are the ones responsible for making sure, with the project manager, that we do these reviews*. This is more about site and less about safety. It is more about where is the site, what sort of plant we are building, effluence, how far is it from neighbours, what have been the past uses of that site, these sorts of criteria.
>
> Then we have an SHE review which is also done with the Technology Centre responsible . . . So they are the technology people for the process, we are the overall SHE review from an area perspective. Then we go into engineering design when you get to mechanical, civil design. When that is completed we do an SHE review and then a pre-start up review during construction, which includes SHE and technology and all the other people get involved too. Post start-up is usually at about three to six months. We go back and do another SHE review to see how it is doing and are we really doing what we thought we were going to do. This is not compliance or anything, just a review of the process and the data collected etc. *In these reviews we don't just look at technology, but management systems,*

> *procedures, training. When we do a pre-start up order, we check all training records, where we can interview operators though this is not always possible.*
>
> Trying to interview operators in our plant in China was not very feasible, but we did interview engineers and other process related people. As you saw, a lot of our engineers really aren't very competent in English. A lot of them can read OK, but speaking is a different matter. *So all the way through from the project initiation through to post start-up, my area environmental health and safety group is responsible for ensuring that it meets the corporate and area requirements. It is a line management responsibility to make sure that it happens, we are the check system.* The guy responsible for the project was also responsible for ensuring that this was all achieved. But, we as a group are a support group to him and he is required to come in and do this. He does not have an option to say we cannot do it. So that is the process. We have to make sure that the facility that we build, and the management system we put in place, meets the requirements of the corporation.
>
> Regional SHE Manager, Eghbalian Pacific

Control is desirable, as is innovation. The contradictory mentality of the corporate headquarters is well illustrated in the following excerpt. Senior Romanowski managers are sent to the United States for training, which is a normal indoctrination procedure. However, the corporate headquarters were also interested in the ways that these locally trained managers could initiate beneficial changes, i.e. to improve on current practices. From another perspective, the dilemma actually contributes to resolving the issue of dominant control. If the locally initiated measures could prove to be useful and profitable, the corporate headquarters might be willing to relax its grip to allow for more innovation.

> There are two processes for manufacturing bleaching chemicals, one is using sulphide, the other using chlorine. We use a mature technology in the chlorine process, which is better than the standards set by the environmental law. When we started employing people for our new factory in Taiwan, nobody from Taiwan had any experience in manufacturing bleaching chemical using the chlorine process. *So we thought all the personnel in charge, from grass-root, to middle and senior levels should go through training to see how they use rules and regulations in America, and what we should improve on.*

> These key personnel go through training from a period of three months to one year, depending on their positions. Before the factory started operation, *all our key personnel in operation, maintenance etc. had run through their functions in America at least once.* When I came, I quickly got involved in engineering design, including the issue of resource, how to transfer the technology. *I think the headquarters in America made the right policy in engineering and SBU. It was a systematic strategy.*
>
> SHE Manager, Romanowski Taiwan

Adapting to local standards

A common enigma of internationalising production and manufacturing is the inconsistency of engineering codes among different countries. Conversions of measuring units is one of the least troubling issue. The need to re-design the entire process line brings the concern of maintaining the integrity of the original design. Inadequate local infrastructural support, which impacts on the manufacturing process directly, tends to inhibit the enthusiasm for an investment project. MNCs' desire for control further complicates the situation. In Niesler's case, the anxiety was eased by hiring an international engineering consulting firm with experience in dealing with both the home and host country requirements.

> *There is a lot of detailed negotiation, and in parallel with what we were doing, detailed engineering design work and participating in an environmental assessment which was necessary for approval.* As well as doing our internal feasibility study we are also doing the PRC version of the feasibility study, using the same basic data but a different accounting convention and different forms of presentation. So all of those things were going on in parallel . . . *You are obliged to deal with a Design Institute and the way we managed the project was to employ a Hong Kong-based engineering consultancy who, acting on our behalf, worked with the local Design Institute to do much of the detailed design work and present the various building approvals to the authorities . . . The Hong Kong consultants were contracted to us but they contracted the Design Institute to do a large part of the detailed design work for them. There is a cost benefit to using local designers, but there is also a benefit in terms of that they know the building room codes and requirements and standards and the manner in which approvals have to be presented, and this is a much more cost-effective way of doing things.*

> *Our reason for not working exclusively through a Design Institute, which is the other option, was that we hadn't built a factory in China before and would have had a problem with language and so on. So we used our in-house expertise to develop the engineering brief of what it was we wanted to build and gave that to the Hong Kong-based consultants whom we could communicate with in terms of the standards we wanted to achieve, and they contracted on our behalf with the Design Institute to do the detailed work* . . . One of the problems is that in many instances, from a starting position you have to say what is the standard that we have to comply with in some particular aspect of design. Say it is the flame-proofing of electrical switch gear in the factory: sometimes there would be a Chinese code and I would say there it is and know exactly what to comply with. In other cases they would say, tell us what you want to do and we will tell you whether or not that meets our needs, and in many instances where they haven't got a code, they will shock the world and pick the most severe standard around the world to adopt, or they might take a blend of say British standards and American standards and come up with a hybrid standard which you have no direct experience with. So it is a bit of a labyrinth to find your way through in terms of what standard should apply (. . .). So we have had to employ some design elements that we really don't believe had any value but in the end we had to concur in order to gain approval. I would say those instances were relatively small, not fundamental, more peripheral.
>
> Operations Manager, Niesler China

A comprehensive set of engineering codes requires a good supplementary management system to embellish its functions, especially when linked to SHE protection. *Adaptation* of engineering codes is often necessary in the case of operating away from the home locations. Even in the industrialised countries, such as the United States, different MNC subsidiaries are subjected to different state rules, excepting that the conflict or the degree of adjustment may not be as great as in the host countries. Regardless of the MNCs' intention to achieve standardisation in their process design, local conditions recurrently command revision of MNCs' global practices. Change in engineering designs generally cajoles changes in the associated management system. *The management standards are, in addition, moulded by the local circumstances.* The resultant changes are hence of a higher magnitude than the MNCs are willing to accept. The coercive 'pull' and 'push' phenomenon is not an unusual occurrence, and is in fact to be expected in a MNC's business venture into an unfamiliar territory.

8.2 Management standards

The need for local adaptation, either for cultural or regulatory reasons, is a perennial problem confronting MNCs. Cultural adaptation is difficult and there exists no simple solution. Management styles vary with culture and an MNC's management preferences are not always compatible with the host country environment. A realistic expectation, according to the informants at Niesler, is the first step towards balancing the conflicting demands.

> We have got to go in there with some real expectations. Where the people are and what their expectation from life is, and what are our expectations, are different by a large step and we have got to be prepared to take it a little bit at a time and pull them up to our standard. It will take time and will be frustrating, and it is easier for me on the outside, than it is for the plant operations manager who has to face it every day. China is probably more difficult than most other countries, from the educational level of people, even though they have degrees, it is not necessarily to the same standard as we would have expected, and I just think of this as an overall general approach of the value of life, the general safety requirements. You see them driving down the roads – good God – you take your life in your hands every time you step outside the door. We will get there. I think what we have is a good solid foundation with people like our plant manager in China, with lots and lots of years of experience. People like Thomas with lots of experience and these other ex-pats that we are bringing in will gradually make a change. If we think we are going to make sustained step changes, huge step changes, we are not. It is going to go up, slip down a little, it is going to be a very gradual process to where we need to be. I am convinced that if you talk to the Regional General Manager of Niesler Group, and if you have been through a similar thing in Korea by the way, it wasn't exactly the same because the work ethic was probably there, but a similar thing in terms of bringing people up to standard, is frustrating but can be done. I have seen it in Indonesia and Thailand, and I am sure we can do it in China.
>
> General Manager, Niesler China

Control and flexibility

Management standards impact on the quality of SHE protection directly. As the need to conform to the internal guidelines on management excellence increases, the tension due to incorporation of local factors becomes more apparent. Management standards, contrary to the engineering standards, are heavily culturally dependent. MNCs rely on a comprehensive set of guidelines and minimum standards to implement their SHE programmes. The emphasis is on the minimum standards, but those are subject to interpretation. MNCs are becoming more sensitive to the local needs, as evident in their *global team* approach to develop the standards. MNCs have also to a certain degree allowed their local subsidiaries freedom in management, as long as the subsidiaries manage within the boundary of headquarters' control.

> The next level down is management standards. *All of this is done corporately through input from all of these people, including business people and various others, but functionally we are responsible to do this on a global basis. Not by someone sitting in our US corporate headquarters, but by a team of people with global representation.* The management standards which take these must do's and translate them into activities is so much as it says, you must have a product stewardship programme, the management standard says that this translates into: you must do the following sixteen things to be in compliance. So it is a more detailed document than the other one is. It is a little different across disciplines . . . We have a set of guidelines which are more detailed how-to's, so if you do not know what to do, it helps you decide how to do it, but *it is not a requirement* . . . So all of these here are more corporately developed, and the site specifics need the technology requirements and fulfil all the requirements of these up above. There are lots of documents. The guidelines section contains hundreds of documents. *This is how we interact.*
>
> In this sort of document here, it stipulates the management system you must have . . . If we cannot use some equipment in handling hazardous material, there must be a certain technology requirement or equivalent. So we would say it sets *performance standards . . . The performance standard is the important part of it, the technology: they can use what we suggest or equivalent.* In a place like China, if we said they had to use a specific equipment, you just cannot get spare parts and cannot service them once they are there, so you have to allow some flexibility. But our criteria of not using that particular equipment remains. They cannot do that because it does not meet our performance standard, so they have to find alternative ways to meet it. It varies from side to side *depending on the infrastructure available.*

There were the area people who were responsible for helping everyone do it, so we operate from a real matrix organisation. These were the realms of responsibility of people, this is how it is going to integrate with our existing programmes, description of Responsible Care, who needs to know what about Responsible Care, what our objectives are and implementation, the processes for updating, revision, etc, how the Material Safety Data Sheet (MSDS) is going to be presented, the reporting system and a report format for interviewers. We then went to each one of these codes which are in the CMA version of Responsible Care, which is the chemical industry initiative to improve environment, health and safety. *There are six codes and for each one of these there are a number of management practices underneath that you could say defines the best management practice. This is not technology, it is more about management systems.*

So this is how we use it, the company says we have to do Responsible Care globally, we said OK and took them and translated it into actions in the Pacific . . . *The communities in Asia are not ready for the same ideal of interaction as the communities in the United States. Just think of the sorts of activities they do in the US where they go out and talk to people about worse case scenarios or probable scenarios. Can you imagine going to the farmers in China and talking to them about probable scenarios of accidents on your site. Get real.* But it does not mean we don't go and talk to the local elected officials, the mayor of the city. We bring them to our site and show them our operations, our emergency response factor, but we don't go as far as the worse-case scenario. *You have to adapt it to your local culture, which is what we have done here.* You cannot say you are not going to do anything, because that is not acceptable to us. We accept that you are not going to talk to the farmers about worse-case scenarios, or educate the Chinese media, but you are not going to do nothing.

So we have set a minimal set of standards of how we can interpret this community awareness activity in the Pacific. It doesn't matter whether you are in China, South Africa or Poland or where ever. Eventually you are going to get to the point where you are going to be doing, this is what we are after. By the end of 1997, this is where we are intending to be. For example there is a mechanism to listen to concerns of the community and the data obtained is used to assess the concerns. We have an outreach programme so we will make donations, sponsor programmes, visit with schools, have open days so people can come and see. *Where we get data relating to community activities or concerns from*

> *say newspapers and various other things, it is fed into a central database and this is reviewed annually to see if the community is changing so that we need to make more activity.*
>
> One of the things that tends to happen is that on our site, not so much in China but in some of the other places, the local mayor likes to play a round of golf. So we take him out for a golf game. That's fine, all we say is that the half hour before they play golf, they need to sit down and talk with him about our environment, health and safety programme and document that they have done that and is there any of these concerns or issues that he might have about our facility. That extra half hour before or after they play golf is a little facetious but it is the sort of level that we need to be at right now and I believe that if you are dealing with the right people: the elected official of the local community, as *community concerns go up you will automatically have to increase your activity because they will start asking for more stuff. We are then hooked into the process and hope our management system will take us along with the community concerns so we do not end up in a situation like in the US.* That's the process that we use. Obviously China is in its infancy and one of our issues in places like China, you can only ignore a direct environment . . . Community awareness comes after you have employee awareness. *If you look at the activities in China you won't see community awareness going on yet. It is just not right with the maturity of the site, but if you went to Hong Kong or even in Taiwan, you saw a lot of outreach activities like dealing with the government, emergency response and various other things, and that's just because of the maturity of the site and the country in terms of these sorts of activities . . .* We have to make sure that we translate the corporate desires into actions that they can take at a site level.
>
> Regional SHE Manager, Eghbalian Pacific

In balancing the corporate versus local demands, a compromise was reached by the creation of a set of *performance standards*. Performance standards are sometimes known as equivalent standards and should carry no less commitment to SHE protection. These standards are frequently criticised by environmental activists and the host country government for lacking rigour and falling short of the intent of the original standards. The balancing act is unusually challenging, because the host country stakeholders examine MNC behaviour with keen suspicion, and a departure from the MNCs' home-country standards can only raise more questions. It is exactly this kind of public policing that keeps the MNCs loyal to their home-country standards, which besides serving the function of quality 'control', also renders MNCs invulnerable to questioning. Flexibility in adapting to local conditions does not always confer legitimacy in the international arena and tight management control is sometimes necessary in venturing into a new country.

> There is this textile company in Thailand, in that area, it is the worst looking plant. Don't ask me what the technology is, I don't know, but there is waste all over the back yard, weeds growing in the waste treatment plant, the whole thing is disgusting. Japanese companies have in the past done a good job of exploiting technology. I read an impact statement from a Japanese company that basically said, this is the environmental condition of this country, here is the standard we will build in Japan, but if we did that we would be cleaning up the river so here is the standard we are going to build in this country. If any one of my people wrote something like that, I would hang them from the nearest tree. That was an environmental impact assessment report that went to an Asian government from a Japanese company. I was disgusted, I thought it was hypocritical. They did not say it in those words but I read through the chapters and I am sure the government felt the same. I have never seen an American company do anything like that, *so despite all the things said about American company ethics, I really think as I look around that I see most American companies, mostly large ones, meeting the same standards, not trying to build shoddy plants or cheaper plants or any of those sorts of things.* I think most European companies are pretty good too. Ciba Geigi for example have an ethic that I see applied throughout the world. Hoechst and Bayer have incinerators in their plants in India for example, where it is not really required, but that is their standard of operation, we use them for contract manufacture, which is why I know that they are there. So I see that and yet the environmentalists have a very different view and it is generally because there aren't enough companies. For everyone that I can find doing it right, they can probably find one that is doing it wrong. They have a valid point, if you see some of these places in China, they are disgusting.
>
> Asia-Pacific SHE Manager, Niesler Group

Corporate culture indoctrination

Corporate culture indoctrination is another control mechanism favoured by the MNC. Routine training courses are organised on a world-wide basis and trainers, often regional SHE managers, are certified by the MNC corporate headquarters. These trainers are known to offer the same courses voluntarily or for a small fee, for their peers and home-country regulatory agencies. The objectives are hence twofold: to 'standardise' SHE protection practices of MNCs' own employees, and to transform the attitudes of local institutions. A convergence in behaviour pattern will ultimately ease the demands for local adaptation.

> *We have a Romanowski China Environmental Programme and we have a set of minimum requirements which our people have been trained on and indoctrinated on, so it spells out the minimum requirements.* In general our people take a lot of pride in the fact that they are working for this company, and that we are part of the Romanowski world, and we have very very strict environmental and safety principles. In general acceptance is not a problem. In a place like China that is a totally different story because there have been a lot of bad practices of just dumping things outside and it takes a lot of training and emphasis by the management of this company for people to understand. There have been a lot of those in the operating discipline of the company, a lot of which is in the kind of systems that we have put together. For example in doing small capital projects for plant improvements, etc, we have established a system for people to go through to get the proper authorisation. *But in order to get the authorisation they have to take the safety, environmental and industrial hygiene into consideration before sending the project out, it then has to be signed off by the people, supervisors who are responsible for those areas.* When you do that and add something onto the plant, you have to follow all those guidelines and minimum requirements, otherwise we are not going to do it. *So local people will slowly learn the requirement discipline.* We are still struggling and have infringement and still have to watch very closely and educate and re-educate, but by and large our performance and the willingness of people to participate has been much much greater than any of the state-owned companies around here.
>
> General Manager, Romanowski China

8.3 SHE standards

Effective engineering design and management systems magnify the effectiveness of SHE standards, but incompatibility between global SHE standards and local conditions remains a major source of friction between corporate headquarters and subsidiaries. On one hand, the need for adaptation in MNCs' engineering and management standards according to local demands raises the need to re-appraise the feasibility of applying the associated SHE standards. On another hand, the SHE standards adopted by the host countries may differ from the MNCs' own. Adopting the most stringent SHE does not always make sense and is not feasible most of the time.

> *In the past, we stated that we wanted to meet the most stringent SHE standards world-wide. Then, we changed our mind. This is not because it's the California standards, which are known to be very stringent. The words 'most stringent' are problematic.* For example, in certain developing countries, the standards may even be higher than the California ones and meeting such standards can be quite difficult. As you probably are aware, in rule-making TEPA often neglects to consider cost-benefit analysis, best technology evaluation. TEPA lacks such policy research projects. In a short period of 3 to 4 years, TEPA, formulated 56 environmental laws. This is incredible considering the normal speed of TEPA. The laws were taken from different countries. This scenario can also be observed in countries such as Thailand and Indonesia. In Indonesia, there is a law that forbids noise level in the factory boundary to exceed 55 dbA. Any background noise can easily exceed this level! It's not practical for us to gather all the laws in the world and therefore we decided to drop the words 'most stringent' from our commitment. *This is also a possibility that certain regulations are established based on the special local needs. It might be difficult to meet such standards. However, if we want to set up our plant there, we need to comply with the regulatory demands.* We hence decided to adopt the 'highest standard' of that particular operation world-wide. For example, our speciality chemical plants. They exist all over the world. If you are considering building a new plant, we will use the 'highest standards' amongst these countries. The words 'most stringent' sound very nice but it's almost impossible to achieve.
>
> Asia-Pacific SHE Manager, Niesler Group

Unlike most other companies in the Greater China region, the MNCs studied all renounced the local 'standard' practice of entering via the 'back door'. Adaptation of this form will invite severe attack and punishment from the corporate headquarters and the greater international communities. MNC informants in China complained bitterly about being 'disqualified' from the market competition for not 'expressing gratitude' towards the local authorities.

In Romanowski, [globalisation versus localisation] is not a dilemma, nor is it a compromise. We call it reconciliation. We have a terminology call PIP, meaning Property Information Protection. Within Romanowski, there are a few of Heaven's commandments that may not be violated. Ethics is the first principle. If someone wants to treat you for dinner, you must refuse. *Romanowski never takes the 'back door' approach. This is why sometimes Romanowski cannot strike a deal with manufacturers because we will not compromise our principle. This is especially true in the developing countries.* We regard the 'back-door' business as amateur, and we'd rather lose business than lose our integrity. This is ethics. The second value is SHE – Safety, Health and Environment. There can be no compromise in SHE. In particular, safety always comes first. If any incident happens, the person responsible will be punished, i.e. fired. Of course this style of sticking to principles may affect our business. But this is the way Romanowski does its business. If you are pitched against Romanowski, you will find there are things that Romanowski can compromise and reconcile and there are things that cannot be compromised or reconciled.

Being an employee of Romanowski, my personal perception is that if you want to survive in Romanowski you have to stick to two principles. First, you have to have a *deep understanding of Romanowski's core values*. It doesn't matter if you don't have the ability because you can be trained. But if you don't possess this understanding then you'd better start looking for jobs elsewhere because you will have a hard time at Romanowski. Secondly, you must have the *flexibility and adaptability*. Changes, you know, this is a global concept. You never know which position you will be assigned to tomorrow. *Romanowski's guidelines are implemented world-wide. You have to implement them into your own thinking*. Then you will be able to adapt to whatever position. So, adaptability is very important, especially in the most harsh conditions. Second is flexibility, including the whole external environment and the organisation's infrastructure. Romanowski's infrastructure is very interesting, it's a matrix organisation. There are many bosses, many resources, many support functions, and also leadership. How do you adopt a pro-active approach and drive your champion under such circumstances? You have to look into the resources to solve a problem. I have seen this many times in America. Apart from the one person working in Romanowski, his brothers, uncles, father also comes to work for the same company. So, we often make jokes that if you've upset somebody in Romanowski, you've upset his whole family. *Therefore, the thinking*

> *and philosophy has not only sunk into the individual employee, but can also affect the whole family and even the whole community.* Even the neighbours could be working for Romanowski. This is also what I'd like to see in Taiwan.
>
> SHE Manager, Romanowski Taiwan

Despite the corporate sensitivity to local demands, there is still a coercive force of conformity as exemplified by instituting various corporate-wide SHE programmes and audit tools.

> We try to do environment one year, health one year and safety another so they have a yearly visit from an audit team. Otherwise every three years you tend to get your spike in. Three years in which to do it and a huge amount of action, so what we are trying to do is do it a little more like this. It varies, in the Pacific we are doing it differently than in the US. Then we have the next level down here, which is a site- or country-driven audit process, where more details are entered of implementation. We use the rules of evidence up here just like you would for an ISO audit, but here you start to get down to a more in-depth look at what are the exact things that we need to do, and then you get down to a site and down to a plant type audit . . . As you go down here it becomes much more operational. Here we use a check list approach where we look at: do you have a management system to make sure that you understand the regulations? Now tell me what are the regulations that you have to comply with. Show me how you ensure that you comply. In the US they have a checklist that says here is your TOSCA requirements and they detail pages and pages of TOSCA requirements. *We cannot do that country by country, that is not feasible.* So we say, show us the management system. Show me the last new piece of legislation that came through. Show me how you view that and how you have now implemented and made change in the management system. So we require to show that they have a management system in place. When they get down to their own site audit, then they get down to these more detailed steps here. In these documents there are a whole lot of things you must do. Even though they are called guidelines you will see things like 'each facility will have . . . ' that is a requirement. We go and check whether you have done all these things that you are supposed to do, then we will go and check the documentation to make sure that you really are doing what you have told us you are doing in your procedures. We do a score, and at the end of the time we will

say 'here are the five major areas where you need to make some change or you are not in compliance. Here are some improvement opportunities that you may want to look at'. Then these people are required to come back to us with a plan to implement these changes.

Regional SHE Manager, Eghbalian Pacific

We conduct our own quarterly safety assessment. There is a checklist that we use. We review our instructions, procedures, auditing, training and overall compliance. We also look at how we performed during the past two years and if we have met our target for that year. At the same time, we set the target for the next year. We hope to achieve 100% of our target. *There are certain Niesler procedures which we have not yet implemented due to their general irrelevance. Niesler has its internal set of procedures.* Regarding safety reporting, it's very much the same. We look back to our targets in 1992, 1993, 1994 and determine if we have met our target for 1995. We use the injury statistics of both our employees and contractors. As for the environmental side, we look at the total number of accidents, non-compliances, emission quantities, etc. We report these numbers to our sponsoring business on a monthly basis. Our sponsoring business then compile all the statistics (SHE, financial data, etc.) for its global operation, starting with the SHE data, followed by customer service, the global business leader's comments, financial data, etc. The SHE section is further classified into reportable injuries, classified injuries. For us, we have to be *in compliance with the official regulations as well as our own internal standards, whichever is higher.* Niesler headquarters sends personnel to audit our facility on a monthly basis. We can't just pay lip service to SHE. We have to implement it. Action shouldn't just be limited to the upper level. The entire company needs to be involved. We implement SHE through various channels. The success of Japanese companies lies in the fact that they mobilise from the very bottom level.

Business Director, Niesler Group

The audit team is chosen by the Site Manager, the Operations Manager and I would like to think we would choose one or two other people who can be perhaps a little more objective. The value of the external audit is that it is objective. We have housekeeping checklists where at the end of each day the area people are meant to check that the plant has been checked properly, which includes basic safety

> items as well as housekeeping items. *We are trying to make even the lowest paid employee aware of safety and to be proactive.* It is incredibly slow, but at the end of the day it is down to experience. Giving the workers the right kind of experience and the right kind of exposure, that's what is going to move it forward. The more they see people practising the wrong things, the more they think it is the right thing to do. That's what we are trying to stamp out.
>
> General Manager, Niesler China

Managing SHE compliance with dual obligation, i.e. global and local, is a querulous task. Translating top-level commands into bottom-level action is equally exigent. Even though SHE protection has gained prominence and attention in the modern board room, it encounters the identical dilemma of the other pressing management issues awaiting an optimal solution. The expansion of MNCs has provoked questions and challenges to the managers and management scholars – it is a mature field to be harvested.

8.4 Summary

MNCs' SHE protection, other than the corporate commitment, rests upon a tripod – engineering, management and SHE standards. 'Globalisation' of these well-researched and developed standards begets the advantage of minimising transaction costs and demonstrates the MNCs' commitment of transferring the state-of-art technology from an industrialised to a developing setting. The establishment of such standards is normally handled by a committee of representatives from different regions of the world and diverse business constituents within the MNCs. It is normal to find that considerable negotiation is required to attain an acceptable compromise in this rule-setting process. A few key personnel at the regional or functional level will act as intermediaries in this case. The MNCs studied all expressed their intention to apply their global standards wherever they invest. However, specific local conditions may hinder their intention. Globalisation versus localisation issues are perennial favourites in corporate planning and discussion. The insistence on utilising the MNCs' standards is best exhibited in joint venture situations, where joint venture partners are bound by contractual agreements to observe and adhere to the MNCs' way of dealing with SHE protection. This is achieved through the means of periodic internal and external audits together with corporate-wide training programmes conducted to ensure a high degree of conformity. International consultants, with extensive experience in the host countries and prior association with MNCs in their home countries, are routinely retained to serve as mediators between the local stakeholders and the corporate headquarters in balancing the conflicting demands. Performance or equivalent standards are popular solutions to satisfy these needs, but regularly invite criticism from both the formal and informal regulators. In upholding and amplifying their invaluable reputation world-wide, several MNCs adopt the known 'highest' standards of operations to appease the concerned stakeholders.

9
Responsive Local Firms?

> There are lessons to be learned from the past experiences. During 60s and 70s when most of the setting up and expansion work was taking place, environmental problems were not such a big issue. As most equipment and installation were imported from abroad, we always tried to save money by leaving out pollution control equipment, thinking we could obtain these in China for much less money . . . Looking back now, we didn't do enough and a lot of damage was done during those years. It was around the mid-80s when an incident happened that people were awakened to the harsh reality of the effects of pollution. There was a riot by the local farmers. It happened during the period of our large-scale expansion. A large quantity of effluent had to be disposed of and it was discharged into the surrounding farming land. This became the fuse that touched off the explosion and the police and army had to be called in to settle the dispute. At the time this was the largest scale of army mobilisation to settle a domestic dispute under the new communist government . . . Although an unhappy memory, the incident helped to awaken our consciousness towards environmental protection.
>
> General Manager, Lin Chemical, China

Local corporations exhibit distinct features that are salient in their own right. Chinese state-owned enterprises (SOE), as the name suggests, rely heavily on state sponsorship. The surge of larger-scale manufacturing facilities in Taiwan can only trace its history back two to three decades, essentially under the 'patronage' of the United States. Local corporations are relatively free from international scrutiny of their environmental stewardship and few enjoy golden brand names such as GE and Westinghouse. Despite the swift expansion of SINOPEC, which is fast expanding and counts virtually all the big Chinese chemical SOEs under its control, including Wang Chemicals, few local chemical manufacturers can emulate the size and the influence of international chemical conglomerates. SHE protection, for most local corporations, used to be as foreign as an MNC operating in the region. For Chinese SOEs, SHE protection effort is tied to the national policies and reflects the conditions of trade internationally, such as in the case of the World Trade Organization (WTO) membership and most favoured nation (MFN) status. For the majority of the local corporations, SHE protection is a direct response to institutions, or more broadly speaking, contextual factors.

Local corporations, however, are well connected in their respective communities and in many ways understand the local needs better. They enjoy closer relationships with the formal regulators and are more experienced in finding their ways around the regulations. The implication that most local corporations are interpreting the laws in the most liberal sense is not entirely fallacious. SHE protection, for local corporations, is characterised and deemed sufficient by meeting the published standards. The pursuits of economic efficiency and maximum return-on-investment surpass other interests. *Cost-benefit analysis* is normally executed to check the feasibility of compliance. Payment of penalty charges to avoid comparatively costly SHE investment and relocation of manufacturing sites to municipalities with loose law enforcement mechanisms are accepted practices. Economic consideration looms high and the situation is exacerbated by the government's silent endorsement of development at the expense of physical environment. In this chapter, I seek to portray the behaviour patterns of two local corporations studied. I adopt the usual pattern of presenting the 'context' and 'response' of local companies' in reacting to the SHE demands.

9.1 Context – economic considerations and institutions

CEOs vision and sense of mission aside, the level of local corporations' SHE commitment is largely determined by *economic factors*. Their business strategies focus primarily on gaining a healthy market share and cost saving in production.

> Engineering plastics . . . if it's something for practical and everyday use, we should be able to manufacture at large quantity and low cost. We managed to make breakthroughs in production concept and techniques and were apt to lessen the cost of production, bringing

> the price down to about one-fifth. The whole system in Wang is the one of producing and selling in large scale, and we've been expanding in the last 10 years. Our annual output was around 2000 tons at the beginning with a monthly output of around 200 tons. Now our monthly output has increased to 600–700 thousand tons.
>
> Assistant Manager, Wang Chemicals, Taiwan

Wang's success is achieved by positioning itself in a niche market and following a route of large-scale production to outperform its competitors with low prices. Avoiding environmental protection expenditure in the early years as a cost-saving measure hence helped it to secure a stronger market position.

> At that time, businesses in Taiwan were experiencing tremendous pressure in the aspects of land, electricity, water shortage and environmental protection. *Everybody was busy running business and no one cared about environmental protection. We had outrun our Japanese and American competitors because we did not have an environmental cost like they did.* We were aiming at making profit and therefore economic growth came first and environmental protection second . . . But now we see environmental protection as a must.
>
> Deputy General Manager, Wang Chemicals, Taiwan

The importance of SHE protection is commonly acknowledged in the local business communities, as a response to *the active international green movement and greater public awareness*. The rules of the game then changed to establishing production bases that promise access to large markets and ease of compliance with SHE protection demands. As some Taiwanese firms are rapidly internationalising, they begin to realise the importance of being 'green' and the *power of various stakeholders*. In Wang's case, the firm was prevented from investing in the United States by its past questionable SHE protection records. Ironically, Wang's decision to withdraw from the United States was also partially due to the high costs associated with the country's tight environmental legislation. Economic considerations still predominate.

> So, we had to think about where we should set up our second base? We bought about 50 acres of land in another site in Taiwan, because we could not expand any further here. So, we turned our attention to the mainland. Currently, we import our raw materials from America and sell our finished products in the mainland. The new base should ideally be close to the source of the raw materials or the

> market. We had to make a decision . . . At that time, the Taiwan government was ambiguous about its policy on the mainland. So, we decided to set up near the source of raw materials . . . Our intention to set up a manufacturing operation was protested heavily by our competitors and several threatened to take hostile actions. We then began to examine our past business records. *Our environmental protection record could easily be used as a negative campaign. There were other issues, such as violating industrial patents, on which they could sue us.* Once the factory is set up, we are immobile. *We also considered the high cost of environmental protection. US has very strict environmental laws* . . . Having considered all the pros and cons, we returned to the option of the mainland . . . As for the main reason for us to move part of our production line over to China, *it was not on the grounds of circumventing regulations on environmental protection by the Taiwanese authorities, but the attributes of the market.* The market potential of engineering plastics is tremendous, particularly in Asia where China accounts for much of the market.
>
> General Manager, Wang Chemicals, Taiwan

Peer pressure and the action of *archetypal competitors* also influence the willingness of the local corporations to engage in SHE protection. The progression of an SHE-orientated mindset over time is quite obvious in the following excerpt, and the economic consideration has been tinted with environmental pragmatism. This progression is probably accelerated by the greater public awareness of 'greening' and the *presence of non-governmental organisations* (NGOs).[52] NGOs are widely recognised, by both the regulatory authority and the general public, to be the catalyst of the environmental movement and have contributed much to restrain the profit-oriented mentality of the local corporations.

> *We have survived in Taiwan whose environmental law is far more rigid. The thing is, requirements on some aspects of environmental protection are fairly high in China, but even the SOEs are unable to meet all the requirements. Hence they would not be so demanding in this regard.* However, we will not ignore or do less on environmental protection. We always bear environmental protection and ecological issues in mind. For my company, which is a chemical manufacturer, we take this as our responsibility. *We don't try to avoid costs on environmental protection so as to promote our competitiveness, because competition in our industry comes primarily from Japan and the United States where the environmental costs are as high. If we were to compete with the producers from*

> *Vietnam or Philippines where the environmental cost is negligible and labour cost low, we might need to take it into consideration.* It depends on who your competitor is. Surely you can hold back the cost on environmental protection and save it as profits, but it is a matter of conscience. Wang has established a good reputation and we are very conscious about the right and the wrong. We do not speculate on real estate and stock markets, or collude with gangsters or politicians. We do not bribe our ways through the standards required for environmental protection.
>
> General Manager, Wang Chemicals, Taiwan

Economic sufficiency emerges to be a pre-requisite for SHE protection. *Regulations, effectual law implementation, and tough enforcement* guarantee optimal levels of environmental protection, which would otherwise be exchanged for maximum economic gains.

> *For large- and medium-scale state enterprises such as us, as long as we have enough funds, we are willing to invest in environmental protection.* It is the same with the nation as a whole – with the national economy getting stronger and stronger, environmental protection has become more important. If a nation is very poor and its primary goal is to feed its population, who would care about fresh air? This is often the case in developing counties. *Without a sound economic base, it is very hard to carry out environmental protection.* It is a tricky business to get the right balance between production and environmental protection. The basic principle is to focus on production while at the same time minimising the pollution level. All our new production installations are based on the principles of 'using new installations to pay off the debts by the old' (this means that new installations have to be cleaner and more advanced and will make up for the inadequacy of old installations), and 'increase the production output while at the same time reduce the total waste discharge level'. *Because of the more stringent environmental regulations and better awareness of environmental issues at the management level in all companies, more and more money is being invested in environmental protection.* In recent years, our company has invested a total of 2800 million in expansion of plants, of which 160 million was for building a waste disposal plant. Plus other environment-related facilities such as water storage facilities, monitoring equipment etc., the total investment in environmental protection is close to 200 million yuan. This is quite a large proportion in relation to the total investment. *Lin is a special case in China.*

> *At present development stage, to invest so much in environmental protection would be beyond the ability of most companies in China.*
>
> In previous years, environmental protection was regarded as an expenditure, not an investment for the future. *But now, people are beginning to understand that environmental protection has economical benefits too.* As discussed before, if you put in some efforts at the source of pollution, you can save money at the treatment end . . . *In the context of overall profitability of a business, environmental protection inevitably occupies a low priority position because it doesn't bring profit to the business.* But in the West, where profitability counts for everything, companies also achieved good results in the area of environmental protection. Why is that? *It is the same binding force of environmental law.* In our company, environmental awareness is generally very high . . . In our company, the number one assistant general manager who is responsible for technical improvement also makes decisions on environmental protection. We are lucky to have our present number one assistant manager who previously worked as environmental manager and thus has a very good awareness of the issue. He is very supportive to us.
>
> Chief Environmental and Process Engineer,
> Lin Chemicals, China

> As I've pointed out, *our basic objective is to comply with the standards set by the government*; we are encouraged to try every means to achieve this goal. Hence, there are no constraints over the budget of my department. The main consideration here is to avoid penalties as well as opposition from the neighbourhood, which otherwise would be a pain . . . As long as the standards have been met, opposition from the neighbourhood or social organisations will fade out.
>
> SHE Manager, Wang Chemicals, Taiwan

The involvement of foreign enterprises, each eager to gain a good share in the Chinese market place, has produced interesting an phenomenon – 'voluntary' donation of equipment and services. The motivation of the foreign companies may not be simple, but their marketing strategies clearly provide incentives for SHE protection.

> The overall environment protection situation in our company is on a par with the national standard grade II level, which is not a bad situation considering the alternating site layout – in some cases, the plant and residential area are only one street away from each other.

For people like yourself coming for a visit, the odour may be apparent, but we are used to the smell. Most importantly, the monitored results are within limits . . . We have never obtained separate loans for environmental protection. *Environmental projects always go hand in hand with major expansion projects* . . . Although we've never obtained separate loans, we sometimes receive gifts from Western companies. For example, *an Italian company donated 1 million US dollars for us to spend on environmental protection mainly for training. A total of 70–80 people from our company went over to Italy for training at different times. Other companies from Japan, Australia, etc, have all donated money for training and producing feasibility studies.*

Chief Chemical Engineer, Lin Chemicals, China

9.2 Strategic response or 'ethical' proactivity?

The preceding sections cited '*pragmatism*' as the prime motivating factor for local corporations to pursue SHE protection. 'Ethics' was another explanation given by the informants. Different cultural and political systems give rise to different forms of 'ethics'. Chinese ethics are heavily family-orientated and form a contrast to the traditional Western value system. Caring for the fellow family members acquires a precedence over protecting the physical environment, and here, a deliberate separation of SH and E may be evident. Nevertheless, commonalities exist between the East and the West, a universal rule-of-thumb suggests that a deep appreciation of ethics can ordinarily be equated to concerns for societal issues.

Well, I cannot say to what extent the morality has been developed. *Our general manager has been concerned about the environmental issues and thus keeps very close relations with my department.* In other words, we can channel our opinions of any kind directly to the management. Our policy is: externally, we stress smooth communication; internally, we are strict with the prevention and control of pollution . . . *A further note on morality, a commitment to SHE protection signals a belief in social equality. Everyone should have the same rights to clean air, water and soil.* The company is a microcosm of society and management is a tool to ensure that every voice can be heard and complaints concerning our careless behaviour in SHE protection can be handled immediately and efficiently . . . Let me put it this way. Take a look at those high-level managers in European or US firms. Most of them join non-profit organisations, such as Rotary, and are pretty much engaged in socialising for their own good. How much time of theirs is left devoted to their companies? Furthermore, there have been too many theoreticians, like the MBAs, and too few practitioners. When business goes sour, managers start the game of acquisition and merger, or seek to bring a lawsuit. This is the Western logic. And there is also a problem of hierarchies in firms. High-level managers are treated very differently from low-class employees.

In Wang, even the chairman has to queue in the dining hall for lunch. This is the genuine democratic spirit. The life and death of a company lies in the front line, which means quality of product, improvements in quality, quantities of production, etc. Running and managing a company is not like attending festivity. For many owners and managers of businesses in Taiwan, once their companies grow significantly in size, they would be eager to set up a head office in Taipei, and join non-profit organisations, or run for a post in the board of the non-profit organisation. Do they do it for real social causes? Do they care about our physical environment? They do so in the hope that good connections bring about good business. This, in fact, damages their businesses. Some entrepreneurial groups have someone within group elected as legislator, wishing that the 'chosen' legislator would guard their interests, such as lenient measures on environmental protection. Yet it turns out to be efforts for nothing . . . Many of the second generation of entrepreneurial groups have been educated abroad, particularly in the United States and Britain; they are to transplant the Western logic here. The way Western people do business indicates no trust in their customers or suppliers; this is different from our way here in the East, which emphasises mutual trust. Will companies operating in the Western way survive the increasingly keen competition? Surely, in the United States, giant multinational corporations do survive, but the issue here is whether it is necessary to expand your company into a multinational.

At Wang, we never thought of being a multinational. Imagine that you are the owner of a company; what do you run a business for? The first thing is for a living; and upon achieving this, you cannot quit and walk off because you think of taking care of your employees. Would you expand your business into a multinational at the expense of your employees' welfare? This is a subject of life philosophy. Our chairman used to cite Karl Marx's philosophy: the very first one million may save you from hunger and the second one may enable you to lead a luxurious (comfortable) life. Yet the third one may kill you . . . Wang goes about things steadily. For the moment, some enterprises have been talking of projects of NT$ thousand billions. I, being a financial manager, cannot but wonder where the money comes from. Where is their conscience? *Businessmen are suffering from image problems, because of a few noted black sheep who ironically are considered as successful businessmen.* It is our obligation to help the society as a whole work in a healthy way. At Wang, 85% of employees hold 15% of Wang shares, which amounts to NT$ 126 million; unlike others, we put the so-called 'employers and employees as a whole' into action. *We take very good care of employees, financially as well as in their safety and health. We would strive to do the same for the environment.*

General Manager, Wang Chemicals, Taiwan

Chinese SOEs ensue a different line of thinking. There are some interesting parallels hinting that a common cultural lineage could profoundly influence ethical reasoning despite the difference in political environment.

In my opinion, to achieve good results in environmental protection in our company, *the most important factor is the awareness at the leadership/management level.* Only if the leadership places emphasis on environmental protection, can the work be easily carried out at base level. Secondly, awareness on the employees' part also plays an important role. If every employee has awareness and pays attention to details such as turning off any leaking valves whenever you see one or paying great attention to reducing waste in your particular part of operation, the overall pollution will be greatly reduced. *Another important factor is the environmental legislation which acts as a binding force. This binding force can help raising people's awareness . . . On ethics issues, I think our company pays great attention to this area, especially after the lesson we learned from the mid 80s incident.* During that incident, the rioting peasants surrounded and barricaded our headquarters office for a whole month. They also blocked all our sewage wells in the residential area so we couldn't discharge any water. The riot was triggered off by a sudden, huge increase of effluent discharged into the surrounding farming fields as a result of an expansion construction project. Because of technical problems and mis-planning, the effluent disposal system broke down completely and effluent passed through to water reservoirs without undergoing

> the necessary pre-treatment. After this incident, the leadership/management of the company realised the importance of environmental protection. They realised that their responsibility is not only churning out products, but they also had a responsibility for the society and its people.
>
> General Manager, Lin Chemicals, China

Whether a business can be ethical remains debatable, as does whether a profit-making company can be SHE friendly. There is a fine line between verbal and action ethics. It is, however, ubiquitously accepted that through highly publicised episodes of ugly confrontation arising from industrial pollution, local companies have become sensitive to the diffusion of green mindset within the population and the increasingly unbearable consequences of violating the law. Sensitivity does not necessarily translate into ethical actions. It only presses the business to ponder cautiously about its behaviour and act pre-emptively. The notion of ethics is thus fairly fuzzy in business management, as the starting and the ending points of profit calculation and ethical consideration are hard to define. An outstanding SHE protection effort can be perceived as a means for greater social legitimacy and businesses are well poised to benefit from it. In spite of its goals for maximising profit making, Wang Chemicals has been praised for its SHE protection effort. It would be tough to judge if economic well-being induces SHE protection or vice versa, as businesses in an increasingly democratic and affluent society are beginning to experience the same strict criteria for operating in a responsive and responsible manners as the MNCs. Failure to comply can have severely negative financial implications. In general, local corporations are in the phase of reassessing their policies on SHE protection. The prevailing ethical principle has advanced from pure self-interest to market- and law-based. Though the approach toward SHE protection is highly utilitarian, local corporations have begun, in a piecemeal manner, to comprehend the intrinsic benefits of the nature of the method.

9.3 In search of a win–win response

The rapprochement of SHE protection and profit maximisation can not be achieved easily. Local corporations lack the appropriate incentive to behave responsibly and if the mentality of pursuing short-term gains persists, SHE protection will never be properly addressed.

> It is the general case in China that once a decision is made at the top, we just carry it out. This doesn't mean we are always happy about the policies that are handed down on us. For example, I'm not very happy about the fee-charging system for waste discharges. In theory, the amount of fee charged should reflect the performance of pollution control of the company. But in reality this is not always so. *Some companies do very badly in this area of work but because they are on very good terms with the authority they can get away with it.* Our company was charged over a million yuan a year a few years ago. We have done a lot of work in recent years and our pollution has reduced considerably but instead of coming down, the pollution fee we have to pay now has gone up. The measurement is based on concentration of pollutants. If the concentration limit is exceeded, a certain amount of fee will be charged. *The trouble is they (i.e. the district bureau of environmental protection) don't come and do sampling every day, probably once a month. As a result, if we exceed the limit just one day, we will be charged for the whole month.* If you exceed the limit every day in the month, you will be charged the same amount. This is unfair. They seem to charge people for the sake of charging money. They don't tackle the pollution problem in a positive way.
>
> General Manager, Lin Chemicals, China

Integrated management and longer-term business strategic planning is gaining popularity in both China and Taiwan. Being green and competitive requires considerable strategic thinking, as the local corporations have learned gradually.

> We didn't know the financial benefits that could be achieved by Cleaner Production. The financial benefits were arrived at by calculation after the implementation of Cleaner Production. But there are specific targets for auditing in terms of pollution reduction, for example, COD [Chemical Oxygen Demand] reduced by 30% . . . They first form an auditing team, and then work out an auditing plan, which is based on data collected. And then, they conduct analysis on material balance, including input of main and auxiliary materials and the process used to turn them into products, etc. Through this analysis, they can establish where the weak points lie in respects of environmental protection. When the weak point is pinpointed, the management of the workshop would invite suggestions from all staff members on how to solve the problem. In one instance, fifty or

so suggestions were received within one workshop. These proposals go through a screening process and the number is reduced to twenty or so proposals. After the second and the third screening there are only three proposals left. These three proposals undergo technical, environmental and financial evaluations. Financial evaluation is the most important part.

As Prof. Zhang put it, like all other enterprises selected for the project, we are in the process of learning . . . The financial evaluation is done within the technical department. For the first few years, financial evaluation was carried out by rough estimation. But in recent years, there have been tighter controls and higher requirements . . . *There is no separate financial department to do the financial part of estimation. Everything, including environmental protection, is done together. Consequently, the economic evaluation for Cleaner Production was done on a very rough basis. The benefits only become clear as the project progresses* . . . When pollution occurs, we try to find a way to solve the problem and designate tasks to the relevant plants. At the corporate level, each of us is responsible for a specific plant so we know each plant well and can pinpoint the weak area of environmental protection in each case. When we find a problem, we report to the head of the environmental department and tackle the pollution problem at an appropriate time . . . There is also a 60% repayment from the Pollution Charges every year. This money is put back into environmental protection. In fact, this sum can only be used for environmental protection and is not allowed to be used elsewhere. This is not a huge sum and thus can only be used in some small projects ranging from 200 to 300 thousand yuan.

General Manager, Lin Chemicals, China

Strategic planning engenders management reforms and management reforms demand much soul searching. For local corporations, this entails a renewal of mindset and a willingness to embrace that being green is good for the business. Such an ideal can be far-reaching, but Chinese SOEs may be in a better position to experiment with new ideas for improvement if the State selects corporations for demonstration purposes and mandates speedy a overhaul of the existing management system.

I believe it was first initiated by the NEPA under the guidance of UN's Office of Environmental Planning. The NEPA was initiating a project with the purpose to obtain loans from international organisations such as the World Bank. NEPA submitted a report on some pollution control related projects from ten state enterprises to the World Bank. But the World Bank didn't give the approval. The requirement was that these enterprises must have a Cleaner Production auditing system. This is how the concept was accepted here. NEPA picked five enterprises in Beijing to implement Cleaner Production. We came to know about this when one day a group of officials from Beijing Municipal Bureau of Environmental Protection led by its director came to Lin for a three-day meeting. Our manager received them and came to know about the Cleaner Production. He thought this was a good idea and ask if we could join in as well. This is how Cleaner Production got started here.

When one tries to solve a problem, one has to look at the fundamental cause . . . Our first goal was to meet the targets set by the government. We in turn set targets for each plant. A 'financial punishment' policy was adopted which had great results. The second change was to include the responsibility of installation and management of pollution control systems into the production system. *The benefit of this was that plant directors have to involve themselves in environmental protection, unlike before when they didn't care much about the issue* . . . A 'reward and punishment' policy has been adopted. If both the concentration and the tonnage of waste discharge are reduced over the year, the plant will be rewarded for its work and vice versa. *Competitions are held sometimes to see who achieved the lowest waste discharge*. The fourth measure was to initiate the 'target achieving' programme for installations. The campaign is organised by the NEPA and is one of the six targets set for installations . . . *We have put great effort into the monitoring of environmental conditions*. We set up a lot of monitoring stations which submit daily reports on monitoring results to the headquarters. Production controllers and managers from each department and plant are called in to look at the data to find out which areas are not up to standard so that improvements can be made.

Chief Process and Environmental Engineer,
Lin Chemicals, China

Besides process evaluation and management system reform, Wang posits that speed of strategy implementation has a bearing on the successful outcome. The following excerpt contests the merit of longer-term planning, and stresses the importance of flexibility.

The art of management at Wang is distinct from that of the enterprises in the West. Some scholars specialised in management, such as professors from National Taiwan University and National Chengkung University as well as their students, have realised, after interviews with our chairman, that what they learned from management theories originated in the West is hardly applicable in the case of Wang. For our chairman, expenditure on marketing or management consultancy is redundant; he would rather give the money over to his employees, in which case the payoffs are higher . . . One thing special about Wang, whose current businesses are worth of NT$ 280 billion, operated by 1400 employees, is that we make decisions quickly; say, a meal time for an expansion project of NT$ 20 million or so. *There is one thing which should be always borne in mind: markets exist where the price of product is low and its quality is satisfying.* In particular, for the industrial sector, markets always exist, as long as the source of raw materials is not being cut.

Set procedures for proposal and assessment of investment projects are the symptom of a highly civilised society. Those who are responsible for planning, very well paid, are not involved in the real business world where the secret to win is to be quick. At Wang, we don't have a so-called long-term scheme, but the confidence in ourselves. Of course, we have the insight to what product is in need and opt for the right one. Once it is confirmed that the market is booming, go for it; whether the Japanese or US firms are expanding is a matter of minor importance . . . In addition, to designate a long-term plan requires a huge team of people; this increases the labour cost and may become a financial burden during recession, which leads to the layoff problem (essential). Flexibility is essential. It wouldn't do any harm to have a long-term scheme, but to be strict with implementation of the scheme would. For instance, Wang wouldn't be able to survive if it followed the usual procedure of budgeting and were rigid with executing the budget. Management is art, pretty much like painting; you follow your instinct . . . *The same management philosophy applies to SHE protection. As long as you have good ideas in your mind and discuss them with your supervisor, the projects can then be put into motion. We don't put much weight on paper work here in Wang. It is not easy to estimate the price and hence to propose the budget. What we do is to invite equipment suppliers, through the procuring department, to do presentation.*

Deputy General Manager, Wang Chemicals, Taiwan

Wang's ability to react fast and its adaptability to the markets conditions garnered the company handsome profit. An impressive profit dwarfs the hefty SHE protection cost.

> The fixed cost amounts to NT$1.5 or 1.6 billion, including land and depreciation; alternatively, it amounts to NT$1.1 billion with the land cost deducted. I suppose the expenditure per year is around NT$300 million, including depreciation and working cost. Say, disposal of one ton of waste water costs NT$30 and we dispose 300 thousand tonnes every day. The cost for a year is a considerable figure. We consider this type of expenditure as unavoidable; we attempt to save every penny we can, but in a reasonable way.
>
> SHE Manager, Wang Chemicals, Taiwan

Acting ahead of the SHE regulations saves on future equipment upgrading and process re-alignment, the cost of which is several magnitudes higher than the 'proactive' measure. Interviews with both the local environmental protection bureau and the TEPA revealed that Wang is equally fast in adopting the most up-to-date clean production technologies, which firmly established Wang as an award-winning leader in SHE protection. Wang is among the very few which has effectively managed a 'win–win' scenario due to its capability to maximise profit-making through quick decision making and contribute positively to the protection of SHE.

> All of our expansion projects have been driven by the need for technological breakthrough. When production technology is being advanced, it is possible to produce more, at lower cost; this means profits. Wang has been characterised by non-stop development of its own technology, distinct from others who import foreign technology and rarely try to improve it. We consider our technology of the time as the second best and thereby are always in the never-ending pursuit of the best.
>
> General Manager, Wang Chemicals, Taiwan

It is true that when compared to the medium and small, less resourceful companies, Lin and Wang are fortunate to have generous SHE budgets. A large number of the local companies, in particular, the TVEs in China and the small entrepreneurs in Taiwan, have been operating 'above the law'. Sadly enough, the future of SHE protection in China and Taiwan is heavily dependent on the co-operation of such firms. The pursuit of profit maximisation will continue and the state of the environment is expected to deteriorate, as illustrated by the results of Rio + 5 meeting: the battle is tough and ongoing.

9.3 Summary

Local corporations are different from the MNCs in their fairly 'provincial' approach to SHE protection. The natural instinct to maximise profits and the absence of keen international observers, coupled with the relatively low risk of world-wide boycott on their production activities render the local corporations reluctant to engage the issue seriously. Their close relationship with the local communities better acquaints them with the local regulatory needs and often leads to strong bargaining positions.

For the larger-scale local enterprises studied, the days of avoiding SHE costs in exchange for straight business investment are over. Greater public awareness of SHE issues and newly acquired wealth, as in China and Taiwan, impel the general public to be more sensitive to the conduct of local corporations. Peer pressure and the increasingly strict SHE regulations may force a number into migration but coerce the rest into compliance. The role of business ethics in local corporations SHE effort cannot be discerned clearly. An 'ethical' behaviour may be a direct outcome of the fear of punishment. In most of the cases, the degree of 'ethical' commitment varies with the nature of economic consideration. The recent trend of strategic environmental planning may be an answer to effective balancing of economic and SHE demands. Process management system audits contribute to the minimisation of pollution output. Speedy implementation of strategies often promises greater economic gains. The age of 'win–win' may in fact be within reach.[53] To avoid taking the path of non-sustainable development. Chinese and Taiwanese corporations should look to the West for examples.

Part III
Conclusions

10
Contribution to Knowledge

> The problem of ensuring the appropriate structural reallocation of resources to meet new environmental perceptions and needs is increasingly facing national governments and the international community. It demands both national and supranational macro-environmental measures – which in many ways may be thought of as paralleling macro-economic measures in the economic area. These measures take account of [MNCs] as one of the many instruments by which environmental goals may be promoted. Indeed, they may place particular emphasis on these corporations to incorporate environmental issues into the planning and execution of their international operations.
>
> Dunning 1993: 540–1

The interview excerpts, presented in Chapters 6 to 9 are relatively free from interpretational analysis and represent an essential component of a story that is in the process of unfolding. A supplementary component is my random audits on the MNCs' facilities, most of which had been scheduled 'spontaneously' at the conclusion of the interviews. These data, while not explicitly presented here due to the confidentiality agreement,[54] in conjunction with the archival research results and the interviews with other major stakeholders, enabled me to render a validity check on the materials supplied by the MNCs and shape the manner by which I selected the representative informant responses for inclusion in this book. The audit observations can thus be considered as a triangulation of the information gathered from interviews (see Chapter 4) and this procedure is crucial in establishing credibility for the following discussion of the MNCs' behaviour.

I make a conscientious attempt in this chapter and in Chapter 11 to reflect upon the outcome of this research, referencing the essential elements of both societal[55] and organisational fields[56] (see Chapter 3). I have adopted the interorganisational field model for analysis. This particular model lends itself to the consideration of the broader societal fields[57] or 'institutions themselves', in which the individuals, corporations, and states all engage and assist in defining and extending the meaning of different 'capitals' (social, cultural, and material) (Giddens 1984, Bourdieu and Wacquant 1992, Jennings and Zandbergen 1995). I further place emphasis on the nature of relations, both horizontal[58] and vertical,[59] linking a collection of chemical MNCs and the associated organisations, i.e. the concept of an inter-connected social system or network, in a specific area (see Chapter 3) (Warren 1967, Turk 1970, Scott and Meyer 1992). The analysis recognises the false dichotomies between so-called task/technical and social environments and, by contrast, seeks a balance by addressing both. In SHE protection, an organisation is expected to be subjected to both the technical and social forces for adaptation. This chapter consists of two parts. The first responds to the research questions posed in Chapter 1 and the second summarises the contribution of this research to modern management.

I. Responses to the research questions

The behaviour of the three MNCs studied – Niesler, Eghbalian, and Romanowski – were fairly homogeneous. The responses given by the informants from different organisational levels were fairly consistent. This can be seen as evidence of an institutional conformity effect. This group of MNCs, together with several other diversified MNCs, actively subscribe to membership of the American Chamber of Commerce (Am Cham) in the Greater China region, through which monthly breakfast meetings are organised on a routine basis to address issues of common concern (see Chapter 6). The organisation is sophisticated, with various functional, industrial, as well as issue-orientated sub-committees, and mimics influential lobby groups in Western society, i.e. there is structural isomorphism to home country environment. The information exchange and sharing, in addition to the 'crisis prevention' mentality and a desire for cross-learning, foster greater inter-organisational connectivity and a sense of 'brother-/sisterhood' among the member organisations that is extremely conducive to the mechanisms of normative and mimetic isomorphism.

A contributing factor to the ease of inter-organisational information flow (or the micro- and macro-processes of knowledge diffusion in the societal and organisational fields), besides perceived similarity of interest (Strang and Meyer 1994), is the suspected practice of 'collusion', also as a representation of increased connectivity, within the global chemical industry. The three MNCs engaged in no direct competition for market shares, given their highly differentiated and specialised product lines. The three are noted international chemical giants and it is inconceivable that they could avoid competition so effectively without some prior negotiation. The observations in China and Taiwan thus yielded an interesting hypothesis that 'collusion' enhances 'co-operation'. Since MNCs maintain global operations with efficient intra-organisational communication channels, it is further surmised that such a phenomenon is not unique to the Greater China region. Beside the sentiment of familiarity and co-dependency among the old 'allies' in a foreign environment, the irony of the flourishing existence of Am Cham in a different institutional and cultural setting can additionally be attributed to the world-wide influence and wealth status of the home countries.

Institutional theory can also be used to account for the 'weakened' roles of MNCs in their local trade association membership.[60] As products of another societal field, or institutional environment, gradually adapting to the local conditions, MNCs in many aspects defy the 'norms' of local business culture. Scott (1992:174) explained that

> organisations are affected by the structure of relations of the interorganisational systems in which they are embedded, and these systems are in turn affected by the societal systems in which they are located. All of these systems are evolving over time, and each is composed of elements created at different points in time.

MNCs in foreign countries encounter the confusion of changes, or overlaps, in environmental boundaries. MNCs are embedded in both the international and the local environments and this creates different and contradictory demands, or isomorphic pulls, for conformity, as correctly predicted by Westney (1993:60–61) (see Chapter 3). The penalties accompanying non-conformity to the greater world environment can have a larger implication for those MNCs that aspire to be 'major players', as witnessed by Union Carbide in the Bhopal case. Non-conformity with the local environment has its immediate costs – MNCs are rendered relatively voiceless and powerless in comparison with their local counterparts and competitors. Niesler and Eghbalian greatly resented not receiving invitations from the trade association in Taiwan, which serves as an information distribution channel between the government and industry, to comment on the draft SHE regulations.

The behaviour patterns of the three MNCs studied, due to their homogeneity, are addressed collectively in the succeeding sections, unless specific circumstances justify separate discussion of each. It must be emphasised that despite the resemblance in their behavioural patterns, the MNCs maintain their own distinct SHE protection programmes (see Chapter 6). There is, however, as mentioned earlier, cross-training and mutual adoption of each other's 'norm' setting programmes, as in the case of Niesler modifying Romanowski's safety procedures for its internal use. The behaviour of Wang and Lin Chemicals differs sufficiently, from one another and from the MNCs, to warrant separate discussion. However, the responses rendered by the informants, from various organisational levels at each of the two companies studied, displayed consistency, with no obvious contradictory statements. The differences between Wang and Lin support the pertinence of institutional theory from another angle: namely, different national environments embody differing institutional environment and induce corresponding isomorphism. The shared cultural heritage between China and Taiwan is reflected, to a certain degree, in their management philosophy, though the differences in political systems (communist versus pseudo-capitalist) and stage of economic development (newly industrialised versus developing) tend to dilute the similarities.

10.1 Research question 1: How do MNCs balance their strategic intent and institutional constraints in respect of SHE protection?

The time horizon concept

Strategic intent defines where the top management desires the organisational unit to be in the future. It may be termed the corporate mission or vision, and an inherent interest to prosper and survive, i.e. 'to win', is palpable (Hamel and Prahalad 1988, 1989). There can be disagreements between top management, divisional managers and business unit leaders on what the appropriate strategic intent should be for a given business unit or locality (Lorange 1993:90) (see Section 10.3). Strategic intent is a built-in function of strategic change, which is dependent on the context (Pettigrew 1987). The variability of context, such as resource availability and relevant regulations, with time necessitates much attention. In commenting on the multidimensional view of resource allocation process within diversified MNCs, Doz and Prahalad (1987:65) asserted the importance of time frame and speculated that 'distribution and technology investments often have a longer time frame than manufacturing and product market investments'. Hamel and Prahalad (1988:7) reiterated the significance of the time horizon in their analysis of the Japanese experience, in which a call was made to understand the 'missing link' of 'long-term' strategic intent along with costs and scale. SHE protection, when treated as a strategic issue (see Chapter 3), is certainly dictated by the time dimension of MNCs' strategic intent.

MNCs are well-established global citizens and their strategic intent is to strive to be the global leaders. In Chapters 3, 6, 7 and 8, the fact that being green is essential for the long-term survival of an organisation has been emphatically sustained. MNCs, in seeking longer-term stability and legitimacy, opt for environmental stewardship. In entering a new market and dealing with an alien institutional environment, acting as a responsible global citizen may be the key to greater access to the local resources and the way to longer-term minimisation of vulnerability costs. This contrasts sharply with the local corporations whose strategic intents are of a more shorter-term nature. As SHE protection investments can be exceedingly expensive, most of the small-to-medium local enterprises would choose to pollute and then relocate or declare bankruptcy upon facing financial penalties. It is only when the time horizon of strategic intent changes that a local corporation will consider devoting resources to SHE protection (cf. Wang Chemical in Chapter 9).

More on contextual factors

On institutions. MNCs are bounded by a wide disposition of institutional or contextual constraints, and institutions are vital in governing SHE protection. Scott (1995) defines institutions to encompass three elements: regulative, normative, and cognitive. Balancing strategic intents with the myriad of institutional demands is consequently difficult, especially when referencing Scott's (1995) scheme. MNCs' strategic intents can be traced to their roots in maximising profit-making (Dillon and Fischer 1992). Maximum economic gains do not presume fulfilling social obligation, even though Friedman (1962:133) may argue otherwise, 'there is one and only one social responsibility of business – to increase its profits', provided that the corporations stay within the rules of the competitive 'game', which are defined as competing freely and openly without deception or fraud. The integrity of MNCs is constantly under close monitoring by their stakeholders. Interviews with the MNCs suggested that a utilitarian mode of reasoning predominates, at least at the surface level, when evaluating SHE protection-related activities. Cost–benefit analysis was mentioned repeatedly by the MNC managers in the initial phase of the interview. This should not be a surprise, for even the defenders of the stakeholder model based their problem-solving rationale on assessments of consequences to indicate 'which of the available alternative actions will bring about the very best results by maximising aggregate welfare' (Donaldson 1987:46). As the interviews progressed, the informants were usually able to supplement the early impression of benefit-orientation with full accounts of corporate social responsibilities (Kellman 1981). Judging from the company records and the external reviewers' comments, there was no doubt that MNCs take their SHE obligation seriously. The existing level of performance was clearly influenced by the occurrence of 'critical events' both within the MNCs studied and their peers. The progression from pure self-interested rationality through market ethics to law ethics, both formal and informal, was accelerated by such events. The ethical reasoning moved from an internal self interest-seeking to an external environment-restrained, and from a competitive to a co-operative dimension. The 'higher-level' self-motivating ethics of respect (Goodpaster 1991), which can be expressed as voluntary and co-operative actions, were manifested in all MNCs' promotional literature but difficult to appraise in the field. Nonetheless, the procedure ethics of the MNCs requires full responsibility of the personnel in charge should an accident occur and the MNCs will undertake their obligation to compensate. Prevention is generally regarded to more desirable than cure.

This lends itself to the pragmatic perspective of considering good ethics or satisfying institutional constraints (in the strict sense of Scott's (1995) definition) to be coinciding with good economics in the long-term. Hechter *et al.* (1990:4) noted that. 'Norms and institutions affect the behaviour of actors by altering benefit/cost calculations'. The managers at Niesler discussed the dreaded consequences of having their licence to operate revoked by the greater society. SHE protection is an indispensable component of such a licence. The costs accompanying non-conformity for a highly visible organisation with global operations is enervating and may altogether defeat the essence of MNCs' strategic intents. The critical events experienced by Niesler and Romanowski in Taiwan are solid examples. The oversight of Niesler not conducting a proper SHE audit on its waste disposal contractors ultimately led to temporary closure of its manufacturing facility as a result of a violent public protest against the unintentional pollution of the environment. Niesler must be commended for sharing the responsibility with its contractors and adopting a drastic but effective measure, however, the cost of which, according to the informants, was exceedingly difficult to recover. Romanowski, on the other hand, under-estimated the extent to which public participation would enter into its decision on where to site a manufacturing plant and chose to rely solely on government approval. This again demonstrated the significance of an all-inclusive approach in SHE protection, but the realisation occurred too late. The company was forced to halt its investment at a tremendous cost. In both episodes, the opportunity costs, such as antagonising customers due to inability to supply and eventually resulting in the loss of precious market shares, critically damaged the MNCs' longer-term strategic intents.

On transaction costs and game theory. *Transaction cost perspective.* Increasingly, MNCs have become sensitive to the implications of transaction costs on their strategic intents and have sought to economise such costs through alternative instruments of markets and hierarchies collectively termed 'governance mechanisms' (Williamson 1975, 1985, 1991, 1994). The market-based form of governance relies on prices, competition and contracts to inform the parties engaging in an exchange of their rights and responsibilities. When viewed with a social and relational contracting perspective (Donaldson 1989:47–64, Boisot and Child 1996), the corporation that championed the concept of SHE stewardship, is said to have devoted effort in fulfilling its contractual obligations. It could therefore avoid the associated severe penalty charges for impairing a socially and financially productive relationship and violating the 'public rights to a clean environment' (Donaldson 1989:64). This concept is embodied in the MNCs' 'licence to operate' and can be considered as to be a disguised form of serving the self-interest seeking element of strategic intent (Williamson 1975:26).

Hierarchical forms of governance, on the contrary, bring parties, in this case various MNC subsidiaries, to an exchange under the direct control of a third party, say, the corporate headquarters. The authority then informs the parties participating in an exchange of their rights and responsibilities and the corporate managers have the right to directly resolve conflicts emerging from an exchange (Barney and Hesterly 1996). The standardisation of MNCs' world-wide SHE protection effort with appropriate streamlining of the applicable technologies, i.e. global integration of manufacturing processes and technologies, contributes to a reduction of transaction costs. The boundary of the technical environment was enlarged to remove the cross-boundary obstacles, i.e. communication and engineering design concept inception barriers due to national and geographic variations. The structure facilitates greater technology transfer. Environmentally friendly technologies are much coveted by developing countries and could be utilised as a bargaining chip for better access to resources and government support. This, in turn, re-introduces a market-based form of governance and constitutes an interesting positive feedback system. For instance, the Chinese NEPA has recurrently urged Eghbalian and Romanowski to supply their green know-how and is prepared to offer financial incentives. Leadership in SHE protection can thus lead to a decrease in the investment project approval time by the host country governments and less scrutiny by the concerned residents in the immediate neighbourhood of the proposed plant.

Game theory perspective. On the other hand, if this form of dynamic interaction between the MNCs and the host governments re-introduces a market-based form of transactions, then it is distinctly oligopolistic in nature rather than 'free market' in nature, since only two large negotiating players are involved in playing the transaction game. MNCs and the host governments are engaged in 'co-option', in which co-operation is needed for both parties to maximise their strategic benefits and some order of competition to 'outperform' each other is also evident. According to Child and Faulkner (1997: Chapter 2): 'The dilemma is that while co-operation will maximise joint interests it does not maximise self-interest – at least for a particular transaction at a particular moment of time'. In the realm of SHE, the interest of the host governments and the MNCs are interconnected and interdependent (Zagare 1984:7). The host countries desire MNCs' advanced technical knowledge and their contribution to the economy of their countries but at the same time resent their pollution-intensive activities. MNCs value government support and resources in the host countries but hesitate to transfer their most advanced technologies. If MNCs' strategic intents are sufficiently long-term and thus involved in an iterative game, they cannot pursue the strategy of defection (Axelrod 1984). The retaliation of a host government, or in a broader sense the international community, on failure to comply with SHE protection demands can result in complete dismissal from the marketplace. A forgiving co-operative strategy cannot be reasonably expected. Again, Union Carbide in Bhopal is the prime example. As the game ceases to be zero-sum and as soon as both parties recognise the impracticality of defection, a strategy of co-operation will be considered (Axelrod 1984, Child and Faulkner 1997). MNCs in Taiwan have been co-operating with the government, in the case of Nielser, over a few decades. 'Iteration improves the prospect for co-operation by encouraging strategies of reciprocity' (Parkhe 1993:799). Their trusting relationship serves to realise both parties' strategic intents. However, in the case of China, due to the authorities tendency to defect, co-operative strategies cannot be formulated satisfactorily. MNC operations managers alluded to the 'treacherous' behaviour of local environmental protection bureaus. The authorities, using the reasons of SHE audits, requested the confidential engineering process designs for their own SOEs.

This discussion of game theory supports the validity of the co-operative strategic response typology advanced in Chapter 3 and supports the view that the demands of both the strategic intents and institutional constraints can be fulfilled simultaneously.

On creating and changing institutions. Costs aside, the benefits of being SHE friendly can be manifold. A pioneer in SHE protection is generally in a good position to establish the norms of the industry, i.e. to become the change agent. Romanowski's acclaimed safety programme has been widely imitated by its 'socially responsive' peers. As more organisations adopt the programme, a 'take for granted' mentality evolves among the patrons and diffuses to their business relations, in the words of Liblebici *et al.* (1991:342) the programme 'became institutional practices by acquiring a normative character, when sustained through some form of legitimacy'. Subsequently, non-conformity with such a set of 'industrial standards' threatens the legitimacy and the long-term stability of an organisation. Romanowski's strategic intent has always been maintaining its leadership role, or orthodoxy, in safety protection. In pursuing this goal, it debilitates the competitiveness of its less progressive (in the sense of SHE protection) business rivals by raising public expectations. Once public awareness becomes attached to certain SHE performance standards, through an organisation's active publicity effort and the co-option strategy of appointing influential primary and secondary stakeholders to its advisory committee, the expectation of the official regulatory agency would respond correspondingly and new regulatory demands would soon ensue.

The corporations that trigger the cycle not only fulfil their strategic intents but also receive rewards, both tangible and intangible, for staying ahead. The reputation of Niesler and Romanowski has enjoyed a revival after their painful experiences in Taiwan and they are actively shaping, via constant audits of their suppliers and contractors as well as contrived attempts to influence policy making, the direction of SHE protection in the Greater China region. Such a strong pull of coercive isomorphism for 'norm' setting is rarely observed among the industrialised countries.[61] The MNCs claimed that their desire is to create an environment for fair competition, but this can also be regarded as a statement that engaging in SHE protection impedes their ability to compete. This may be true to a certain degree, however, with the vast resource backing and a determination for norm-setting, it is difficult to determine if there will ever be a 'fair' competition.

In sum, MNCs balance their strategic intents with the institutional constraints by a 'reconciliation' of several factors. Since economic consideration is by far the most important, MNCs 'rationalise' their SHE expenditure with a calculation of the cost involved and such 'rationalisation' is highly dependent on the time horizon of their strategic intents. If cost, which is broadly defined to include 'soft items' such as stakeholder interests, MNCs' world-wide reputation, and social obligation in general, far exceeds benefit, then it is unlikely that MNCs will actively embrace greening. The balance demands pragmatic thinking and reasoning. MNCs are gradually abandoning their static viewpoints of SHE protection. A few noted SHE tragedies also served to induce this new kind of 'balancing act'.

10.2 Research question 2: How do MNCs from industrialised countries respond and adapt to local institutional pressures for SHE protection in developing countries such as China and Taiwan?

Based on the framework developed in Chapter 3, MNCs' responses to local conditions in a developing country context can be examined via two sets of lenses – passive and proactive. The combination affords a better and more systematic appreciation of institutional dynamics. Despite the fact that a given MNC's focused levels may display multiple types of responses concurrently, a well-formulated strategic response typology can constitute a useful basis for assessing the responses of an organisation to the SHE demands. The merits and the flaws of the continuum/progression and categorical models were presented in Chapter 3. The field data confirmed those characteristics and the historical accounts of MNCs' SHE protection development, as rendered by the informants, supported the relevance of both models (see Chapter 7). The continuum/progression perspective has been used to guide the future directions of the MNCs, even though MNCs maintain different criteria for what a 'leading edge' company should be.[62] The categorical model is especially valuable in studying the responses in a task/issue-oriented environment. The adapted model of Oliver (1991), as advanced in Chapter 3, has proven to be satisfactory in accounting for field situations. An explicit analysis will be provided in this section. The analysis also recognises Scott's (1995:124–125) comment on Oliver's (1991) typology that

> institutional environment influences and delimits what strategies organisations can use. Just as institutions constitute organisations, they also constitute what are their appropriate ways of acting, including acts that are responses to institutional pressures.

Reference will be made to the connectiveness of societal, i.e., nation state, and organisational fields and the increased interaction of vertical and horizontal dimensions. Regulatory instruments within societal fields – SHE regulations (CAC and market-based models), law enforcement and implementation mechanisms – are of exceptional importance here.

In Oliver's (1991) original model, institutional and resource dependence theories provide the primary, *passive* explanation for both the response by MNCs to SHE issues as well as the fact that such responses are largely dependent on the context of operation. However, it is apparent that the more *proactive* dimensions, strategic choice and bargaining power, are also important, especially for understanding the specific ways in which MNCs respond to the institutional context within which they operate.

Responses to local pressures – the passive dimension

MNCs, in this study, are considered by host governments to be the models in SHE protection. The 'positive' responses can be attributed to the greater external institutional pressure experienced by MNCs for responsible behaviour. Three general types of institutional pressure, corporate headquarters, host government and 'informal legislators' (national and international NGOs/media), are identified as the key forces behind MNC responses to SHE issues in developing countries. The first factor, i.e. forces relating to the corporate headquarters, will be addressed in the next Section. The other two factors can be treated as coercive exogenous isomorphism with national systems and culture, legislation, and enforcement mechanisms. This institutionalised form of societal and organisational field interaction is crucial for achieving legitimacy of an MNC entering and operating in an unfamiliar territory. The interest of survival in a foreign territory leads MNCs to 'accede to the demands of other actors on which they depend for resource and legitimacy' (DiMaggio 1988). The strategy of *acquiescence* is thus the preferred option.

In both China and Taiwan, MNCs face greater scrutiny from local regulators than other types of companies. MNCs' 'foreignness' denotes uncertainties and raises questions on their 'trustworthiness'. The absolute size of MNCs, as well as the actual size and pollution-intensive nature of the projects undertaken, provide regulators with a good rationale for ensuring that MNCs comply with any relevant environmental legislation. It was not until recently that China and Taiwan, under the coercive pressure of the greater world system, began to take their environmental protection responsibilities seriously. More often than not, as part of this more rigorous approach, MNCs and the associated industries are at the top of the list being scrutinised. In China and Taiwan, for instance, the governments prescribe strict guidelines on the submission of environmental impact assessment as prerequisites for investment project approval. The Chinese NEPA, on the other hand, imposes different SHE compliance schedules for MNCs. The underlying rationale was the predominance of MNCs within their societal sector and the relative ease with which they could be made to comply with SHE legislation. MNC informants indicated that legislators would make an example of MNCs, to provide an indication to the rest of the industry that they are serious about environmental protection. MNCs, relative to other types of companies, are more easily identifiable and likely to comply with any penalties for non-compliance. As a consequence, the regulatory authorities *impose* their policies upon MNCs, with the intention of *inducing* the rest of the industry to *incorporate* responsible environmental business practices. With these tight constraints, the strategy of *avoidance* is clearly improbable. MNCs sometimes chose to *defy* (in terms of challenge) the unreasonably tough regulations, as in the case of chemical registry taxes in China, and then exercised the option of *compromise*. These actions were predicted accurately in Chapter 3.

At the same time, MNCs experience a coercive isomorphic pull from 'informal legislators', such as local and international NGOs and media organisations, who may impact upon their public profile. MNCs tend to be much more concerned about their global reputation than local companies or small- and medium-sized overseas companies. Incidents linking MNCs with negative environmental experiences, such as Union Carbide and the Bhopal chemical leak (Bowonder *et al.* 1985, Bowonder and Linstone 1987, Gladwin 1987, Shrivastava 1987, Weir 1987), the Exxon Valdez oil spill (Cairncross 1992, Rich 1994:277), and Shell Petroleum and the offshore oil-rig disposal controversy in the UK (*Financial Times*: June 22 1995:21), have clearly indicated the negative impact, financial and otherwise, that poor environmental management can have for MNCs. The globalisation of international pressure groups and the revolution in global telecommunications further means that it is much more difficult for MNCs to behave responsibly only in a developed country context. This pattern was evident in the case study area of Greater China where the negligence of a waste disposal contractor's environmental management practice caused considerable cost to Niesler. On another occasion, an SHE manager at Romanowski offered the following explanation for their SHE behaviour.

> Look at what happened to Union Carbide. It took them years to be in the black again. In this day and age, when information diffuses at a more than rapid speed, we can't, and let me repeat, we can't afford to make this kind of fatal mistake. We need to be in a leading position in our dealing with SHE matters.

Moreover, in those countries where legislation appeared weak, MNCs attract the largest share of attention from the 'informal legislators'. For instance, in Taiwan, despite relatively comprehensive legislation, enforcement can be a problem and NGOs play an important monitoring role, especially of the large MNCs. Again, coercive isomorphism is evident. In ordinary times, MNCs adopt a *manipulative* strategy against the informal regulators. This encompasses tactics such as engaging in large and extensive public relations campaigns and frequent media exposure to their SHE protection effort. In the period of crisis, the strategy of *compromise* has been proven to be effective.

Responses to local pressures – the proactive dimension

While MNC response can be explained primarily in terms of the greater institutional pressures relative to other types of companies, there is also a complementary proactive explanation, which is based upon the strategic choice and bargaining power perspectives. In general terms, the relatively large size of projects implemented by MNCs in countries such as China and Taiwan means that the technical and financial resources and strategic choices available for these projects are greater than those available to local companies.

A number of the MNCs considered appeared to perceive good SHE behaviour as a strategic opportunity (operationally and otherwise) and not necessarily a threat (see Section 10.1). This was especially the case for those MNCs with new or recently established operations, where the flexibility in choice and strategic benefit from selecting the most up-to-date environmental technologies and practices is greatest. For instance, MNCs in China with manufacturing operations configured to global standards are able to save in process-design time and adhere to a set of resource-saving maintenance codes. This enhances central planning capability as operations become streamlined on a world-wide level. The practice encompasses the essential ingredients to reduce transaction costs and improve the overall organisational efficiency (Williamson 1975, 1985, 1991, 1994) (see above).

Within a broader context, MNCs also appear to view good environmental practice as being as strategically important as part of their integration strategy to the host country. It is at this level that the bargaining power perspective becomes important. For instance, the Greater China region is regarded as a key strategic geographic area by many MNCs. By positioning themselves as responsible global citizens, MNCs hope to increase their 'bargaining power' with local government on such issues as manufacturing site selection and accessibility to crucial local resources. A strategy that has received much success is to *co-operate* or enter into partnership with the local governments. MNCs are routinely invited to organise courses for the TEPA, MNCs' suppliers and contractors in promoting SHE protection. The benefits are coupled, winning the trust and favour of the host governments as well as seizing the opportunity for 'norm-setting' (see above), which ultimately entails some competitive advantage.

10.3 Research question 3: What are the dominant modes of interaction between MNC headquarters' demands and the local needs in the realm of SHE protection?

Globalisation and localisation are topical themes in the international management literature and have been popularised by the work of Ohmae (1990) among others. Most of the research, which tackles the tension[63] between corporations and subsidiaries, adapts a 'contingency' perspective and focuses on the extent to which corporate-wide integration can be maintained when different strategies are adapted within the various units, and at the different levels of the modern large MNC (Doz 1976, 1979, 1980; Bartlett 1979; Prahalad and Doz 1987; among others). The global integration–local responsiveness (I-R) framework (Prahalad and Doz 1987), though primarily addressing global market and competition issues, represents an area of congruence with the new institutionalism in its explicit recognition for the need of an 'integrative optimisation between multiple and often conflicting pressures in a business'[64] and it facilitates assessments of whether the 'management systems form a context consistent with external demands, given business conditions and competitive positions' (Doz and Prahalad 1994:521–522).

It is important to know whether the corporate policies towards SHE protection are subject to modification, even with a degree of undermining, by the units operating within specific national or regional contexts. In fact, Lorange (1993:130) advocated that 'management control process should be sufficiently tailor-made to realistically cope with local circumstances'. This draws attention to the potential for 'control loss' (Williamson 1964) within MNCs and its relevance to their ability to implement corporate environmental policies on the ground. With regard to headquarters control over the affiliates, the existing theories (Negandhi 1980a,b; Hedlund 1981; Negandhi and Baliga 1981; Doz and Prahalad 1984; Ghoshal and Nohria 1989) complement the essence of institutionalist thinking, as Doz and Prahalad stated (1994:508): 'the research . . . considered both the adjustment of subsidiaries to their environment and to the culture and style of parent company, thus raising issues of institutional isomorphism which are closer to the institutional school of organisation theory'.

Indeed, the work of Westney (1993:67) suggests that the

> question of standardisation versus local tailoring of [MNC] organisation can better be understood as the result of a larger range of potentially competing isomorphic pulls. The MNC organisation is the source of strong isomorphic pulls towards similarity across the organisational structures and processes of subsidiaries; these pulls are not altogether a matter of conscious choice or imposition.

In line with this train of thought, MNCs in China and Taiwan exhibit various forms of isomorphism with their corporate headquarters, manifested primarily in terms of engineering design codes, internal management guidelines, SHE policies and audits. Nearly all MNCs, within sectors such as chemicals, have in recent years developed strict internal SHE policies intended for global application. In China and Taiwan, all the study subjects made particular reference to their global standards. The impact of these policies is that MNCs and their subsidiaries are regularly audited along a number of business functional dimensions, including environmental management. Thus, MNC headquarters exert an endogenous coercive isomorphic or 'ritual conformity' (Meyer and Rowan 1977) pull on their subsidiaries.

Global versus local MNC responses – the passive dimension

Institutional and resource-dependence theories can be used to explain why the level of MNC response to environmental issues is not uniform – with MNC subsidiary behaviour largely dependent on the local context of operation. The differing strengths of the three identified institutional pulls can be used to explain this non-uniformity in response. MNC subsidiaries have to balance the different isomorphic pulls from host countries, corporate headquarters and 'informal legislators'. In general, the two stronger pulls come from the host country legislators and the corporate headquarters. On the one hand, the corporate headquarters of MNCs exercise control over their subsidiaries through a 'loose-coupling' system (Meyer and Rowan 1977) that endeavours to produce consistent global behaviour. On the other hand, subsidiaries must be responsive to local legislation, culture, norms, and stakeholders in general.

Although a number of MNC managers stated that their corporate policy was to comply with their own internal policies, unless local legislation was more stringent, in reality, the research suggests that of the two competing isomorphic pulls, whatever the context of operation, local legislation is the more important determinant. The underlying need for legitimacy and a desire for stable operations by the MNC subsidiary within the host country perhaps explains why the local pull is so important. Unless MNC subsidiaries align to the same extent as they do with the local institutions, they risk losing their licence to operate. This is not the case if MNC subsidiaries fail to align themselves with their headquarters. Indeed, in those cases where there was strong local legislation, environment managers found it much easier to justify the importance of responsible environmental behaviour to the rest of the company. Also pressure comes from corporate level to maintain corporate-wide standards when the local situation is less demanding, because of MNCs' need to demonstrate long-term institutional integrity. The very role of large MNCs as global 'citizens' gives then this institutional type of responsibility. Isomorphic pull of corporate standards is in terms of maintaining a threshold SHE standard.

This does not completely negate the importance of the endogenous isomorphic pulls created by MNC headquarters. The centralisation of engineering process design and the need for headquarters' approval on capital investments above certain figures give support to the fact that MNC subsidiaries are much influenced by their internal policies. This form of procedure design is to safeguard the 'integrity of MNCs' corporate names or their brands in the world marketplace' (Child & Heavens 1997). In addition, the role of regional offices, besides consolidating upward information and co-ordination among different business units, is to ensure compliance with the corporate standards. MNCs' regional SHE managers often report directly to the headquarters as well as to the sponsoring business units of various subsidiaries and are routinely co-opted into various headquarters' SHE policy formulation committees. Even with this strong level of control, when there is a conflict with the local SHE legislation, MNC subsidiaries will tend to submit to the local isomorphic pulls when these require higher standards or additional expenditure. On another level, in circumstances where MNC headquarters might insist on applying a global SHE standard, the dependency of the MNC subsidiaries on external resources, such as contractors, for many of their operations makes this a difficult goal to achieve.

Global versus local MNC environmental response – the proactive dimension

Strategic choice and bargaining power perspectives provide further explanations of why MNC behaviour is dependent on the operational context. This includes the observed variations between both MNC subsidiaries operating in different countries and in the same countries. Although all MNCs' subsidiaries operating in a particular developing country are governed by the same local legislation and similar internal guidelines, they retain the option to respond differently according to their strategic intent. For instance in Taiwan, MNCs placed considerable emphasis on shaping or influencing SHE legislation and are frequently invited to do so by the keen legislators. If MNCs succeed in introducing their own standards, this could become the easiest way to solve the dilemma of succumbing to either one of the two distinct and often conflicting SHE standards. In contrast, the same MNCs in China did not accord the same emphasis on assisting the local legislators, for the conflicting and confusing orders of the laws diminish the strategic value of the exercise. In China, some MNC subsidiaries saw a strategic advantage in applying the latest environmental practices, while others saw no benefit. The variation in perceived strategic advantage was often dependent on such factors as previous experience and future plans within the host country.

Finally, the importance of good environmental performance as a bargaining chip can vary between countries. In some countries where emphasis is placed on good environmental performance, such issues as environmental technology transfer can be important. For instance, in the wealthy coastal Chinese provinces, MNCs were able to exercise a fair amount of 'bargaining power' *vis-à-vis* local governments in siting their manufacturing plant based on their prospect of applying the most up-to-date environmental technologies, among other factors. In contrast, in the poorer inland provinces, local governments appeared more than willing to sacrifice environmental well-being for greater material wealth.

Innovation and learning

The tension between MNC corporate headquarters and local subsidiaries often yield innovative solutions to long-standing problems (Hedlund 1986, Lorange 1993, Child and Heavens 1997). Niesler, for example, was able to devise a system in Taiwan to satisfy the corporate desire of controlling the SHE protection behaviour of the contractors and simultaneously maintain a productive relationship with them. The system of adding a penalty clause in the work contract was deemed effective and rapidly diffused to other MNC subsidiaries. The swift diffusion was achieved, ironically, via the mechanism of communication (intermingling vertical and horizontal intra-company organisational and communication networks). MNC subsidiaries in the same locality exchange valuable 'learning events' or 'focused learning' (Child and Heavens 1997) on a regular basis through periodic meetings in the regional office. Focal actors, normally present at those meetings, then act as mediators between the local and corporate levels, filtering and communicating the 'adaptational' demands. The prime focal actors for SHE matters are regional CEOs and regional SHE executives:

> This reconciliation, as China is concerned, is dependent on a relatively few focal factors. They are located at the interface between business units and higher corporate levels, playing a mediating role somewhat akin to that of divisional managers in the resource allocation process of the multi-divisional firm. (Child and Heavens 1997)

The Niesler example thus validated the universalistic-particularistic model in Chapter 3 and posed the challenge of attaining a 'simultaneous tight-loose coupling' (Peters and Waterman 1982) to facilitate innovation without losing control.

SHE protection is no longer a controversial issue in the board room and is a well-accepted requirement to secure the 'licence to operate' (RSA 1995). Consequently, the tension for globalisation versus localisation has become minimal. As a result, the elaborate control mechanisms described by Doz and Prahalad (1992) cannot be readily detected in this case. Interviews with the MNC managers demonstrated that the corporate headquarters has increasingly been sensitised to local needs (cf. 'I-R model' (Prahalad and Doz 1987)). MNC focal actors at the regional level have been given authorisation to approve SHE investment projects up to millions of US dollars, as have regional SHE executives and CEOs, depending on the level of expenditure involved. They also serve as the advocates for 'adaptation' to local conditions if the situation warrants it, especially if it is under legislative demands, in which there would be no room for 'negotiation' between corporate and local levels. In recent years, MNCs have also been engaging in indoctrinating their employees with 'corporate culture', even in culturally distinct China and Taiwan. The first day of the new employee training contains a module entitled 'corporate culture' and employees are required to attend annual refreshers and to participate in exams. The net result is impressive: of all the informants (managers and workers), a strikingly high percentage could recite the company's SHE mission statement. Niesler China further boasted an exam average of over 90% (I was allowed the privilege of extracting the results from the personnel files). The interview excerpts in Chapters 6 to 8 are witness to this phenomenon. Maybe MNCs have discovered a new key to success – that 'normative' isomorphism is decidedly more potent than 'coercive' isomorphism; in Child and Heavens' (1997) words: 'the corporate culture, supported by formalised corporate routines, contributes to 'pattern maintenance' – i.e., consistent world-wide standards'.

10.4 Research question 4: How do the same MNCs respond under different institutional pressure in China and Taiwan? What are the similarities and differences in comparison with the local corporations?

China and Taiwan, collectively with Hong Kong, have been termed the Greater China region. Politically, with regaining sovereignty over Hong Kong, China is building a powerful nation-state. Economically, the region has generated miracles and commercial activities blossom. China is in transition between socialist and free-market economies and Taiwan has been trading in the free market for decades. The country profiles of China and Taiwan were presented in Chapter 5. The description spawns a disturbing indication that the region may not be developing in a sustainable manner. China and Taiwan are each in a different stage of development. Despite its rapid growth, China can expect to maintain developing country status for the next decade or so. Taiwan is firmly in the league of newly industrialised countries and its large enterprises, mostly family-owned, are entering the phase of internationalisation. China is actively considering privatising its big state-owned enterprises and at the same time, the SOEs are spawning their influence beyond China's national boundaries. The setting for research is more fascinating than ever.

Orru *et al.*'s (1997) work[65] on East Asia is one of the first to adopt an institutional framework for examining the phenomenon of economic growth in that region. A central theme of their work proposed the convergence of institutional and competitive isomorphism (Orru *et al.* 1997:151–187) (see Chapter 1). This concept indeed complements the analytical framework advanced in this research and provides a different perspective from which to view the 'corporate self-greenewal' (Shrivastava 1992) process, however, it conveys a sense of passivity and is largely dependent on market competition. 'In the heat of competition, organisations adopt efficient structures and practices or risk defeat by relatively better-adapted rivals' (Orru *et al.* 1997:152). Competitive isomorphism is most relevant for those fields in which free and open competition exists, such as manufacturing firms in a market economy (DiMaggio and Powell 1983:150). The Chinese market is still steps away from affording open competition, even though under the economic reforms of Deng Xiaoping and later Zhu Rongji, the circumstances are changing. In this section, I have deliberately altered the structure of my discussion from revolving around the passive and proactive mechanisms (which should appear to be rather redundant by now) to differentiating responses and gauging the relative contribution of various environmental factors.

MNC China versus MNC Taiwan

China and Taiwan can be surmised as two distinct societal fields with overlapping cultural boundaries. The two localities have been separated for 50 years and each follows a different set of political ideologies. The institutional environments are different, and yet the essential Chinese cultural elements are identical. This observation is indeed paradoxical. In Child's (1994:285) description of China, which could also include Taiwan as in the Greater China concept:

> China is a particularly complex society, by virtue of its deeply embedded and multi-layered cultural heritage, the vicissitudes of its sociopolitical development (especially in this century), its rapid rate of recent modernisation and its vast scale which encompasses strong local identities as well as distinctive languages. This complexity, combined with the present rate at which the country is changing, makes it extremely difficult to reach anything like an adequate understanding of contemporary developments, even in a specific field of activity such as industrial management.

The complexity deserves an 'institutionalised' treatment and the roles of state, regulations, historical and political events, and culture are paramount in explaining the organisational behaviour, since such institutions exert demands for isomorphism. Given these pre-conditions and the simultaneous embeddedness in two paradox-bearing fields, MNCs' responses in each societal field are expected to be non-uniform. The research findings suggest otherwise, even though at a superficial level, there are observable differences.

The subsidiaries of the same MNC operating in China and Taiwan submit to multiple reporting lines, or control channels, linking the corporate headquarters, regional office, and sponsoring businesses. As the same focal actor in the regional office oversees the operations in both localities, the 'core' of the SHE practices varies little. In fact, the responses concerning SHE protection furnished by different informants, across business function and hierarchical levels, in both localities are fairly homogeneous. This substantiates the presence of coercive isomorphism with the corporate standards. As the subsidiaries depend on the support of external resource providers, the chance for interaction at the organisational level avails itself. MNCs' isomorphic pulls in Taiwan with respect to regulations, NGOs and contractors are much greater than in China. The societal field in Taiwan is considered to be more transparent and connected. This may be attributed to the isomorphism of its societal and organisational fields to the ones of its long-time Western trading partners (some may argue that it is a result of 'over-dependency' on its foreign allies). Federalisation (Meyer 1979, Scott and Meyer 1982) of informal links between state and city to the county level is correspondingly higher. The MNC in Taiwan, in general, takes an active interest in community relations and regulatory advising. It 'willingly' seeks a leadership role in SHE protection (ultimately for competitive advantage) and often engages in promotion of its innovative and strategically benefiting initiatives. It has succeeded in creating a mimetic isomorphism among the peers in same industrial sector.

MNCs in China, on the other hand, due to an unfamiliarity and incompatibility with institutions nurtured within the socialist traditions, and their presumed 'superiority' in SHE protection, function as an 'island of SHE excellence'. Compliance with the local regulations is beyond doubt, but deciding the right law-enforcing authority to submit to is a problem. The sparse linkages among SHE policy-making bodies affect the diffusion of laws and regulations and stand as the major source of criticism among the law-abiding MNCs. The strategic choice options in SHE protection are few and may not even be necessary, as the government's attitudes are overwhelmingly pro-development and the competition is far from being perfect. MNCs in China, compared to their counterparts in Taiwan, appear to be more inward-looking, and because of the ambiguity in SHE laws, MNCs in China are more cautious in their behaviour and subject themselves more to the guidance of the headquarters. The absence of benchmarking and the lack of high expectation from the law enforcers oblige the MNCs to revert to the rules and values of their familiar and 'superior' environment for justifying their actions. Expatriate informants reminisce about 'wonderful' and 'efficient' home-country systems. This may confer evidence that MNCs' organisational boundary is expanding rather than straddling two fields.

Despite the differences, MNCs in China and Taiwan do not seem to be less protective of SHE compared to their siblings in the industrialised countries. MNCs in China and Taiwan are similar in their management styles (an indication of standardisation) and show concern for their international reputation. Both are extremely risk adverse, as induced by their own perceived 'foreignness' and a desire for greater organisational stability and legitimacy and would comply with the local demands if their own functioning principles are not compromised. Most would not engage in the practice of bribery or paying the environmental charges in China to relieve their SHE obligations.

MNCs versus local enterprises

MNCs in general are much more progressive in SHE protection than the local enterprises. Informants in both Chinese and Taiwanese regulatory agencies complimented MNCs for introducing responsible SHE stewardship into their regions. Representatives from Taiwanese environmental NGOs, though wary of MNCs' presence, failed to find fault in MNCs' dealings on SHE-related matters. It would be misleading to compare MNCs with the small or medium local enterprises, for they lack the essential capital to invest properly in SHE protection. When compared to the largest of the Chinese SOEs (Lin Chemicals), MNCs' SHE protection performance was several magnitudes better. As an SOE, Lin Chemicals' capital investment (including SHE protection facilities) needs multiple levels of approval, i.e. a lengthy and bureaucratic process, and its SHE protection initiatives rely on the national policy guidelines and the state's priority list. Its responses to SHE demands were therefore 'mediated' and followed the patterns of passive acquiescence; it practised little strategic choice or bargaining. As a 'target' enterprise, Wang is constantly audited by both the state, through TEPA, and the local authority, to ensure full compliance with all applicable national SHE standards, but the standards are limited in scope. A quick site walk-over of Wang's 'award-winning' hazardous waste disposal facility – an exposed landfill – demonstrated deficiency in the sophistication of design and could itself be a safety hazard. The facility managers and engineers were well-intentioned but inexperienced in SHE protection. They were further handicapped by their inability to gain direct access to the latest technologies.[66] The responsibility for selecting an appropriate technology rests upon the 'higher authority' and there was much 'suspected' corruption at the senior manager–technology provider interface. The recent scandal at Capital Steel that led to the imprisonment of its charismatic leader provides a clear example. SHE protection was of lower priority in relation to maximum personal and organisational economic gains, which was the de facto goal of most Chinese SOEs.

When evaluated against the best (Wang Chemicals) of Taiwanese private enterprises, MNCs' records were in the same league or better. It must be clarified here that Wang is an oddity among the Taiwanese enterprises. The company is successful and returns a generous profit annually. Its investment on SHE protection is vast but proportional to its earning, i.e. Wang could afford it without much struggle. It would be naive to assume that Wang is truly proactive in SHE protection. The informants at Wang readily admitted to pursuing economic objectives first in the early years of the company. A low-cost position, free of SHE expenditure, enabled Wang to price aggressively and resulted in a high sales volume. Only at the realisation of economic objectives and when confronted with an array of strong isomorphic pulls from both the formal and the informal regulators, did Wang start to strategically invest in SHE. Wang's waste water treatment plant, in addition to its practical functions, had been serving as an educational tool to engineering students in nearby universities and technical institutes. Whether this was a strategic move to please the local stakeholders or an action to fulfil its social obligations, Wang had received commendation for its effort. The fusion of societal and organisational fields expedites responsive behaviour via interlocking networks and promotes symbiosis of linking nodes.

MNCs are disadvantaged in competition relative to local corporations – they lack a huge self-propagating relational network, i.e. *guanxi*. Local enterprises are inherently embedded, via state or family ties, in constructing meaningful *guanxi* and are in enviable positions to rely on stable or familial relations during crisis periods (Boisot and Child 1996, Orru *et al.* 1997). MNC informants complained about the favouritism shown by the regulatory agencies towards their local rivals but could do nothing to alter it. This problem may be specific to the areas studied, as the turnover rates for the bureaucrats are low. Consequently, a favoured company may enjoy competitive advantages over its rivals for years. In SHE protection, the situation can be acute if the favoured companies could 'anticipate' policy changes far in advance to gain strategic benefits. However, the pre-emptive approach should not affect the competition much if MNCs are consciously 'competing for the future' (Hamel and Prahalad 1989, 1994) and apply 'advanced' SHE standards regardless of the market situation.[67]

II. Summary of contributions

10.5 Environmental management

This research project is a direct response to Gladwin's (1993) plea for adapting organisation theories to evaluate the phenomenon of greening or corporate self-greenewal (Shrivastava 1992). Environmental management is a young discipline; perhaps, because of its youthfulness, 'researchers have not yet produced after two to three decades of attention, what anyone could rightfully consider as a great wealth of high quality empirical findings' (Gladwin 1993:43). The need for knowledge building is much empathised by colleagues in the more traditional business disciplines, 'the ideas of being environmentally friendly, or "green" will have an impact on all aspects of the business – from the conception of products and services to use and subsequent disposal by customers' (Prahalad and Hamel 1994:8). The review in Chapter 2 further confirmed the need for in-depth, systematic studies, which are relatively free from ideological preaching, to assist the management scholars in gaining an understanding of the greening process in the modern corporations.

The contribution of this study rests on its *pioneering nature*. It is the first of its kind conducted in an emerging market setting of Greater China. It is ethnographic, or qualitative in a broader sense, which is rare in contemporary management research. A total of four years was spent in collecting and sorting data. In this respect, the study offers an insight into dynamic processes, which forms the basis for a long-term study as result of looking at different levels and at MNCs in their context, and also as a result of investigation over a period of years, although an explicitly longitudinal designed was not adopted. That again, is rare in a field in search of an identity, as Gladwin (1993:43) rightly observed 'researchers have not explicitly incorporated dynamics into their study designs, relying overwhelmingly instead on static, cross-sectional methodology – no programmatic, long-term, longitudinal research efforts on greening appear to exist'. Sizeable research funding is hard to obtain, since both governments (excepting the Northern European ones) and a majority of the profit-making organisations still judge environmental management to be a trivial subject. Moreover, good business consulting opportunities often distract researchers from devoting a substantial period of time to a single topic. The study can therefore be regarded as a pioneering contribution to an emerging field of research.

The *international dimension* – two contexts, three MNCs, and one local firm in each context – of this study helps to clarify fundamental issues concerning: (1) strategic choice versus institutional constraints, and (2) inter-MNC isomorphism versus institutional isomorphism. Most of the studies in the field, as discussed in Chapter 2, covered only the 'home' or 'industrialised' country issues and a greater number focus on ideological issues without paying respect to the reality outside of theorisation. The present study questions the validity of their assumptions when applied internationally, particularly those bearing deep green traits in viewing the natural environment as infinitely more precious than the well-being of human kind. Such assumptions can only arouse controversial debates and can easily be dismissed in developing countries where a staple meal is difficult to acquire. Along the same line of thinking, I have developed serious doubts about the practicality of deep green[68] management guidelines. Greening principles taken to this extreme are noble, but at present, appear to be primarily a public relations instrument and a good corporate mission statement, which informants in China considered to be 'futile'. The sentiment may be harsh but it reflects the reality that companies, MNCs and locals alike, assume a utilitarian approach and endeavour to attach a price value to greening and business ethics. Sadly enough, the practice is entirely against the intention of the ideological stance of the formulation, as 'researchers have not always distanced themselves from advocacy and ideology' (Gladwin 1993:43).

Another contribution is in relation to the *cultural perspective*. I regard the more culturally neutral stakeholder model (Freeman 1984, Freeman and Gilbert 1988, Hosmer 1994), which is mentioned in Stead and Stead's (1996) influential book *Management for a Small Planet*, but has seldom been adopted by the environmental management researchers, to be more akin to the mindset of corporate executives. The relative values of the stakeholders and their potential impacts can be incorporated into an equation: 'it is generally agreed (. . .) that the interests of shareholders are to be given greater weight in the decision making of corporate managers than those of, say, suppliers or members of the general public' (Donaldson 1989:46). Notwithstanding the subjectivity and difficulty of value assignment, I extended the model with social contract (Donaldson 1989:44–65) and transaction cost (Williamson 1975, 1985, 1991, 1994) perspectives to account for the behaviour of the companies. In this way, I considered the corporations to be fulfilling their contract obligations, i.e. to contribute positively towards SHE protection, to the society in exchange for long-term stability and resource provision. The underlying message is that all firms pursue a dominant goal, profit, but some are more capable of adapting ethical standards to match their strategic intent. The inquiry into 'ethics' is again, one of the first attempts in this line of research and fills the need of appropriating the research into 'broader streams of organisational research dealing variously with change, quality, ethics, globalisation, leadership, transaction cost, and so forth' (Gladwin 1993:43).

A further contribution of this study lies in the debate about, and evolution of, *MNC power*. I would challenge the perspective that MNCs are all powerful (Korten 1995) and tend to be prime agents for pollution transfer. The findings, on the contrary, indicate that MNCs are constrained by a variety of institutional pressures and can indulge in environmentally harmful practices on a limited and bounded basis. To balance their strategic intent and institutional demands, MNCs are forever searching for pragmatic solutions. The use of institutional theory (DiMaggio and Powell 1983, 1991; Meyer and Scott 1983; Zucker 1986; Scott and Meyer 1989, among others) is not novel in environmental management – researchers have recognised the contributions of institutions, notably formal regulatory agencies, to SHE protection (Gladwin 1993:47–48, Jennings and Zandbergen 1995: among others). However, I have introduced two distinct societal fields, i.e. China and Taiwan, in interaction with MNCs' home environment, to determine if a variation in environment was reflected in different corporate SHE responses as a result of different and competing isomorphic pulls. This approach took the research to the firm–environment interface and afforded insights into how a corporation balances its SHE protection effort against other unfamiliar, country-specific demands and marks a departure from the conventional inquiries into the interactive dynamics between a single societal field versus one or multiple organisational fields. This partially answers Gladwin's (1993:43) criticism that 'researchers have not conducted very much systematic comparison of their discoveries across industries, across firm size, and across societies'.

The topic of *globalisation versus localisation* of SHE standards has been pursued and should lead to a greater appreciation of MNCs' tension in control versus flexibility (Child 1988) and standardisation versus variation. Even though my contribution here may be more aligned with the thoughts of organisational theorists, an assessment of country-specific factors along with the stages of development and the associated spread of SHE awareness, assists an understanding of the greening mechanism in the developing countries. To this end, this study is valuable in offering a description of MNCs' behaviour in their early phase of market entry and how the two distinct and related countries embrace the increasingly global trend of environmentalism.

Complementing Hart's (1995) framework of a 'natural-resource-based view' of the firm, this study incorporated the perspectives of resource dependency (Pfeffer and Salancik 1978), strategic choice (Child 1972, 1997) and bargaining power (Blodgett 1991) with institutional theory in addressing competition-induced proactive behaviour. The data from this study, when interpreted with the aforementioned theories, support Porter and Linde's (1995) viewpoints that being green can enhance a firm's competitiveness.[69] Modifying and validating Oliver's (1991) work with the combined perspectives, the study contributed to the cognition of firms' greening behaviour by generating a set *strategic response typology*. The option of co-operation was added to explicate proactivity. The adoption of an existing model for studying greening movement thus qualifies Gladwin's (1993:43) comments that 'researchers have not worked very hard at building and validating general models, instead being content to operate at the level of historical particulars' and 'researchers have not systematically built on one another's work – scholars of greening suffer from a "bias of the present", failing to cumulate research findings'.

To summarise, this research has contributed towards the integration of organisation and strategic management theories with environmental management. The path I am taking may not be particularly green in comparison with the deep ecologists. As a consultant turned academic, I am much more concerned with practical and operational management issues. I subscribe to the ideal that business can be intrinsically good, which counters the central theses of both the ancient Eastern and Western philosophers, and that MNCs can exert some positive influence in the host countries. The findings in China and Taiwan demonstrated that the degree of SHE awareness and the protection effort is directly proportional to the country's GDP level and that MNCs are acting as catalysts in promoting the host countries' SHE protection effort.

10.6 International and strategic management

Much of the contribution to the field of environmental management also applies here. As the topic of this study is inter-disciplinary, a hard subject boundary is difficult to define. Greening and the internationalising of strategic management is one of the main goals of this study and this section presents the contribution specific to this aim. To avoid being repetitious, I limit myself to the main themes of strategic management terminology and challenge the conventional wisdom of 'strategic fit'.

The discussion thus far has supported the virtue of environmental adaptive theories and indicated the potential value of contingency theory in offering an alternative perspective on the issue of globalisation versus localisation within MNCs with respect to the greening demands (see Section 10.3). The contingency framework (Lawrence and Lorsch 1967, Thompson 1967, Woodward 1965) emphasises the 'differentiated responses to diverse environments and integration of action across environment', but leaves the issues of 'change and adaptation to new environmental demands' unanswered (Doz and Prahalad 1994:508–509). This is a major drawback for research that focuses specifically on the phenomenon of greening strategic change. Moreover, Doz and Prahalad (1994:509) warned that 'an explicit use of contingency theory may lead to simplistic dichotomous thinking in considering the management of diversified MNCs, in particular to polarising one's understanding of MNC management into an opposition between responsiveness and integration categories when, in fact, a fusion is needed'. This ultimately leads to a critical examination of the functional top management-driven perspective, 'in which adaptation is primarily organisation design and development', and raises a further question of how 'top management perceives the need for adjusting the 'fit' or for responding to new environmental conditions' (Doz and Prahalad 1994:509). Despite this criticism, the work of Prahalad (1975), Doz (1976, 1979), and Doz and Prahalad (1981, 1987), though cast in the contingency framework, proved that with some modification, the static and functionalist traditions of contingency theory can accommodate research on the change process.

Since the popular and influential concept of 'strategic fit' was largely a derivation of contingency theory, a review of the dominant criticism of the 'source' perspective helps to build a basis for my contention. Strategic fit stipulates that in order for a 'strategy to be successful, it must be consistent with the firm's goals and values, with its external environment, with its resources and capabilities, and with its organisation and systems' (Grant 1995:31). The importance of achieving a fit between the environment and a firm's strategy has been asserted by Mintzberg (1979: 287):

> the environmental variables also seem to be the most important ones at, and near, the strategic apex. . . . Among those apexes of structure

most strongly influenced by the environmental contingency factors are the amount of decision-making power that must rest at the strategic apex, the speed and flexibility of the organisation's strategic responses.

This is a further elaboration of Child's (1975:13) statement that 'successful performance is likely to depend on a company having the capacity for intelligent adaptation to changing circumstances'. However, it must be pointed out that Child (1972, 1984, 1997) rejected out-and-out contextual determinism in his strategic choice model. Incorporating his viewpoints but with partial abandonment, Donaldson (1987) proposed the SARFIT (structural adjustment to regain fit) model to study structure and strategy, and again, the need to align strategy with the environment is emphasised.

Similarly relying on Child (1972), but shifting its attention away from structure, the observation from this study provides another perspective to strategy formulation and strategic re-adjustment. The role of environment is recognised in one of the central theses of this study, i.e. the 'embeddedness' of the organisations (Granovetter 1985), and the contextual factors were indeed proven to exert influence on strategic change (Pettigrew 1987). The finding suggests, instead of *fitting* to the environmental demands, corporations were devising strategies to *shape* the environment, particularly the institutional environment. Strategic *fit* assumes a certain degree of passivity, while strategic *transformation* infers proactivity. Corporations would engage in shaping the environmental demands if they can readily perceive the associated benefits. A leading MNC in the area of SHE protection would seek to promote wide adoption of its highly acclaimed programmes in an effort to alter the norm of the industry, and possibly even influence the formulation of the host countries' SHE standards. The motivation is self-interest serving and consequently the corporations with longer-term strategic intents are vying with each other for the leadership position. There is ultimately a certain amount of rationality involved (March and Simon 1958, Simon 1957, Simon 1960, March 1981). The mechanism is dependent on competitive isomorphism and hence consists of the essential elements of strategic choice. This corroborates March and Olsen's (1989) proposition that following rules and making choices are not necessarily incompatible. Institutions act as carriers for this proactive behaviour, through which norms are shaped and transmitted. The societal field carries the context within which individual organisational fields exist and interact, shaping them both as agents of change and environment

(Scott 1995:141). This promises a fresh look at the greening phenomenon, which is often postulated as the outcome of the institutional coercive isomorphism. Greening is undeniably led by the legislative demands, but within the defined boundary, i.e. the limits of the 'legal' constraints, corporations can and are exercising active choice behaviour.

The attempt to shape the environment is inclusive of both the internal and external environments. A consistent corporate culture and a firm acceptance among the employees of a standardised SHE-protection programme reduce administrative costs and minimise work hour loss due to accidents. Financial and strategic incentives are again the initiators for the construction of new institutions and the transmission and diffusion of existing institutions. MNCs often encourage their employees to earnestly embrace company values and are often adamant about applying certain sets of core values irrespective of the geographic locations (cf. the top-down model). This mechanism may be mediated by a group of focal actors who have the power to filter information in either direction. However, it was also observed that in the developing country setting, where local conditions prevail and unfamiliarity looms, if the lower level of the hierarchy could present a rationally sound (in both financial terms and otherwise) SHE initiative, institution forming can assume a model of bottom-up process. Thus, in China and Taiwan, there exists a bi-directional flow of institutional construction and transmission. This form of hybrid is conducive to learning and contributes towards invention and innovation. Niesler in Taiwan, for example, has been experiencing cultural indoctrination in both directions. Some of its best SHE initiatives, especially the culturally sensitive ones, such as safe work practices, which in Taiwan was promoted through an understanding of Chinese familial relationship, have their roots in the local operations. This forms a positive feedback to the home country where family values are enjoying a revival.

Strategies to shape the environment to gain tangible benefits originate from a rational choice perspective and are often products of intense bargaining among the agents capable of initiating changes for 'good' causes. The concept of strategic transformation supplements the static construct of 'strategic fit' and can also be used to explain the simultaneous tight–loose coupling systems among the MNCs. Corporations which seek profits will strive to shape the environment in harvesting competitive advantages. The mechanism is best observed in an open free-market system where winning the competition cannot be realised through the involvement of a higher authority that has the legal power to control, i.e. in a planned economy setting. The study demonstrated that in Taiwan, where the market economy dominates, MNCs are keen to participate in norm construction activities to enhance their competitive status. In China, where government still maintains control, albeit diminishing, over business transactions, MNCs are less enthusiastic and even wary of the positive impact of their 'voluntary' activities, such as commenting on regulations that might not be enforced equally on all types of business organisations, on gaining a competitive edge. It is after all a meticulously calculated move.

III. Future directions

10.7 Recommendations for further research

The pioneering nature of this study implies the need for further research, and the results of this study help to identify a number of issues requiring the attention of the academic community. The first is the endorsement of environmental management as a rightful discipline within the confines of management schools. This calls for greater synthesis of environmental issues with the more established branches of management inquiries, such as organisational theory and behaviour, and business policy. The findings of this research have in many ways revealed the fact that the existing management theories are inadequate to address the greening phenomenon fully. The pervasive and diffusive nature of greening necessitates a better understanding both at the interfirm and the intrafirm levels. Interfirm analysis should include the consideration of various types of institution and their interactive mechanism. The natural choice would be to continue this investigation for another prolonged period of time, as the effect of institutionalism is best observed on a longer-term basis. Also, the youth of environmental management calls for more in-depth and systematic case studies to gain rich insights into organisations before a set of meaningful hypotheses can be generated.

The second issue concerns the cultural dependency of greening. A majority of the existing studies focus on greening in the affluent Western countries. The Scandinavians, as well as the Germans, are the noted champions in producing superb research work dealing with environmental management issues within their own country context. Cross-country studies are rare (Castleman 1987, Brown *et al.* 1993; among others) and this is probably attributable to the difficulties in overcoming language and cultural barriers in conducting research. If greening is global, there is no reason to ignore cross-national and cross-cultural dialogue. An extension of this research can hence be designed to enlarge the home-country components. Compared to the firms or MNC subsidiaries in the developing countries, organisations and MNC headquarters in the industrialised countries are generally more accessible to researchers. An extension of this kind promises greater appreciation of the tension between centralisation and variation, control and flexibility, as well as globalisation and localisation. The control mechanisms can best be observed in the headquarters and the political interaction of different coalitions to ascertain power and control is likely to be the most dynamic in the corporate environment. The home country corporate headquarters context also makes identifying research issue easier, since most of the SHE programmes implemented world-wide originate from the corporate headquarters. My experience with the GE Corporate Environmental Programmes attested to the omnipotence of its 'think tank' power and assisted in the refinement of my research agenda.

The third issue centres on home country (usually industrialised) involvement in the developing countries. Interviews with the foreign trade commissions in the home country can help to determine the roles of home country government in promoting or prohibiting potential pollution transfer. The findings from this research disclose the involvement of home country government in shaping the laws of policies of China and Taiwan. Both the US EPA and Environment Canada routinely send their representatives to 'lobby' for (or more appropriately 'market') the adoption of their SHE standards. The Australian government has approached China to supply pollution abatement equipment free of charge in exchange for the future patronage of maintenance and the associated consulting services. The loans to construct the controversial dam in the ecologically sensitive and culturally important Three Gorge area in China were secured from various 'private' sources with the consent of different foreign governments in seizing the business opportunities created by the sanctions of the World Bank and the Asia Development Bank. The German government has openly permitted bribery as a tax deduction item in order to increase the competitiveness of its businesses in a global environment and German corporations are benefiting tremendously from such ruling.

A fourth promising line of inquiry would be the investigation of similar issues in another developing region, such as Latin America. A companion study to this one is being undertaken in the Judge Institute and examines the MNCs involvement in the Peruvian and Colombian petroleum industries (Moser and Tsai 1997) and their responsiveness to environmental and social issues. Even though the methodology employed in that study falls into the ethnographic tradition, a more ideal research design would be to keep the industrial sector, i.e. either petroleum or chemical, constant between the two culturally distinct geographic regions. In this manner, the cultural effects on greening can be much better differentiated. Despite the 'imperfection', the findings of the two studies evince similarities in terms of MNCs' greater response to environmental legislation and their dealing with local contractors. This yields an early support that MNCs have standardised their SHE protection effort globally and the force of mimetic isomorphism is visible among the leading MNCs.

Fifth, cross-sector studies within the same country can also be useful in providing insights for policy making. Researchers have seldom engaged themselves in this endeavour. Rappaport and Flaherty (1992) are among the few to accept the challenge. Cross-sectoral studies can assess the consistency of industrial responses to the uniform SHE protection demands. Different industries can be viewed as different societal sectors constituting a single greater societal field. In this case, the greater environment is fixed and the number of the dependent variables is thus eliminated. As each industry possesses a set of distinct characteristics, the responses to greening are expected to vary from each other in the initial phase of greening. However, within each societal sector, the behaviour of each corporation is expected to converge through formal and informal networks. These hypotheses require the validation of further research. The effectiveness of cross-sectoral studies is highly dependent on the researchers' expert knowledge in several industrial sectors, which can be a major deterrence in considering this type of study.

The sixth issue relates to the strategic aspect of greening. This research has identified realising financial goals, both long and short term, as the principal driving force and that companies often 'invent' pragmatic approaches to achieve a balance between fulfilling institutional demands and self interest. However, the detailed processes involved remain poorly understood. This line of research can adopt the methodologies and concepts of traditional decision making, whereby key actors are identified with stages of the process clearly delineated along a time line. The process is important in understanding how greening permeates different levels of a firm and how each key actor responds to the demands with their perceived orders of priorities. This would afford another dimension of assessing greening within a firm and answer Gladwin's (1993:43) call for more research to establish causal directionality in determining the antecedents or consequences of greening in organisations.

Taking this train of thought further, the strategic response typology advanced in this research requires further validation via quantitative research methodologies. A large sample of companies could be obtained in both China and Taiwan and the survey results could be differentiated by type of company (MNC-wholly-owned, MNC-joint venture, local), size (small, medium, large – defined by the number of employees), age, and so forth. This analysis should shed light on defining the strategic patterns of the companies and most importantly, the results would be much more generalisible.

The list of potential research opportunities could easily fill many pages of this book, as a reflection of the urgency for further theory development in environmental and international strategic management. It is hoped that this exploratory research work has identified the issues requiring immediate and additional attention. The field is ripe for exploration.

11
Policy Implications

> Tokyo Disneyland – owned, operated, and licensed by a Japanese company – claimed to be a '100 percent' copy of the American original, but Raz found a much complex 'local adaptation and active appropriation of Disney by the Japanese'.... 'Dreamers' rides that rely on narrative and atmosphere effects, necessitate a cultural rewrite, Raz explains. Jungle Cruise, for instance, resurfaces in Tokyo with a brand new wrapping: its script or 'spiel' is replete with Japanese puns in place of the American wisecracks.... The *prima facie* evidence suggests that Disney has simply finished the job begun by Commodore Matthew Perry. In 1853, Perry anchored four ships of the U.S. East Indies Fleet in Tokyo Bay and demanded the right to trade with Japan, effectively ending Japanese isolation and spurring modernisation. These infamous 'black ships' quickly became the symbol of coerced Americanisation and foreign influence, Raz says, explaining why Tokyo Disneyland was nicknamed kuro-fune (black ship) by its Japanese competitors. But 'we can't really speak of Americanisation here,' he argues, 'because what we see is not cultural imperialism but local adaptation' (The current buzz-word, he notes, is 'localisation'). Tokyo Disneyland, he says, allows us to redefine globalization, the spread of cultural homogeneity, as 'the dynamic, bilateral flow of culture among first-world cores such as Tokyo and Los Angeles.
>
> Hodder 1997: 10–12

The aim of every purposely designed management research project springs from a desire to explore the unknown and contribute towards better management practice. The findings presented thus far, though seemingly interesting, may appear to be abstract in the eyes of active practitioners of management. However, this is not my intention, for I value practical knowledge and endeavour to contribute to the field in a realistic and 'ecocentric' way. The management implications derived from this study are many and may at times seem controversial. However, to fulfil my obligation as a responsible researcher of 'hands-on' knowledge, I have been obliged to organise my thoughts in two broad categories – implications for the policy makers and implications for the industrial leaders. The sections are written specifically for a third world readership, but the principles apply universally.

11.1 For policy makers

National policy makers often display a 'love–hate' sentiment towards MNCs. A sizeable investment initiative from MNCs represents confidence in the government's ability to maintain a thriving business environment. On the other hand, MNCs are difficult to control and many are arguably more powerful than leaders of state. Taming the MNCs requires much experience and practice. It would be foolish for policy makers to assume that MNCs will voluntarily contribute towards their national SHE protection effort. MNCs are neither charitable organisations nor philanthropists. They seek real profit and are forever searching for the means to gain more market share. Dealing with MNCs can be portrayed as playing *go*, in which strategies and stamina determine the winner. In the light of my present study, I propose the following guidelines on environmental policy *vis-à-vis* MNCs.

Policy makers should develop realistic long-term and short-term goals for SHE protection and integrate SHE demands into their overall strategic planning. Immediate and pressing needs have to be considered along with the long-term objectives. Policy makers should prioritise their policy agenda and devise a longer-term plan for achieving them. Tools such as cost-benefit analysis, should be deployed as a reference, but not as a decision-making determinant. Policy makers need to understand the financial impacts on the market for implementing their goals. Thus, the ability of the market to absorb the costs associated with new SHE initiatives needs to be incorporated into the planning. Public, industrialist and expert participation in formulating goals and time tables are essential. Policy makers tend to be detached from reality and prefer instead to realise their ideals. This is prohibitive in policy formulation. A set of unattainable regulations not only damages the reputation of the government, but also raises doubt on the competence of policy makers. According to a MNC informant:

> Taiwan is no longer an ideal place for establishing a manufacturing plant. Its wages are high, manufacturing sites are difficult to obtain and costs are high, and government regulations are ambiguous. This combined with irrational environmental protection in pursuit of high compensation and the shortage in labour supply can drive potential investors away. There are regulations and official procedures to deal with public hazards but they have never been implemented. When hazards occur, the affected population will ignore the regulations and proceed with requests for financial compensation or blockade manufacturing plants. The lack of a convincing public authority further complicates the issue. The government fails to ensure that the manufacturing plants are in full compliance with various regulations. Once a hazard occurs, it seeks to stop public protests. This of course won't work. The public has no one to trust and therefore listens to no one. The public authority fails to serve its functions completely. The public should also learn to employ the legal means rather than using blockade. An effective communication channel with the public and a clean and a full compliance record can certainly help the situation.

Policy makers should ensure good regulatory machinery and strive for the comprehensiveness of SHE laws and regulations. This can be difficult for leaders of the third world countries, where SHE protection is a recent demand from the greater international community. The desire for a rapid promulgation of laws should not be translated into a blind adoption of the corresponding laws from the industrialised countries. Policy makers need to assess the local conditions carefully. Corporations respond foremost to laws and regulations. However, unreasonable regulatory demands will only repel them from compliance. Policy makers in the developing countries should also certify the integrity of their law enforcement and implementation mechanisms. The roles of these mechanisms should be properly recognised and taken into the consideration when enacting policies and regulations. The effects of thoughtfully designed and well-intended regulations can often be dampened by inefficient and corrupted mechanisms.

Policy makers should also use the market mechanism. Permits, charges and taxes are commonly employed market-based instruments for regulation. Taxes, if the rates are properly assigned to reflect the market conditions, can raise revenue for the government and increase the awareness of the need to exercise responsible SHE protection behaviour. They can also lead to a better appreciation of the costs accompanying environmental policies and pose the question of how much the society is willing to pay for a clean environment (Cairncross 1995).

Policy makers should engage MNCs in SHE protection. It is true that MNCs enjoy technological advantages over the local competitors. However, their capability might be impeded by the lack of infrastructural support. The routine requests from the host government for transfers of most up-to-date technology are often unreasonable and unrealistic. One of the MNCs studied was forced into a complete shut-down because it transferred the latest manufacturing technology which was incompatible with the local infrastructure. This is counterproductive to the overall desire to achieve a 'win–win' scenario. Instead of requesting the cleanest and the best available technologies, policy makers should engage the MNCs in upgrading domestic SHE procedures in the host countries. Advantage should be taken of the MNCs' concern for maintaining a leadership position in both technology and SHE protection. MNCs' competence in educating the public through their elaborated designed public relations programme should be referenced and utilised to raise the level of public awareness of the importance of maintaining a safe and sound environment.

11.2 For industrial leaders

SHE protection should no longer be regarded as a threat. Even though being a responsible SHE steward is increasingly crucial for the survival of an organisation, SHE-friendly initiatives could bring extra income and boost the morale of the employees. SHE protection is an integral part of the present-day management functions and should be treated with the same mentality. Consumers are gradually differentiating eco-friendly products, and a company with a good SHE reputation can gain an advantage in certain market sectors. Cosmetics and fast-food industries are good examples. In balancing the cost-benefits and in realising competitive advantage from SHE protection in the developing country setting, an industrial leader should consider the following advice.

Industrial leaders should build SHE-friendly measures into their business policy planning. Developing countries are under tremendous pressure from international organisations to take on SHE protection. This will ultimately result in more stringent regulations and greater community awareness. Industrial leaders should participate actively in the public debate on SHE protection, anticipate and shape the direction of SHE policy promulgation, and share their strategic visions with the community. Niesler, Eghbalian, and Romanowski have all achieved success in merging strategic business objectives with SHE goals. Their company reports showed successive reductions in waste output and pollution in all environmental media and yet the companies remain fairly profitable. A proaction pays. A corporation which is able to combine long-term strategic intents with SHE protection will emerge as a victor in the market place.

Industrial leaders should exercise management control mechanisms to assist the SHE protection effort, e.g. building an SHE protection record into the annual performance appraisal. This can be implemented at two levels: plant[70] and personal.[71] Such means will give managers a greater incentive to engage in SHE protection acts. As for an MNC, such practice, when supplemented with effective annual SHE audits, can serve as a tool to assure complete implementation of corporate SHE standards in the local subsidiaries.

Industrial leaders should show commitment to SHE protection. A clear mission statement is useful in illustrating the attention given by the corporate to SHE protection activities. Industrial leaders should also commission a more detailed guidance document to set forth the requirements clearly and succinctly. Authority should be given to the regional or local managers to transform the guidance document into local operating procedures taking into account the specific local factors. Allowance should also be made for meeting seemingly obscure local SHE regulations. SHE protection is a culturally dependent social issue and the rationale for engaging in certain practices may not always be clear. The corporate level needs to trust its informants at the local level to maintain the integrity of its reputation.

Industrial leaders should be pragmatic in approaching SHE protection demands. More effort should be devoted to the study of how innovatively to reduce high SHE expenditure. This may entail the examination of current processes to identify potential points for waste minimisation, a greater budget for SHE-related R&D activities, and a greater involvement of community residents in the discussion of proposed pollution reduction schemes. The protocol to ban the use of CFCs enhanced the competitiveness of both ICI and Du Pont, who had had the foresight to engage in CFC-substitute research. A 'win–win' scenario is indeed possible.

SHE protection is in its adolescence. There is still a long way to go. The success of SHE protection rests upon the willingness of policy makers and the industrial decision makers to undertake certain measures in partnership with each other. In the past, there have been both tragedies and successes. There are lessons to be learned and they should be learned in collaboration.

Notes

1. Development that meets the needs of the present without compromising the ability of future generations to meet their own needs (WCED 1987).
2. The Montreal Protocol (16/9/1987) is another influential legal instrument which bans the use of chlorofluorocarbon (CFC).
3. Mitsubishi Kagusu and E. Merck are just two of many companies attracted to the region (Hunter 1996).
4. General bargaining tends to proceed in stages, with each stage centring on different level of government and different aspects of the enterprise.
5. Environmental policies often developed and implemented by local and regional authorities, while the licensing process and the accompanying negotiations are led by central authorities.
6. Host country institutions often suffer from lack of experience, poor access to technical information, short planning horizons, narrowly defined missions, and lack of vision.
7. Present-day thinking may not regard these 'boundaries' as well defined or substantial, in observing organisation-institution inter-penetration via joint committee memberships, etc.
8. It states that any damage to the environment is morally questionable. Two shades of environmental ethics are in existence: light- and deep-green.
9. This group is represented by bodies whose manifest mission is to care for the planet. These include national or local green pressure groups and high-profile individual champions in society.
10. Surveys show that about three out of four US corporations have ethics codes. Their purpose is to provide guidance to managers and employees when they encounter an ethical dilemma. Some companies – about one in three Fortune 1000 companies, according to a 1989 survey by the Ethics Resource Centre – have even created an ethics committee to give guidance on ethical matters. Dow Corning and Hewlett-Packard have both instituted ethics audit programmes.
11. Isomorphism is defined as a process through which organisations in the same business lines become homogeneous (DiMaggio and Powell 1991).
12. Normative conformity with government agencies and professional organisations is, to a large extent, passive. Mimicry as a form of direct learning from competitors and other related organisations is considered by Lu and Lake (1995) as an active and willing act.
13. Bailey (1994) made a distinction between typology, which is conceptually based, and taxonomies, which is empirically based.
14. These encompass the internal operations of the company including the materials, technologies, processes, and human resources used in manufacturing and distribution (Rondinelli and Vastag 1996).
15. These risks are determined by the company's external world: its location, the ecological characteristics (biodiversity, winds, topography) of the physical environment in which it operates, location demographics (population

density, age, income distribution), infrastructure (roads, telecommunication networks), education levels of the population, and public attitudes toward environmental hazards (Rondinelli and Vastag 1996).

16. See Chapter 2.
17. From the MNC's perspective, 'particularistic' and 'universalistic' may be reversed as it views its range of international operations.
18. Convention on Nature Protection and Wildlife Preservation in the Western Hemisphere, Washington DC, 12 October 1940, in force 1 May 1942 (Sands, 1993).
19. The UN noted that there is an emergence of certain minimum international environmental standards relating to the following: (a) the use of natural resources; (b) production processes; (c) emissions into the atmosphere; (d) emissions into the marine environment; (e) management of waste; (f) the carrying out of appropriate environmental impact assessments; and (g) the provision of information to citizens, national authorities and, where appropriate, international authorities.
20. In almost every country, CAC efforts have been aimed separately at the air, water and land media. The major US environmental laws such as the Clean Air Act (CAA), the Clean Water Act (CWA), and the hazardous waste statutes were each written to address one environmental medium. Many regulations address one pollutant at a time.
21. Also, because they carry with them their own isomorphic organisational culture and routines.
22. Competitors in the same industry, or even across industries, are in their perennial search for a competitive advantage in being green.
23. Command and control, market-based, or a mixture of both, as discussed elsewhere in this chapter.
24. This refers to 'those organisations that, in the aggregate, constitute a recognised area of institutional life: key suppliers, resource and product consumers, regulatory agencies, and other organisations that produce similar services or products' (DiMaggio and Powell 1991).
25. The issues pertaining to globalisation versus localisation will be examined in Chapters 8 and 10.
26. Such practice has been criticised for its lack of contribution to knowledge advancement as the 'data of research is always interpreted as reinforcing or verifying the existing perspective of the researcher. Thus it is very difficult for genuinely new theory or forms of explanation to emerge if the research data is simply labelled or conceptualised in terms of the favoured framework' (Layder 1993: 52).
27. This government organisation bears the responsibility of advising the industries in wide ranging issues including environmental protection technology, evaluation for installing pollution control and monitoring systems in various industrial parks.
28. This unit ensures the general welfare of the labour force, and promulgates as well as enforces occupational safety regulations.
29. NGOs are non-existent in China. The laws forbid such establishments.
30. They were not as recent as to justify the use of 'protocol analysis' (Easterby-Smith *et al.* 1991: 91–93).
31. The concept was first proposed by Denzin (1978).

32. These may be treated as the dependent variables.
33. I must confess to not taking the full advantage of the softwares such as NUD·IST and ATLAS/ti. I discovered the software too late in the data analysis phase, and my limited financial resources prevented me from pursuing the option further.
34. A preoccupation with selecting and defending methods to the exclusion of the actual substance of the story being told.
35. Percentage change on year earlier.
36. As of 30th June 2001.
37. As of 31st July 2001.
38. This group includes suppliers of crucial electronic manufacturing ingredients, i.e. chemicals, and sub-micron electronic components.
39. In 1991, there were 19 million TVEs that employed 96 million workers and produced 1100 billion yuan of output, accounting for one-third of the social industrial output value. While the industrial output of TVEs now total 850 billion yuan, rural industries have also become a major polluting source (PRC National Environmental Protection Agency and State Planning Commission 1994).
40. Based on the translation of NEPA.
41. This principle refers to the three main phases in the building of new industrial facilities: (1) projection, (2) construction, (3) operation. The principle is intended to guarantee that suitable pollution abatement equipment will be developed and constructed parallel to, or simultaneously with, the development and construction of new industrial facilities over these three phases.
42. These include environmental quality targets for 37 cities and treatment targets for each province, autonomous regions, and municipalities.
43. NEPA consists of nine departments: Planning and Financial Affairs (Divisions of Programmes, Annual Plans, Investment, Statistics, Planning and Finance), Policies, Laws and Regulations (Secretariat of the Environmental Protection Commission under the State Council, Divisions of Policy Research, Laws and Regulations), Institutional and Personnel Management, Science, Technology and Standards (Divisions of Scientific and Technological Development, Scientific and Technological Achievement, Standards, Environmental Industries), Pollution Control (Divisions of Comprehensive Affairs, Water Pollution Control, Air Pollution Control, Noise Pollution Control, Solid Waste and Toxic Chemical Management), Supervision and Management (Divisions of Development and Construction Management, Monitoring, Environmental Supervision and Management, Environmental Management of Radioactive Substances), Nature Conservation (Divisions of Ecological Environment Management, Nature Reserves and Species Management, Environmental Management for Village and Township Enterprises, Marine Environment Management), International Co-operation (Divisions of Comprehensive Affairs, International Organisations, Bilateral Co-operation), Communication and Education.
44. In March 1993, the National People's Congress set up a Committee on Environmental Protection, and this Committee has the responsibility to lead relevant government bodies to set up new laws and regulations and take measure to guarantee enforcement, including inspection of EPBs at every

level (provincial, municipal and county) (PRC National Environmental Protection Agency and State Planning Commission 1994).

45. The Provincial Government of Taiwan does not possess judiciary power over Kaohsiung and Taipei.
46. With the fees collected from the discharge levy system, the local EPB provides financial support in terms of low-interest loans for enterprises engaging in pollution control. The State Planning Commission will also provide low-interest loans through its local departments.
47. These are degree of protection achievable, technical practicality, long-term cost of ownership, business strategy, level of risk reduction achievable, and economic viability/cost effectiveness.
48. See Chapter 3 for its strategic response model on SHE issues.
49. See Chapter 4.
50. I have italicised the particularly significant sections of quotations as a device to draw attention to these without artificailly abstracting them from the context of my informants' replies.
51. Compliance with the local or internal (whichever is more stringent) standards on gaseous emission, waste water discharge, safety measures, waste disposal procedures, hazardous chemical handling and transport, work-related injury reporting, emergency response, etc.
52. The government prohibits the presence of NGOs in China.
53. Some argue that 'win–win' is only possible up to a point, where SHE problems can be identified and solved easily. Then, SHE protection becomes a real cost. See Walley and Whitehead (1994) and Cairncross (1995).
54. Audit reports become the properties of the MNCs studied. Duplication in any shape or form is not permitted. However, the audits served as 'reality checks' against the MNC executives' claims.
55. External sources of the structuration of the fields tend to be based on supra-organisational bodies that have the power to designate the actors and activities that comprise a subfield (Jennings and Zandbergen 1995:1028).
56. The field is created through four crucial steps of structuration: (a) an increase in interaction among organisations, (b) the emergence of sharply defined inter-organisational structures of domination and patterns of coalitions, (c) an increased information load with which organisation in the field must contend, and (d) the development of mutual awareness among participants that organisations are involved in common enterprise (DiMaggio 1991:277).
57. See also Scott and Meyer's (1992) definition of a societal sector.
58. We shall define a community's horizontal pattern as the structural and functional relation of its various social units and subsystems to each other. The term 'horizontal' is used to indicate that, roughly speaking, the community units, insofar as they have relevance to the community system, tend to be on approximately the same hierarchical level (a community unit level, as opposed to a state, regional, national, or international level of authority, administration, decision-making, and so on) (Warren 1972:162).
59. We shall define a community's vertical pattern as the structural and functional relations of its various social units and subsystems to extracommunity systems. The term 'vertical' is used to reflect the fact that such relationships often involve different hierarchical levels within the extracommunity

system's structure of authority and power. The relationships are typically those of a system unit to the system's headquarters, although several intervening levels may occur (Warren 1972:161).

60. This is more in the case for Taiwan than in China, where the government is currently exploring the potential economic contribution and regulatory benefits of setting up trade associations.
61. Such a phenomenon also has to do with the organisation of the host societies.
62. I remain doubtful if a company will ever fully adopt ecocentric management principles.
63. MNCs face a functional requirement to capitalise on the dynamic tensions created by their inherent paradoxes in ways that promote a coherent adaptation in response to changing environment. There are two salient tensions. The first is that between conformity and a creative deviance from the norm. The second tension is that between hierarchical power and the diffusion of power and initiative within the organisation (Child and Heavens 1997).
64. Pressures for global integration needs, such as economies of scale, universal products, privileged access to raw materials, global customers, technology intensity, and presence of global competitors, and pressures for local responsiveness needs, such as distribution differences, local customs, differences in customer needs, market structure, and host government demands (Prahalad and Doz 1987).
65. The research is largely conducted with their colleagues in Tunghai University, Taichung, Taiwan.
66. Inadequate foreign-language ability hinders the perusal of foreign professional and technological trade journals.
67. These may just be MNCs internal standards but considered to be 'advanced' in a developing country setting.
68. A form of environmental management philosophy which places nature higher than humanity.
69. For instance, informants at Niesler maintained that SHE poses opportunities rather than threats.
70. This may include a rigorous site-wide SHE audit by an external expert.
71. This can be done in conjunction with the pay increase review.

References

Allenby, B. R. (1993) Achieving sustainable development through industrial ecology. *International Environmental Affairs*, 4;1: 56–68.

Alperoxicz, N. (1996) Bayer finalises Taiwan TDI; China hydrazine unit cancelled. *Chemical Week*, 158;12: 20.

Amba-Rao, S. C. (1989) Whither Bhopal: Technological hazards and social responsiveness in the third world. *Social Development Issues*, 12;2: 11–22.

Ashford, N. A. and C. Ayers (1985) Policy issues for consideration in transferring technology to developing countries. *Ecology Law Quarterly*, 12;4: 871–905.

Auty, R. and A. Warhurst (1993) Sustainable development in mineral exploring economies. *Resources Policy*, March: 14–29.

Avila, J. A. and B. W. Whitehead (1993) What is environmental strategy? *The McKinsey Quarterly*, 4: 53–68.

Axelrod, R. (1984) *The Evolution of Co-operation*. New York: Basic Books.

Ayres, R. (1993) *Eco-restructuring: The transition to an ecologically sustainable economy.* INSEAD Working Paper, Fontainbleau, France.

Azzone, G. and R. Manzini (1994) Measuring strategic environmental performance. *Business Strategy and the Environment*, 3;1: 1–14.

Bailey, K. D. (1994) Typologies and taxonomies: An introduction to classification techniques. *Sage University Paper Series on Quantitative Applications in the Social Science*. Series number 070102.

Barney, J. B. and W. Hesterly (1996) Organisational economics: Understanding the relationship between organisations and economic analysis. In Clegg, S. R., C. Hardy and W. R. Nord eds, *Handbook of Organisation Studies*. London: Sage: 115–47.

Bartlett, C. A. (1979) *Multinational Structural Evolution: The Changing Decision Environment in International Divisions*. Unpublished dissertation, Harvard Business School.

Bartlett, C. A. and S. Ghoshal (1989) *Managing Across Borders: The Transnational Solution*. Boston, MA: Harvard Business School Press.

Baum, J. (1996) *Slippery slope*. Far Eastern Economic Review, 159;31: 52.

Biggart, N. W. and G. G. Hamilton (1992) On the limit of a firm-based theory to explain business network: The Western bias of neo-classical economics. In Nohria, N. and R. G. Eccles, eds, *Network and Organisations: Structure, form, and action*. Boston, MA: Harvard Business School Press: 471–90.

Birdsall, N. and D. Wheeler (1992) Trade policy and industrial pollution in Latin America: Where are the pollution havens? In Low, P. ed., *International Trade and the Environment*. World Bank Discussion Paper, 13: 159, Washington, D.C.

Blodgett, L. L. (1991) Partner contributions as predictors of equity share in international joint ventures. *Journal of International Business Studies*, 22: 63–78.

Blumer, H. (1954) What is wrong with social theory? *American Sociological Review*, 19: 3–10.

Boisot, M. and J. Child (1996) From fiefs to clans and network capitalism: Explaining China's emerging economic order. *Administrative Science Quarterly*, 41: 600–28.

Bourdieu, P. and L. J. D. Warcquant (1992) *An Invitation to Reflexive Sociology*. Chicago: University of Chicago Press.

Bowonder, B., J. Kasperson and R. Kasperson (1985) Avoiding future Bhopal. *Environment*, 27: 6–13, 31–7.

Bowonder, B. and H. A. Linstone (1987) Notes on the Bhopal accident: Risk analysis and multiple perspectives. *Technological Forecasting and Social Change*, 32: 183–202.

Bradbury, N. (1996) An island powered for success. *Euromoney*, April: 184–91.

Brown, H. P. Derr, O. Renn, A. White, J. Kasperson and R. Kasperson (1993) *Corporate Environmental Management in a Global Economy*. Westport, CT: Quorum.

Business Week (1996a) Global tremors from an unruly giant: China finally awakens – and the world braces for a new economic superpower. 4 March: 1–5. http://www.businessweek.com/1996/10/b34653.html

Business Week (1996b) Rethinking China: A pattern of disturbing behaviour – from saber-rattling over Taiwan to strong-arming Western business – is causing concern about China's swiftly growing power. 4 March: 1–4. http://www.businessweek.com/1996/10/b34641.html

Cairncross, F. (1992) *Costing the Earth: The challenge for governments, the opportunities for business*. Boston, MA: Harvard Business School Press.

Cairncross, F. (1995) *Green, Inc: Guide to business and the environment*. London: Earthscan.

Carroll, G., J. Delacroix and J. Goodstein (1990) The political environments of organisation: An ecological view. In Cummings, L. L. and B. M. Staw, eds, *The Evolution and Adaptation of Organisations*. Greenwich, CT: JAI Press: 67–100.

Castleman, B. (1987) Workplace health in developing countries. In Pearson C. ed., *Multinational Corporations, Environment, and Third World: Business matters*. Durham, NC: Duke University Press: 149–74.

Castleman, B. and P. Purkavastha (1985) The Bhopal disaster as a case study in double standards. In Ives, J. H. ed., *The Export of Hazard: Transnational corporations and environmental control issues*. Boston, MA: Routledge and Kegan Paul.

Child, J. (1972) Organisational structure, environment and performance: The role of strategic choice. *Sociology*, 6: 2–22.

Child, J. (1975) Managerial and organisational factors associated with company performance – Part II, a contingency analysis. *The Journal of Management Studies*, 12: 12–27.

Child, J. (1984) *Organisation: A guide to problems and practice* (second edn). London: Harper and Row.

Child, J. (1994) *Management in China during the Age of Reform*. Cambridge: Cambridge University Press.

Child, J. (1997) Strategic choice in the analysis of action, structure, organisations and environment: Retrospect and prospect. *Organisation Studies*, 18;1: 43–76.

Child, J. and D. Faulkner (1997) *The New Strategy*. Oxford: Oxford University Press (forthcoming).

Child, J. and S. Heavens (1997) The management of corporate networks: Multinational corporations with operations in China. Paper presented at the 13th

EGOS Colloquium, Sub-Theme 10, Budapest University of Economic Science, July 3–5.
Chinainfobank (2001) http://www.chinainfobank.com/IrisBin/Text.dll?db=TJ&no=105950&cs=11904573&str=
Chinese Security Company (1994) *Taiwanese Industrial Sector Annual – Petrochemical*. Taipei, Taiwan. (In Chinese)
Choucri, N. (1993) *Global Accord, Environmental Challenges and International Responses*. MIT Press: Cambridge, Massachusetts.
Clapp, J. (1994) *Dumping on the poor*. Global Security Programme Occasional Paper No.5, August 1994, University of Cambridge.
Clark, C. (1994) Trends in Taiwan – An economic perspective. *Issues and Studies*, 30;11: 23–52.
Commoner, B. (1990) Can capitalists be environmentalists? *Business and Society Review*, 75: 31–5.
Cook, T. D. and D. T. Campbell (1979) *Quasi-experimentation: Design and analysis issues for field settings*. Chicago: Rand McNally.
Corbett, C. J. and L. N. Van Wassenhove (1993) The green fee: Internalising and operationalising environmental issues. *California Management Review*, Fall 1993: 116–35.
Corporate Location (1996) Philips shifts base to Asia, March/April: 3.
Covaleski, M. A. and Dirsmith, M. W. (1988) An institutional perspective on the rise, social transformation, and fall of a university budget category. *Administrative Science Quarterly*, 33: 562–87.
Crossborder Monitor (1996) Taiwan. May 8: 5.
Cyert, R. M. and J. G. March (1963) *A Behavioural Theory of the Firm*. Oxford: Blackwell.
Daly, H. E. and J. B. Cobb (1994) *For the Common Good: Redirecting the economy toward community, the environment and sustainable development*. Boston, MA: Beacon Press.
Daniel, P. (1991) Editorial: Foreign investment revisited. *IDS Bulletin*, 22;2: 1–6
Denzin, N. K. (1989) *Interpretative Interactionism*. Newbury Park, CA: Sage.
Dillon, P. S. and K. Fischer (1992) *Environmental Management in Corporations: Methods and motivations*. Medford, MA: The Centre for Environmental Management, Tufts University.
DiMaggio, P. J. (1988) Interest and agency in institutional theory. In Zucker. L. ed, *Institutional Patterns and Organisations: culture and environment*. Cambridge, MA: Ballinger.
DiMaggio, P. J. and W. W. Powell (1983) The iron cage revisited: Institutional isomorphism and collective rational in organisational fields. *American Sociological Review*, 48, April: 147–60.
DiMaggio, P. J. and W. W. Powell (1991) *The New Institutionalism in Organisational Analysis*. Chicago, IL: University of Chicago Press
Donaldson, G. and J. Lorch (1983) *Decision Making at the Top*. New York: Basic Books.
Donaldson, L. (1987) Strategy and structural adjustment to regain fit and performance: In defence of contingency theory. *Journal of Management Studies*, 24: 1–24.
Donaldson, T. (1989) *The Ethics of International Business*. New York: Oxford University Press.

Dowling, J. and J. Pfeffer (1975) Organisational legitimacy: Social values and organisational behaviour. *Pacific Sociological Review*, 18: 122–35.
Doz, Y. L. (1976) *National Policies and Multinational Management*. Unpublished doctoral dissertation, Harvard Business School.
Doz, Y. L. (1979) *Government Control and Multinational Strategic Management*. New York: Praeger.
Doz, Y. L. (1980) Strategic management in multinational companies. *Sloan Management Review*, 21;2: 27–46.
Doz, Y. L. and C. K. Prahalad (1981) Headquarters influence and strategic control in MNCs. *Sloan Management Review*, 21;2: 27–46.
Doz, Y. L. and C. K. Prahalad (1984) Patterns of strategic control in multinational corporations. *Journal of International Business Studies*, Fall: 55–72.
Doz, Y. L. and C. K. Prahalad (1987) A process model strategic redirection in large complex firms: The case of multinational corporations. In Pettigrew, A. ed., *The Management of Strategic Change*. Oxford: Basil Blackwell: 63–8.
Doz, Y. L. and C. K. Prahalad (1992) Headquarters influence and strategic control in MNCs. In Bartlett, C. A. and S. Ghoshal eds, *Transnational Management: Texts, cases, and readings in cross-border management*. Chicago: Irwin: 552–66.
Doz, Y. L. and C. K. Prahalad (1994) Managing DMNCs: A search for a new paradigm. In Rumelt, R. P., D. E. Schendel and D. J. Teece eds, *Fundamental Issues in Strategy*. Boston: Harvard Business School Press.
Dudek, P., R. Stewart and J. Wiener (1993) Technology-based approaches versus market-based Approaches. In Sands, P. ed, Greening *International Law*. London: Earthscan Publications.
Duerksen, C. (1983) *Environmental Regulations of Plant Siting: How to make it work better*. Washington, D.C.: The Conservation Foundation.
Dunning, J. H. (1993) *Multinational Enterprises and the Global Economy*. New York: Addison-Wesley.
Dutton, J. E. and J. M. Dukerich (1991) Keeping an eye on the mirror: Image and identity in organisational adaptation. *The Academy of Management Journal*, 34;3: 517–54
East Asian Executive Reports (1996) Moving up in the world of information technology, 15 March: 22–4.
Easterby-Smith, M., R. Thrope and A. Lowe (1991) *Management Research: An introduction*. London: Sage.
Economist (1996) China: A funny-looking tiger – What can the Asian tigers tell us about the future of China? 17–23 August: 17–19.
Economist (2001) *Emerging Market Indicators – Economy*, 15–21 September: 90.
Ehrenfeld, J. (1994) *Industrial Ecology: A strategic framework for product policy and other sustainable practices*. MIT Working Paper, Cambridge, MA, USA.
Ehrenfeld, J. and A. Hoffman (1993) Becoming a green company: The importance of corporate culture in the greening process. Paper presented at the Greening of Industry Network's Conference, Boston, MA, USA, October.
Eisenhardt, K. M. (1989) Building theory from case study research. *Academy of Management Review*, 14: 532–50.
EIU Country Forecast (2001) *China*. July: 4.
Elkington, J. (1994) Towards the sustainable corporation: Win-win-win business strategies for sustainable development. *California Management Review*, Winter 1994: 90–100

Engardio, P. and P. Burrows (1996) *Acer: A global powerhouse. Business Week*, July 1: 94–6.
Etzioni, A. (1988) *The Moral Dimension: Toward a new economics*. New York: The Free Press.
Faure, D. (1994) China and capitalism: Business enterprise in modern China. Annual Workshop in Social History and Cultural Anthropology, 1993. Occasional Paper no. 1, Division of Humanities, Hong Kong University of Science and Technology.
Fineman, S. and K. Clarke (1996) Green stakeholders: Industry interpretations response. *Journal of Management Studies*, 33;6: 715–30.
Frederick, W., J. Post and K. Davis (1992) *Business and Society: Corporate strategy, public policy, ethics*. New York: McGraw-Hill.
Freeman, R. E. (1984) *Strategic Management: A stakeholder approach*. Boston, MA: Pitman.
Freeman, R. E. and D. R. Gilbert, Jr (1988) *Corporate Strategy and the Search for Ethics*. Englewood Cliffs, NJ: Prentice Hall.
Friedland, R. and R. R. Alford (1987) Bringing society back in: Symbiosis, structures and institutional contradiction. Paper presented at Conference on Institutional Change, Centre for Advanced Study in the Behavioural Sciences, Stanford, CA, May, 15–16.
Friedman, M. (1962) *Capitalism and Freedom*. Chicago: University of Chicago Press.
Fuss, D. (1989) *Essentially Speaking: Feminism, nature, and difference*. London: Routledge.
Gergen, K. J. (1985) The social constructionist movement in modern psychology. *American Psychologist*, 40: 266–75.
Gergen, K. J. (1986) Correspondence versus autonomy in the language of understanding human action. In D. W. Fiske and R. A Shewder eds, *Metatheory in Social Science*. Chicago: University of Chicago Press.
Gergen, K. J. and M. M. Gergen (1991) Toward reflexive methodologies. In F. Steier ed, *Research and Reflexivity*. Newbury Park, CA: Sage: 76–95.
Ghoshal, S. and N. Nohria (1989) Internal differentiation within multinational corporations. *Strategic Management Journal*, 10;4: 323–38.
Giddens, A. (1984) *The Constitution of Society*. Berkeley: University of California Press.
Gladwin, T. N. (1975) *Environment Planning and the Multinational Corporation*. Greenwich, CT: JAI Press.
Gladwin, T. N. (1977) *Environment, Planning and the Multinational Corporations*. Greenwich, CT: JAI Press.
Gladwin, T. N. (1985) The Bhopal tragedy: Lessons for management. *NYU Business*, 5;1: 17–21.
Gladwin, T. N. (1987) A case study of the Bhopal tragedy. In Pearson, C. ed, *Multinational Corporations, Environment, and the Third World: Business matters*. Durham, NC: Duke University Press: 223–39.
Gladwin, T. N. (1993) The meaning of greening: a plea for organisational theory. In Fischer, K. and J. Schot eds, *Environmental Strategies for Industry*. Washington, D.C.: Island Press.
Gladwin, T. N., J. J. Kennelly and T.-S. Krause (1995) Shifting paradigms for sustainable development: implications for management theory and research. *Academy of Management Review*, 20;4: 874–907.

Gladwin, T. N. and I. Walter (1976) Multinational enterprise, social responsibility, and pollution control. *Journal of International Business Studies*, 7: 57–74.

Gladwin, T. N. and J. Wells (1976) Multinational corporations and environmental protection: Pattern of organisational adaptation. *International Studies of Management and Organisation*, 6: 160–84.

Glaser, B. and A. L. Strauss (1967) *The Discovery of Grounded Theory: Strategies for qualitative research*. Chicago: Aldine.

Glesne, C. and A. Peshkin (1992) *Becoming a Qualitative Researcher: An Introduction*. Plains, NY: Longman.

Goodpaster, K. (1991) Ethical imperatives and corporate leadership. In Freeman, R. ed, *Business Ethics: the state of the art*. Oxford: Oxford University Press: 89–110.

Gore, A. (1992) *Earth in the Balance*. London: Earthscan Publications.

Granovetter, M. (1985) Economic action and social structure: the problem of embeddedness. *American Journal of Sociology*, 91;3: 481–510.

Grant, R. M. (1995) *Contemporary Strategy Analysis*. Cambridge, MA: Blackwell.

Greeno, J. L. (1991) *Environmental excellence: Meeting the challenge*. Arthur D. Little Prism, Third Quarter: 13–31.

Greeno, J. L. and S. N. Robinson (1992) Rethinking corporate environmental management. *The Columbia Journal of World Business*, 27;3/4: 222–33.

Greenwood, R. and C. Hinings (1993) Understanding strategic change: The contribution of archetypes. *Academy of Management Journal*, 36: 1052–81.

Guba, E. G. and Y. S. Lincoln (1989) *Fourth Generation Evaluation*. Newbury Park, CA: Sage.

Guba, E. G. and Y. S. Lincoln (1994) Competing paradigms in qualitative research. In Denzin, N. K. and Y. S. Lincoln eds, *Handbook of Qualitative Research*. Thousand Oaks, CA: Sage.

Halme, M. (1995) Environmental issues in a product development process: Paradigm shift in a packaging company. *Business Ethics Quarterly*, 5: 713–33.

Halme, M. (1996) Shifting environmental management paradigm in two Finnish paper facility: A broader view of institutional theory. *Business Strategy and the Environment*, 5: 94–105.

Hamel, G. and C. K. Prahalad (1988) Creating global strategic capability. In Hood, N. and J.-E. Vahlne eds, *Strategies in Global Competition*. New York: Croom Helm: 5–39.

Hamel, G. and C. K. Prahalad (1989) Strategic intent. *Harvard Business Review*, May–June: 63–76.

Hamel, G. and C. K. Prahalad (1994) *Competing for the Future*. Boston: Harvard Business School Press.

Hamilton, G. and N. W. Biggart (1997) The economic organisation of East Asian capitalism. In Orru M, N. W. Biggart and G. G. Hamilton eds, *The Economic Organisation of East Asian Capitalism*. Thousand Oaks, CA: Sage.

Harrison, A. (1994) The role of multinationals in economic development: The benefits of FDI. *The Columbia Journal of World Business*, Winter: 7–11.

Hart, S. L. (1995) A natural resource-based view of the firm. *Academy of Management Review*, 20;4: 986–1014.

Hass, J. L. (1996) Environmental ('green') management typologies: An evaluation, operationalisation and empirical development. *Business Strategy and the Environment*, 5: 59–68.

Hassan, A., *et al.* (1981) Mercury poisoning in Nicaragua: A case study of the export of environment and occupational health hazard by multinational corporations. *International Journal of Health Service,* 11: 221–6.
Hawken, P. (1993) *The Ecology of Commerce: A declaration of sustainability*. New York: Harper Business.
Hechter, M., K.-D. Opp and R. Wipple eds (1990) *Social Institutions: Their emergence, maintenance, and effects*. New York: Aldine de Gruyter.
Hedlund, G. (1981) Autonomy of subsidiaries and formalisation of headquarters-subsidiary relations in Swedish MNCs. In Otterbeck, L. ed., *The Management of Headquarters-Subsidiary Relations in Multinational Corporations*. Aldershot: Gower: 25–78.
Hedlund, G. (1986) The hypermodern MNC – A heterarchy? *Human Resource Management*, 25: 9–25.
Hinings, B. and R. Greenwood (1988) The normative prescription of organisations. In Zucker, L. G. ed., *Institutional Patterns and Organisations: Culture and environment*. Cambridge, MA: Ballinger: 53–70.
Hodder, H. F. (1997) Pop-cultural imperialism? Tokyo Disney. *Harvard Magazine*, July–August: 10–12.
Hoffman, A. (1994) Organisational change and the greening process: A case study of the Amoco corporation. *Total Quality Environmental Management*, Autumn: 1–21
Hopfenbeck, W. (1992) *The Green Management Revolution*. New York: Prentice Hall.
Hosmer, L. T. (1994) Strategic planning as if ethics mattered. *Strategic Management Journal*, 15: 7–34.
Huberman, A. M. and M. B. Miles (1994) Data management and analysis method. In Denzin, N. K. and Y. S. Lincoln eds, *Handbook of Qualitative Research*. Thousand Oaks, CA: Sage: 428–44.
Hunt, C. B. and E. R. Auster (1990) Proactive environmental management: Avoiding the toxic trap. *Sloan Management Review*, Winter: 7–18.
Hunter, D. (1996) Meeting semiconductor's chemicals appetite. *Chemical Week*, 158;29: 45.
Hutchinson, C. (1992a) Environmental issues: the challenge for the chief executives. *Long Range Planning*, 25;3: 50–9.
Hutchinson, C. (1992b) Corporate strategy and environment. *Long Range Planning*, 25;4: 9–21.
International Labour Office (ILO) (1984) *Safety and Health Practices of Multinational Enterprises*. Geneva.
Ives, J. H. (1985) The health effects of the transfer of technology to the developing world: Report and case studies. In Ives, J. ed., *The Export of Hazard: Transnational corporations and environmental control issues*. Boston, MA: Routledge and Kegan Paul: 172–91.
Jacob, R. (1995) Pacific Rim: Special Report – Where to Invest in Asia. *Fortune*, 30 October. http://www.fortune.com/magazine/specials/asiaspecial/asia.main.html
Jacobs, M. (1991) *The Green Economy: Environment, sustainable development and the politics of the future*. London: Pluto Press.
Janesick, V. J. (1994) The dance of qualitative research design: Metaphor, methodolatry, and meaning. In Denzin, N. K. and Y. S. Lincoln eds, *Handbook of Qualitative Research*. Thousand Oaks, CA: Sage: 209–19.

Jennings, P. D. and P. Zandbergen (1995) Ecologically sustainable organisations: An institutional approach. *Academy of Management Review*, 20: 1015–52.
Johnson, G. (1992) Managing strategic change – Strategy, culture and action. *Long Range Planning*, 25: 28–36.
Johnston Hernandez, B. (1992) Dirty growth. *The New Internationalist*, 246, August.
Jones, A. (1996) The 10 steps of global trade – Step 4: Matching your capabilities to marketplace need. *World Trade*, 9(8), August: 18–20.
Kao, C. H. C. and C. C. S. Lin (1994) The economic impact of Taiwan investment in the mainland. *Issues and Studies*, 30(6): 16–27.
Kellman, S. (1981) Cost-benefit analysis: An ethical critique. *Regulation*, 5: 1, Washington, DC: American Enterprise Institute for Public Policy Research: 33–40.
Kilburn, D. (1996) Asia rising. *Adweek*, 37(34), 19 August: 22–6.
Kim, M.-J. (1996) A comparative analysis of the information sectors of South Korea, Singapore and Taiwan. *Information Processing and Management*, 32(3), May: 357–71.
Kinlaw, D. (1993) *Competitive and Green: Sustainable performance in the environmental age*. San Diego, CA: Pfeiffer and Company.
Kirchgeorg, M. (1993) Oekologieorientiertes Unternehmensverhalten, Gabler Verlag, Wiesbaden 1990. Translated by Nitsche, C. in Banks and the Environment – A European Comparison, First Year Report, The Judge Institute of Management Studies, University of Cambridge: 16–20.
Korten, D. C. (1995) *When Corporations Rule the World*. London: Earthscan Publications.
Knogden, G. (1979) Environment and industrial siting: Results of an empirical survey of investment by West German industry in developing countries. *Zeitschrift fur unweltpolitik*, 2: 407.
Krueger, A. (1985) Import substitution versus export promotion policies. *Finance and Development*, June.
Lagadec, P. (1987) From Seveso to Mexico and Bhopal: Learning to cope with crisis. In Kleindorfer, P. and H. Kunreuther eds, *Insuring and Managing Hazardous Risks: From Seveso to Bhopal and beyond*. Berlin: Springer-Verlag.
Lawrence, P. R. and J. W. Lorsch (1967) *Organisation and Environment: Managing differentiation and integration*. Boston: Division of Research, Harvard Business School.
Layder, D. (1993) *New Strategies in Social Research*. Cambridge: Polity Press.
Leger, J. M. (1994) The boom. *Far Eastern Economic Review*, 24 November: 174–6.
Leonard, H. J. (1985) Politics and pollution from urban and industrial development. In Leonard, H. J. ed., *Diverting Nature's Capital: The political economy of environmental abuse in the third world*. New York: Holmes and Meier: 263–91.
Leonard, H. J. (1987) *Are Environmental Regulations Driving U.S. Industry Overseas?* Washington, DC: Conservation Foundation.
Leonard, H. J. (1988) *Pollution and the Struggle for World Product*. Cambridge: Cambridge University Press.
Leonard, H. J. and D. Morrell (1985) The emergence of environmental concern in developing countries: A political perspective. *Stanford Journal of Environmental Law*, 17: 281–313.

Levy, D. L. (1995) The environmental practices and performance of transnational corporations. Paper presented at the Academy of Management Conference, Vancouver, Canada, August.
Li, L. (1993) Chinese Environmental Management System. *New Environment Monthly*, October: 14.
Li, P. (1989) Establish a new order in environmental protection in the process of improving the economic environment and rectifying the economic order. In PRC State Council Environmental Protection Commission: 1990. *Chinese Environmental Protection*. Beijing, China: China Environmental Science Press.
Liblebici, H., G. R. Salancik, A. Copay and T. King (1991) Institutional change and the transformation of inter-organisational fields: An organisational history of the U.S. radio broadcasting industry. *Administrative Science Quarterly*, 36: 333–63.
Liu, C.-Y. (1994) The prospects of Taiwanese investment in China. *Management World Bi-monthly*, Vol. 6: 106–13. (In Chinese, translated by author.)
Lorange, P. (1993) *Strategic Planning and Control*. Cambridge, MA: Blackwell.
Lu, Y. and D. Lake (1997) Managing international joint venture: An institutional approach. In Beamish, P. W. and J. P. Killing eds, *Corporate Strategies: European perspectives*. San Francisco: The New Lexington Press: 74–99.
McCoy, F. (1996) Tapping into emerging markets. *Black Enterprise*, 26;10: 80–8.
McCracken, G. (1988) *The Long Interview*. Newbury Park, CA: Sage.
McKerron, C. and D. Cogan eds. (1993) *Business in the Rain Forest – Corporations, deforestation and sustainability*. Washington, DC: Investor Responsibility Research Centre.
Maddox, B. (1993) Pollution: It will get worse. *Financial Times*, 18 November: China 11.
March, J. G. (1981) Decision making perspective: Decision in organisation and theories of choice. In Van de Ven, A. and W. Joyce eds, *Perspectives on Organisation Design and Behaviour*. New York: John Wiley: 205–44.
March, J. G. and J. P. Olsen (1989) *Rediscovering Institutions: The organisational basis of politics*. New York: Free Press.
March, G. J. and H. A. Simon (1958) *Organisations*. New York: John Wiley and Sons.
Maxwell, J. A. (1996) *Qualitative Research Design*. Thousand Oaks, CA: Sage.
Meima, R. (1995) Environmental management and competitive strategy in the information technology industry. In: *Proceedings of the GEMI Conference*, Arlington, VA, USA, March 22–3.
Meyer, J. W. (1979) The impact of the centralisation of educational funding and control on state and local organisational governance. Program report 79-B20. Institute for Research on Educational Finance and Governance, Stanford University, August.
Meyer, J. W. and B. Rowan (1977) Institutional organisations: Formal structure as myth and ceremony. *American Journal of Sociology*, 80: 340–63.
Meyer, J. W. and B. Rowan (1992) The structure of educational organisations. In Meyer, J. W. and W. R. Scott eds, *Organisational Environments: Ritual and rationality*. Updated edition. Beverly Hills, CA: Sage: 71–98.
Meyer, J. W. and W. R. Scott (1983) *Organisational Environment: ritual and rationality*. Newbury Park, CA: Sage.
Miles, M. B. and A. M. Huberman (1984) *Analysing Qualitative Data: A source book for new methods*. Beverly Hills, CA: Sage.

Miles, R. E. and C. C. Snow (1984) Fit, failure and the hall of fame. *California Management Review*, 26(3): 10–28.

Miller, V. and J. Quinn (1993) How green is the transnational corporation? *Business Strategy and the Environment*, 2[1]: 13–25.

Ministry of Economic Affairs (1994) *Statistics on overseas Chinese and foreign investment, technical co-operation, outward investment, outward technical co-operation, indirect mainland investment, the Republic of China*. Taiwan: Investment Commission.

Mintzberg, H. (1979) *The Structuring of Organisations*. Englewood Cliffs, New Jersey: Prentice-Hall.

Moore, J. (1996) Package deal. *Worldbusiness*, 2;4: 12.

Morell, D. and J. Poznanski (1981) Rhetoric and reality: Environmental politics and environmental administration in developing countries. In Leonard, H. J. ed, *Diverting Nature's Capital: The political economy of environmental abuse in the third world*. New York: Holmes and Meier.

Morrison, C. (1991) *Managing Environmental Affairs: Corporate practices in the US, Canada and Europe*. New York: The Conference Board.

Moser, T. (1994) Transnational corporations and sustainable development: the Colombian and Peruvian petroleum industries. Research Papers in Management Studies. The Judge Institute of Management Studies, University of Cambridge, UK.

Moser, T. and S.-H. T. Tsai (1997) Multinational corporations, developing countries, and environmental protection: The case of the petroleum and chemical sectors in Latin American and the Greater China region. Paper presented at the Academy of International Business meeting, October.

Myers, R. H. and L. Chao (1994) Cross-straits economic relations and their implication for Taiwan. *Issues and Studies*, 30;12: 97–112.

Mylonadis, Y. (1993) *The Green Challenge to the Industrial Enterprise mindset: Survival threat or strategic opportunity*. Unpublished doctoral dissertation, MIT.

Nash, J. and J. Ehrenfeld (1996) Code green: Business adopts a voluntary environmental standards. *Environment*, 38: 1.

National Environmental Protection Agency (NEPA) (1994) *An Introduction*. China: Beijing.

Negandhi, A. R. (1980a) Multinational in industrially developed countries: A comparative study of American, European and Japanese multinationals. In Negandhi, A. R. and B. R. Baliga eds, *Functioning of the Multinational Corporations*. Oxford: Pergamon: 117–35.

Negandhi, A. R. (1980b) Adaptability of American, European and Japanese multinationals corporations in developing countries. In Negandhi, A. R. and B. R. Baliga eds, *Functioning of the Multinational Corporations*. Oxford: Pergamon: 136–64.

Negandhi, A. R. and B. R. Baliga (1981) Internal functioning of American, German and Japanese multinational corporations. In Otterbeck, L. ed., *The Management of Headquarters-Subsidiary Relations in Multinational Corporations*. Aldershot: Gower: 107–20.

Newman, J. C. (1993) Opportunity knocks, and leaders answer. *Director and Boards*, 18(1): 32–48.

Nitsche, C. P. (1993) *Banks and the Environment: A European Comparison*. First Year Report, The Judge Institute of Management Studies, University of Cambridge.

Nitsche, C. P. (1997) *Banks and the Environment – Empirical evidence from Great Britain and Germany*. Unpublished doctoral dissertation, University of Cambridge.

North, D. C. (1990) *Institutions, Institutional Change and Economic Performance*. Cambridge: Cambridge University Press.

North, K. (1992) *Environmental Business Management: An introduction*. Geneva: International Labour Office.

OECD (1975) *The Polluter Pays Principle: Definition, analysis, implementation*. Paris.

Ohmae, K. (1990) *The Borderless World: Management lessons in the new logic of the global marketplace*. New York: Harper Collins.

Oliver, C. (1990) Determinants of inter-organisational relationships: Integration and future directions. *Academy of Management Review*, 15: 241–65.

Oliver, C. (1991) Strategic responses to institutional processes, *Academy of Management Review*, 16;1: 145–79.

Orru, M., N. W. Biggart and G. G. Hamilton (1997) *The Economic Organisation of East Asian Capitalism*. Thousand Oaks, CA: Sage.

Orru, M., N. W. Biggart and G. G. Hamilton (1997) Organisational isomorphism in East Asia. In Orru, M., N. W. Biggart and G. G. Hamilton eds, *The Economic Organisation of East Asian Capitalism*. Thousand Oaks, CA: Sage.

Parkhe, A. (1993) Strategic alliance structuring: A game theories and transaction cost examination of interfirm co-operation. *Academy of Management Journal*, 36: 794–829.

Parsons, T. (1953) A revised analytical approach to the theory of social stratification. In Bendix, R. and M. L. Seymour eds, *Class, Status and Power: A reader in social stratification*. Glencoe, IL: Free Press: 92–129.

Patton, M. Q. (1987) *How to Use Qualitative Methods in Evaluation*. Newbury Park, CA: Sage.

Patton, M. Q. (1990) *Qualitative Evaluation and Research Methods*. Second edition. Newbury Park, CA: Sage.

Pearce, D. ed. (1989) *Blueprint for a Green Economy*. London: Earthscan.

Pearce, D. ed. (1991) *Blueprint 2: Greening the world economy*. London: Earthscan.

Pearce, D. ed. (1994) *Blueprint 3: Measuring sustainable development*. London: Earthscan.

Pearce, D. ed. (1995) *Blueprint 4: Sustaining the earth*. London: Earthscan.

Pearce, D. ed. (1996) *Blueprint 5: The true costs of road transport*. London: Earthscan.

Pearson, C. S. ed. (1987) *Multinational Corporations, Environment, and the Third World*. Duke University Press, Durham.

Pearson, C. S. and A. Pryor (1978) *Environment: North and South*. New York: John Wiley.

Penner, W. (1994) The role of issue interpretations, parent companies, and community contexts in the adoption of environmental conservation practice: A broader view of institutional theory. Paper presented at the Academy of Management meeting, Dallas, TX, USA, August.

Perrow, C. (1985) Review essay: Overboard with myth and symbols. *American Journal of Sociology*, 91: 151–5.

Peters, T. J. and R. H. Waterman, Jr. (1982) *In Search of Excellence*. New York: Warner Books.

Pettigrew, A. (1987) *The Management of Strategic Change*. Oxford, England: Basil Blackwell.

Pfeffer, J. (1981) *Power in Organisations*. Marshfield: Pitman.
Pfeffer, J. (1982) *Organisations and Organisational Theory*. Boston, MA: Pitman.
Pfeffer, J. (1992) *Managing with Power*. Boston, MA: Harvard Business School Press.
Pfeffer, J. and G. R. Salancik (1978) *The External Control of Organisations: A resource dependence perspective*. New York: Harper and Row.
Pimenta, J. C. P. (1987) Multinational corporations and industrial pollution control in Sao Paulo, Brazil. In Pearson, C. S. ed., *Multinational Corporations, Environment, and Third the World: Business matters*. Durham, NC: Duke University Press: 198–200.
Pintz, W. (1987) Environmental negotiation in Ok Tedi mine in Papua New Guinea. In Pearson, C. S. ed., *Multinational Corporations, Environment, and the Third World*. Duke University Press, Durham.
Porter, M. (1985) *Competitive Advantage: Creating and sustaining superior performance*. New York: The Free Press.
Porter, M. (1991) America's green strategy. *Scientific America*, April 1991: 96.
Porter, M. and C. Linde (1995) Green and competitive: Ending the stalement. *Harvard Business Review*, September–October: 120–34.
Powell, W. W. (1985) The institutionalisation of rational organisations. *Contemporary Sociology*, 14: 564–6.
Powell, W. W. (1988) Institutional effects on organisational structure and performance. In Zucker, L. G. ed, *Institutional Pattern and Organisation: Culture and environment*. Cambridge, MA: Ballinger: 115–36.
Powell, W. W. and P. J. DiMaggio eds (1991) *The New Institutionalism in Organisational Analysis*. Chicago, IL: The University of Chicago Press.
Prahalad, C. K. (1975) *The Strategic Process in a Multinational Corporation*. Unpublished doctoral dissertation, Harvard Business School.
Prahalad, C. K and Y. L. Doz (1987) *The Multinational Mission: Balancing local demands and global vision*. New York: The Free Press.
Prahalad, C. K. and G. Hamel (1994) Strategy as a field of study: Why search for a new paradigm? *Strategic Management Journal*, 15: 5–16.
PRC National Environmental Protection Agency and State Planning Commission (1994) *Environmental Action Plan of China: 1991–2000*. Beijing: China Environmental Science Press.
Punch, M. (1994) Politics and ethics in qualitative research. In Denzin, N. K. and Y. S. Lincoln eds, *Handbook of Qualitative Research*. Thousand Oaks, CA: Sage: 83–97.
Qu, G.-P. (1994) Challenges facing Chinese environmental protection. Proceedings of the Second China-German Environmental Conference. Beijing: 4–8. (In Chinese, translated by author.)
Rappaport, A. and M. F. Flaherty (1992) *Corporate Responses to Environmental Challenges*. New York: Quorum Books.
Republic of China – Government Information Office (2001) *Taiwan is World's Information Industry Powerhouse*. 22 June. http://publish.gio.gov.tw/FCJ/past/01062282.html
Reyes, A. (1996) Investment: After the war games – Taiwan takes the offensive on China trade. *Asiaweek*, 17 May.
http://pathfinder.com/@@LvgV19ABEAAQNzO/Asiaweek/96/0517/biz1.html
Rich, B. (1994) *Mortgaging the Earth: The World Bank, environmental impoverishment, and the crisis of development*. Boston: Beacon Press.

Richardson, D. and J. Mutti (1976) Industrial displacement through environmental controls. In Walter, I. ed., *Studies in International Environmental Economics*. New York: John Wiley.

Roberts, M. (1996) Taiwan: Technology to boast global fitness. *Chemical Week*, 158;15: 29.

Rondinelli, D. A. and G. Vastag (1996) International environmental standards and corporate practice: An integrative framework. *California Management Review*, 39;1: 106–22.

Roome, N. (1992) Developing environmental management strategies. *Business Strategy and the Environment*, 1[1]: 11–24.

Ross, L. (1988) *Environmental Policy in China*. Bloomington and Indianapolis, IN: Indiana University Press.

Rothenberg, S. and J. Maxwell (1992) Issues in the implementation of proactive environmental strategies. *Business Strategy and Environment*, 1[4]: 1–12.

Royal Society for the Encouragement of Arts, Manufactures and Commerce (RSA) (1995) *RSA Inquiry – Tomorrow's company: The role of business in a changing world*. London: RSA.

Royston, M. G. (1979) Control by multinational corporations: The environmental case for scenario 4. *Ambio*, 8: 84–9.

Royston, M. G. (1985) Local and multinational corporations: Re-appraising environmental management. *Environment*, 27;1: 12–20, 39–43.

Rugman, A. and A. Verbeke (1998) Corporate strategies and environmental regulations: an organising framework. *Strategic Management Journal*, 19: 363–75.

Sandbach, F. (1980) *Environment Ideology and Policy*. Oxford: Basil Blackwell.

Sands, P. (1993) List of treaties and other international acts. In Sands, P. ed., *Greening International Law*. London: Earthscan Publications.

Schein, E. (1992) *Organisation Culture and Leadership*. San Francisco: Jossey-Bass.

Schenk, K.-E. (1988) Comment on the theory of hierarchies and why it is 'relatively underdeveloped' for comparative purposes. *Journal of Institutional and Theoretical Economics*, 144: 849–56.

Schmidheiny, S. (1992) *Changing Course*. Cambridge, MA: The MIT Press.

Schot, J. (1992) Credibility and markets as greening forces for the chemical industry. *Business Strategy and the Environment*, 1(1): 35–44.

Scott, W. R. (1987) The adolescence of institutional theory. *Administrative Science Quarterly*, 32: 493–511.

Scott, W. R. (1992) The organisation of environments: Network, culture, and historical elements. In Meyer, J. W. and W. R. Scott eds, *Organisational Environments: Ritual and rationality (Updated edition)*. Newbury Park, CA: Sage: 155–75.

Scott, W. R. (1995) *Institutions and Organisations*. Thousand Oaks, CA: Sage.

Scott, W. R. and J. W. Meyer (1982) The organisational of institutional sector. Project report 82-A16. Institute for Research on Educational Finance and Governance, Stanford University, July.

Scott, W. R. and J. W. Meyer (1989) The rise of training programs in firms and agencies: An institutional perspective. Stanford University Working Paper.

Scott, W. R. and J. W. Meyer (1992) The organisation of societal sectors. In Meyer, J. W. and W. R. Scott, *Organisational Environments: Ritual and rationality (Updated edition)*. Newbury Park, CA: Sage: 129–53.

Selznick, P. (1949) *TVA and the Grass Roots*. Berkeley: University of California Press.

Sender, H. (1996) Sprinting to the forefront. *Far Eastern Economic Review*, 159;31: 50–1.

Sharma, S. and H. Vredenburg (1994) Environmental response in the Canadian oil and gas industry. In: *Proceedings of International Association for Business and Society*, Hilton Head, SC. USA, March. University of Wisconsin. Madison.

Shrivastava, P. (1987) *Bhopal: Anatomy of a crisis*. Cambridge, MA: Ballinger.

Shrivastava, P. (1992) Corporate self-greenewal: Strategic responses to environmentalism. *Business Strategy and the Environment*, 1(3): 9–21.

Shrivastava, P. (1995) Ecocentric management for a risk society. *Academy of Management Review*, 20: 118–37.

Shrivastava, P. and S. Schneider (1984) Organisational frames of reference. *Human Relations*, 37: 795–809.

Simon, H. A. (1947) *Administrative Behaviour: A study of decision making process in administrative organisations*. New York: Wiley.

Simon, H. A. (1957) *Models of Man*. New York: Wiley.

Simon, H. A. (1960) *The New Science of Management Decision*. Harper and Row, New York.

Smart, B. (1992) *Beyond Compliance*. Washington, DC: World Resources Institute.

Soderbaum, P. (1994) Towards a microeconomics for ecological sustainability. *The Journal of Interdisciplinary Economics*, 5: 197–220.

Solomon, R. (1992) *Ethics and Excellence: Co-operation and integrity in businesses*. Oxford: Oxford University Press.

Sorell, T. and J. Hendry (1994) *Business Ethics*. Oxford: Butterworth-Heinemann.

Spybey, T. (1984) Traditional and professional frames of meaning in management. *Sociology*, 18: 551–62.

Stake, R. E. (1994) Case studies. In Denzin, N. K. and Y. S. Lincoln eds, *Handbook of Qualitative Research*. Thousand Oaks, CA: Sage: 236–47.

Starik, M. and G. P. Rands (1995) Weaving an integrated web: Multilevel and multisystem perspectives of ecologically sustainable Organisations. *Academy of Management Review*, 20;4: 908–35.

Stead, E. and J. Stead (1996) *Management for a Small Planet*. Thousand Oaks, CA: Sage.

Steger, U. (1993) The greening of the board room: How German companies are dealing with environmental Issues. In Fischer, K. and J. Schot eds, *Environmental Strategies for Industry*. Washington, DC: Island Press.

Strang, D. and J. W. Meyer (1993) Institutional conditions for diffusion. *Theory and Society*, 22: 487–511.

Strang, D. and J. W. Meyer (1994) Institutional conditions for diffusion. In Scott, W. R., *et al. Institutional Environments and Organisation*. Thousand Oaks, CA: Sage: 100–12.

Strauss, A. (1987) *Qualitative Analysis for Social Scientists*. Cambridge: Cambridge University Press.

Strauss, A. and J. Corbin (1990) *Basics of Qualitative Research: Grounded theory procedures and techniques*. Newbury Park, CA: Sage.

Strauss, A. and J. Corbin (1994) Grounded theory methodology. In Denzin, N. K. and Y. S. Lincoln eds, *Handbook of Qualitative Research*. Thousand Oaks, CA: Sage: 118–37.

Taipei Representative Office (2001) *Foreign Investment in Taiwan Sets New Record.* 8 March. http://www.roc-taiwan.be/press/20010308/2001030810.html
Taiwan Environmental Protection Administration (1995) *Environmental Information.* Taipei.
Tang, S.-Y., W.-H. Lo, C. Cheung, K.-C. and M.-K. Lo (1997) Institutional constraints on environmental management in urban China: environmental impact assessment in Guangzhou and Shanghai. *The China Quarterly*, 863–74.
Tayeb, M. (1992) *The Global Business Environment: An introduction.* London: Sage.
Taylor, G. and R. Welford (1993) An integrated systems approach to environmental management: Case study of IBM UK. *Business Strategy and the Environment*, 2(3).
Thompson, J. D. (1967) *Organisations in Action.* New York: McGraw-Hill.
Throop, G., M. Starik, and G. Rands (1993) Sustainable strategy in the greening world: integrating the natural environment into strategic management. *Advances in Strategic Management*, 9: 63–92.
Tietenberg, T. (1988) *Environmental and Natural Resource Economics.* Glenview, IL: Scott, Foresman and Company.
Tripathi, S. (1996) *It's Singapore.* Asia Inc., December/January. http://www.asia-inc.com/archive/1296cities/singapore.html
Trochim, W. (1989) Outcome pattern matching and program theory. *Evaluation and Program Planning*, 12: 355–66.
Tsai, S.-H. T. and J. Child (1997) Strategic responses of multinational corporations to environmental demands. *Journal of General Management*, 23;1: 1–21.
Turk, H. (1970) Inter-organisational networks in urban society: Initial perspectives and comparative research. *American Sociological Review*, 35: 1–9.
United Nations (1993) *International Environmental Law: Emerging trends and implications for transnational corporations.* New York: Department of Economic and Social Development, Transnational Corporation and Management Division.
United Nations Conference on Trade and Development (UNCTAD) (1991) *World Investment Report.* New York: United Nations Publications.
United Nations Conference on Trade and Development (UNCTAD) (1992) *World Investment Report.* New York: United Nations Publications.
United Nations Conference on Trade and Development (UNCTAD) (1995) *Recent Trends in International Investment and Transnational Corporations.* UN, Geneva.
United Nations Conference on Trade and Development (UNCTAD) (1996) *World Investment Report.* New York and Geneva: United Nations.
United Nations Conference on Trade and Development (UNCTAD) 1997 *World Investment Report.* New York and Geneva: United Nations.
United Nations Economic Commission for Latin America and the Caribbean (ECLAC) (1991) *Sustainable Development: Changing production patterns, social equity and the environment.* Santiago, Chile.
United Nations Economic and Social Commission for Asia and the Pacific/United Nations Centre on Transnational Corporations Joint Unit on Transnational Corporations (UNESCAP) (1988) *Transnational Corporations and Environment Management in selected Asian and Pacific Developing Countries.* Bangkok: United Nations.
United Nations Economic and Social Commission for Asia and the Pacific/United Nations Centre on Transnational Corporations Joint Unit on Transnational

Corporations (UNESCAP) (1990) *Environmental aspects of transnational corporations activities in pollution-intensive industries in selected Asian and Pacific developing countries*. Bangkok: United Nations.
Ural, E. (1987) Environmental protection and foreign private investment in Turkey. In Pearson, C. S. ed., *Multinational Corporations, Environment, and the Third World*. Duke University Press, Durham: 175–97.
Van Maanen, J. (1988) *Tales of the Field: On writing ethnography*. Chicago: University of Chicago Press.
Walker, T. (1996) Pollution Looms as Economy Booms in China. *Financial Times*, 3 June. http://www.ft.com/hippocampus/12c2a.html
Walley, N., and B. Whitehead (1994) It's not easy being green. *Harvard Business Review*, May–June: 49–51.
Walter, I. (1982) Environmentally induced industrial relocation to developing countries. In Rubin, S. and T. Graham eds, *Environment and Trade*. Totowa, NJ: Allenheld, Osmon and Co.: 127–51.
Wan, B.-L. (1994) Current state, questions and recommendations concerning Chinese environmental law making. Proceedings of the First China-Germany Environmental Protection Conference. Beijing: 23–30. (In Chinese, translated by author.)
Wang, Y. (1994) The main environmental problems in China and its countermeasures. *The World Environment*, March: 3–6. (In Chinese, translated by author.)
Warhurst, A. (1994) *Environmental Degradation from Mining and Mineral Processing in Developing Countries: Corporate responses and national policies* OECD, Paris.
Warren, R. L. (1967) The inter-organisational field as a focus for investigation. *Administrative Science Quarterly*, 12: 396–419.
Warren, R. L. (1972) *The Community in America* (revised edn). Chicago: Rand McNally.
Weir, D. (1987) *The Bhopal Syndrome: Pesticides, environment, and health*. San Francisco: Sierra Club Publications.
Welford, R. (1995) *Environmental Strategy and Sustainable Development: The corporate challenge for the 21st century*. London: Routledge.
Welford, R. and A. Gouldson (1993) *Environmental Management and Business Strategy*. London: Pitman Publishing.
Wescott, W. F. (1992) Environmental technology co-operation: A quid pro quo for transnational corporations and developing countries. *The Columbia Journal of World Business*, Fall and Winter.
Westney, D. E. (1993) Institutionalisation theory and the multinational corporation. In Ghoshal, S. and D. E. Westney ed., *Organisation Theory and the Multinational Corporation*. New York: St. Martin's Press: 53–76.
White, A. L. (1991) Venezuela's organic law: Regulating pollution in a industrialising country. *Environment*, 33;7: 16–20, 37–42.
Whittington, R. (1993) *What is Strategy – And does it matter?* London: Routledge.
Williamson, O. E. (1964) *The Economics of Discretionary Behaviour*. Englewood Cliffs, NJ: Prentice Hall.
Williamson, O. E. (1975) *Markets and Hierarchies: Analysis and antitrust implications*. New York: Free Press.
Williamson, O. E. (1985) *The Economic Institutions of Capitalism*. New York: Free Press.

Williamson, O. E. (1991) Comparative economic organisation: The analysis of discrete structural alternatives. *Administratively Science Quarterly*, 36: 269–96.

Williamson, O. E. (1994) Transaction cost economics and organisation theory. In Smelser, N. J. and R. Swedberg ed., *The Handbook of Economic Sociology*. Princeton, NJ: Princeton University Press: 77–107.

Willums, J.-O. (1990) *The Greening of Enterprise: Business leaders speak out*. Bergen, Norway: International Chamber of Commerce.

Willums, J.-O. and U. Goluke (1992) *From Ideas to Action: Business and sustainable development*. Oslo, Norway: International Environmental Bureau, International Chamber of Commerce.

Wood, D. (1991) Corporate social performance revisited. *Academy of Management Review*, 16;4: 691–718.

Woodward, J. (1965) *Industrial Organisation: Theory and practice*. New York: Oxford University Press.

World Commission on Environment and Development (WCED) (1987) *Our Common Future*. Oxford University Press, Oxford.

Wu, B. and A. Flynn (1995) Sustainable development in China: Seeking a balance between economic growth and environmental protection. *Sustainable Development*, 3: 1–8.

Wu, Y.-S. (1994) Mainland China economic policy towards Taiwan – Economic needs or unification scheme. *Issues and Studies*, 30(9): 29–49.

Wu, Z. (1987) The origins of environmental management in China. In Glaeser, B. ed., *Learning from China? – Development and environment in third world countries*. London: Allen and Unwin.

Xia, Y.-F. (1995) Policies against transfer of pollution intensive industries from foreign investors. *Management World Bi-monthly*, 2. (In Chinese, translated by author.)

Yin, R. K. (1994) *Case Study Research: Design and method*. Second edn. Thousand Oaks, CA: Sage.

Yu, Y. S. (1987) *Chinese Religious and Commercial Ethics*. Taipei, Taiwan: Lian-jing Press. (In Chinese)

Zagare, F. (1984) *Game Theory*. London: Sage.

Zhang, K. (1994) The environmental policies in China. *The World's Environment*, January: 3–6. (In Chinese, translated by author.)

Zucker, L. G. (1977) The role of institutionalisation in cultural persistence. *American Sociological Review*, 42: 726–43.

Zucker, L. G. (1986) Production of trust: Institutional sources of economic structure, 1840 to (1920) In Staw, B. M. and L. L. Cummings eds, *Research in Organisational Behaviour*. Greenwich. CT: JAI Press: 8: 53–112.

Index

Note: f = figure; n = endnote; t = table.